A PROJECT FOR THE THEATRE

NORA
(*A Doll's House*)

JULIE
(*Miss Julie*)

SCENES FROM A MARRIAGE
(*a play*)

INGMAR BERGMAN
A PROJECT FOR THE THEATRE

Edited and introduced by

Frederick J. Marker and Lise-Lone Marker

A Frederick Ungar Book
CONTINUUM · NEW YORK

1994
The Continuum Publishing Company
370 Lexington Avenue, New York, NY 10017

Printed in the United States of America

Library of Congress Cataloging in Publication Data

Bergman, Ingmar, 1918–
  A project for the theatre.

  Contents: Of winners and losers, a conversation with
Ingmar Bergman — Love without lovers, a commentary
on the Bergman project — Nora (A doll's house, by
Henrik Ibsen) / stage version by Ingmar Bergman —
[etc.]
  I. Marker, Frederick J. II. Marker, Lise-Lone.
III. Ibsen, Henrik, 1828–1906. Et dukkehjem.
English. IV. Strindberg, August, 1849–1912. Fröken
Julie. English. V. Title.
PT9875.B533A26   1983   839.7'234   82-40258

  ISBN 0-8044-6040-X (pbk.)

The interview "Of Winners and Losers" appeared, in a preliminary and abbreviated form, in the Back of the Book section of *Theater,* Volume 13/3 (Summer, 1982). © *Theater* 1982

A different version of *Scenes from a Marriage* was published by Pantheon Books, a Division of Random House, Inc., in a translation by Alan Blair, copyright © 1974. The present version is published by permission of Pantheon Books. It has been edited and partially retranslated by Frederick J. Marker. *Nora* and *Julie,* which are published here for the first time, have been translated by Frederick J. Marker and Lise-Lone Marker.

ACKNOWLEDGMENTS

Many willing hands have helped in the making of this book. We owe a special expression of thanks, however, to the artists and staff of the Residenztheater in Munich. In particular, our gratitude goes to Frank Baumbauer, Eva Zankl, and Johannes Kaetzler, formerly Bergman's able assistant and now head of his own theatre in Wilhelmshaven.

The photographs in this volume, reproduced through the courtesy of Ingmar Bergman and the Residenztheater, are all the work of Jean-Marie Bottequin and Eva Titus, whose skill and cooperation we gratefully acknowledge.

The German translation in which *Nora* was produced was by Heiner Gimmler; Peter Weiss was responsible for the German translation of *Julie*. We acknowledge our indebtedness to the fine work of both these writers. We also wish to express appreciation to André Schiffrin and Pantheon Books, a division of Random House Inc., for graciously allowing us to make use, in altered and substantially abridged form, of the original screenplay of *Scenes from a Marriage*, translated for the Pantheon edition by Alan Blair in 1974. On the editorial side, we thank Stanley Hochman of Frederick Ungar Publishing Co. for his helpful suggestions.

Above all, it is a great pleasure for us to be able to acknowledge the generosity of Ingmar Bergman and his wife, Ingrid. Without his customary patience and kindness and her gracious and active interventions on our behalf, our modest involvement in the Bergman Project would not have been possible.

As keenly felt as these and other debts of gratitude are, they must not be allowed to obscure the fact that we bear the full responsibility for the translation and arrangement of all material contained in this volume.

Frederick J. Marker
Lise-Lone Marker

CONTENTS

OF WINNERS AND LOSERS
A Conversation with Ingmar Bergman

Had it been anyone other than Ingmar Bergman who proposed it, the very idea of singlehandedly directing a simultaneous production of Henrik Ibsen's *A Doll's House*, August Strindberg's *Miss Julie*, and a new stage version of the Bergman film *Scenes from a Marriage* might have seemed an unlikely one, to say the least. Even for Bergman, during whose long and versatile career as a stage director audiences have grown to expect the unexpected, this mammoth Project is certain to remain the most ambitious of all his accomplishments in the theatre. Intended by him to be seen side by side, his parallel productions of these three plays were designed to form not a trilogy but what he calls, with a touch of irony, a "triangle," reflecting three facets of the relationship between men and women and the effect that is exerted upon it by the society they inhabit.

On April 30, 1981, the idea became a reality. After more than four months of intensive preparation, often rehearsing ten hours a day and six days a week, the director and his German company opened the Bergman Project, as it was called, at the Residenztheater in Munich. This had been Bergman's theatre since he left his native Sweden in 1976, and here, after five previous productions under his direction, a handpicked ensemble of actors trained in his methods was now ready to undertake the challenging experiment. While the four-hour production of *Nora-Julie* (as the Ibsen-Strindberg couplet was christened) was being performed on the main stage of the Residenz, the couplet's modern epilogue, *Szenen einer Ehe* (*Scenes from a Marriage*), was given a three-hour performance at the intimate Theater im Marstall, just across the street.

Taken individually, none of these plays would be an unusual or surprising choice for Bergman. Strindberg has always been his favorite dramatist—he has directed fifteen of his plays to date—and a production of *Miss Julie* has long been in his mind. *A Doll's House*, too, is an old friend—as far back as 1948 Bergman was commissioned by David O. Selznick to write a screenplay based on Ibsen's drama. (The film was never made, but the handsome remuneration forthcoming from Hollywood enabled the thirty-year-old filmmaker to begin buying Chaplin films and other rarities that formed the basis for his impressive private film collection.) Moreover, the appearance of a new play of his own only serves to remind us that Bergman, who directed half a dozen of his own stage plays during the early years of his career, has never stopped being a playwright at heart. (It was not until 1955, for reasons that are understandable, that he stopped being one in practice when *Painting on Wood*, a one-act play he wrote as an exercise for his acting students at the Malmö City Theatre, provided the inspiration for *The Seventh Seal*.)

Taken together, and seen (or read) in Bergman's highly creative stage versions, the three plays in the "triangle" interact and comment on one another, revealing in the process what Bergman likes to call "new dimensions" and "unlooked-for tensions." One of the most provocative of these dimensions is that created by his juxtaposition of the fates of the three women in the triangle. Nora, Julie, and Marianne—their modern "sister" in *Scenes from a Marriage*—are spiritually related characters, and their contrasting reactions to the pressures imposed by their respective societies stimulated widespread discussion and intense critical commentary. The influential German daily *Die Welt*, to take a typical example, hailed the Bergman Project as a massive pan-Scandinavian contribution to the theme of emancipation. Three women, three ways out, this critic reasoned. The first of the women (Nora) turns her back on her family, the second (Julie) escapes into death, while the third (Marianne) adjusts and finds for herself a new bed to lie in.

Ultimately, however, the spectrum of Bergman's vision is far broader than so evidently limited a view seems to allow. His perception—here as in all his work—is governed by a truly existential sense of human entrapment and isolation, of which bitter sexual warfare and woman's quest for emancipation are only illustrative metaphors. Hell, in Bergman's world picture, is not a place but a condition engendered by the deliberate malice that human beings are uniquely capable of inflicting upon one another. "We can call it original sin or whatever we want—an active evil that human kind, as distinct from animals, is completely unique in possessing," he once remarked. And so the couples in this trilogy are caught in private hells of their own devising, trapped in relationships that are defined and deformed by a litany of recurrent rituals—role playing and demasking, buying and selling, oppression and retaliatory humiliation, in short all those games that human beings play and lose at so disastrously.

"Oh, I'm so tired!" Julie cries out near the end of her ordeal. "I'm unable to do anything any longer! Unable to feel remorse, unable to run, unable to stay, unable to live—unable to die! Help me!" This outcry of human frustration, which was made so prominent and so poignant in Bergman's production of Strindberg's play, articulates a general condition of existential suffering. That condition is shared, in one fashion or another, by every major character in these three plays—and by most of the minor characters in them as well.

Not, however, that Bergman's three-part production sought in any sense to impose an abstract, preconceived pattern of similarities on the plays. On the contrary, his undogmatic method is entirely suggestive and intuitive, and in the interview that follows he makes it abundantly clear that the true purpose of his Project has not been to formulate conclusions, but to provoke thought and discussion on the part of his audiences. This interview is a conflation of two lengthy conversations with him. The first of them took place on a wintery Saturday afternoon late in February, some ten weeks before the opening, following an all-day rehearsal of *Scenes from a Marriage*. Six months later we talked again, this time in the offices of Bergman's film company in Stockholm, just three days before he began shooting his newest film, *Fanny and Alexander*. By then, the Project was already history; the individual productions that made it up had, with the director's approval, been separated and were now being performed by the Residenztheather in repertory and on tour.

IB: Why perform the three plays together? It's an experiment. I want to activize the audience a bit. I want to challenge people to make comparisons. When these plays are seen together, an interesting discussion might arise. What does our society—political, religious, pedagogical—do to the relationship between man and woman? Why does it cripple men and women to such an extent that when they try to live with one another the result is, for the most part, a catastrophe? The important thing to me is to present *A Doll's House* and *Miss Julie* and *Scenes from a Marriage* not as three separate productions, but as one production. What I would have liked to do here [at the Residenztheater] would have been to construct an intimate stage on the big stage, and then play *Scenes from a Marriage* at three in the afternoon, *A Doll's House* at seven, and *Julie* at nine o'clock in the evening. That was my first intention. But it's a factory here, you know (*laughs*)—and it wasn't possible.

LLM: So now they open on the same night, but on two different stages.

IB: Yes. And they will run together in the repertory for a time. And the playbills for all three will appear together in the same program. I think that's good.

FJM: Because you feel they belong together?

IB: Yes. In all three of these plays, you find exactly the same motif—the motif of winners and losers. That's precisely what they're really all about. Marianne is a winner, you know, and Johan is a loser. Miss Julie is a loser, Jean is a winner. Nora is a winner and Helmer is a loser. And that has everything to do with their relation to society. Society is what makes Julie kill herself—her education, the pressure of her father and her social conditions. Yet Nora has the strength to go out and attempt to create a new world. It makes a very interesting contrast. And so I have had this intense desire, you see, to do these plays at the same time, to show how new dimensions suddenly suggest themselves and materialize when you see the plays right beside each other. How entirely unlooked-for and fascinating tensions are created.

LLM: It's been a long time since you directed a play of your own for the theatre, hasn't it?

IB: I think it was—almost thirty years—twenty-five years ago!

LLM: How did you go about creating your new stage version of *Scenes from a Marriage*?

IB: Together with the actors. First we looked at the German translation of the filmscript, and we didn't find that it was very good. So I made a new German version during the summer. Then we sat down, together with the actors, for almost three weeks—working through it, word for word, trying to find out precisely how to say it. There are only two characters, you know, and so you have to be very careful with the rhythm—very careful that it's breathing all the time. The playing time is exactly two hours and forty-five minutes, and there is a fifteen-minute intermission. Three hours. And unless you create the right rhythm, it could easily become very boring. And I hope it's not boring (*laughter*)—it's difficult for me to tell, you see. Having written it and filmed it and cut it and made a motion picture out of it, I now have had to rehearse it and make a play out of it. And to sit there hour after hour and day after day at rehearsal, listening to what you yourself have written—that's terrible!

FJM: Isn't the play very different from the film version, though?

IB: Yes, it's very, very different. The film is weaker, in a way, much more tender.

FJM: All the external scenes in the film, all the incidents and characters operating outside the marriage have been eliminated—Peter and Katarina, Johan's laboratory and Eva, Marianne's scenes with her mother and with Mrs. Jacobi. The play focuses much more relentlessly on the personal crisis of the two isolated human beings, doesn't it?

IB: It's a hell of a job, you know, just to cut out everything that can take away your concentration in the theatre. When you sit there watching this play, you must have the feeling that you are directly involved in it. We try to make the spectator forget everything around him—the other people there, the settings, everything. So that he can concentrate entirely on the human beings—on the faces. It may sound banal, but the most important thing, both in film and in the theatre, is the human being— the study of human beings. What you want above all, whether you are doing film or theatre, is to make the audience experience the result as something absolutely alive. The most important thing of all is to create a reflection of reality—to capture a heightened intensity, a distillation of life—and to guide the audience through that magical process.

LLM: From the very first rehearsal of *Scenes* that we saw, one of the most remarkable things about it was the strong emotional and psychological rapport created between the two actors [Gaby Dohm and Erich Hallhuber].

IB: I'm happy to hear that, because they have never acted together before. And this play depends very heavily on that kind of close collaboration. Everything in this production is built up from very, very small details, one after another, one after another. Normally I don't rehearse a play that way—usually I begin by giving the actors the rhythm of the whole thing. But this time we started out with very small details, building them up slowly, with enormous patience. And the actors were very fascinated by this way of doing it. The collaboration with them made the production bearable.

LLM: In itself, isn't this kind of play quite different from what you have directed for the theatre in the past?

IB: Very different. Normally I work with the classics. It's also been a very long time since I directed a play for a small stage. In this case we have tried hard to achieve a strong sense of intimacy—of an intimate space. That has been very difficult.

FJM: You could almost imagine it being performed right there in the rehearsal room, without costumes, with the same simple screens and the same rehearsal furniture. Actually, hadn't you thought of doing that at one point?

IB: Oh, yes—in a way I've always disliked settings and costumes and makeup and stagehands and all that. I like it best when we have our rehearsal lights—our rehearsal screens—furniture that doesn't belong to the play—actors in their everyday clothes. Magic. For me that's the best way.

LLM: Why is that? Because it focuses attention on the actor?

IB: No—because then your imagination can be the co-creator. Once the settings and the makeup and the costumes are brought into it, it then becomes a fact. Those things bind us.

FJM: A great deal of rebuilding was necessary to achieve the very intimate effect you wanted, wasn't it?

IB: We decided to build up a small, enclosed theatre inside the Theater im Marstall itself, seating one hundred and twenty-three people. And from the stage to the first row of the audience, where the interviewer sits during most of the opening scene, is a bit more than one meter and thirty centimeters [four and one quarter feet]. I think I ruined them financially! Building that theatre in the theatre was terribly expensive—it cost something like 150,000 marks or 200,000 marks. But I hated that vast open space in the Marstall—and for this play it was impossible. All I wanted was a small, protected, quiet room where you could sit comfortably and watch. So we built it.

FJM: Under those conditions you cease to be a spectator. The audience becomes part of the performance.

IB: That's the way it was intended.

FJM: Is the character of the interviewer related to that idea?

IB: Yes, she's a part of the audience.

FJM: And even after she leaves, her empty chair remains. The other chairs in the auditorium become almost extensions of it.

IB: (laughs) Yes, that's true. At first, you know, I had thought of cutting out the interview that opens the play. You really don't need it. Technically speaking, it might have been smoother to begin with the morning scene, when they're in bed and then get up. They could have begun the entire play by saying good morning, and then ended it by saying goodnight. But I think that, as a prologue, the interview is good. It's reality, you know— the reality of women's magazines, the pseudo-reality we all consume every day. Besides, it's humorous and gives the audience a chance to laugh a little. And also a chance to become acquainted with Johan and Marianne. It makes the whole atmosphere a little bit more relaxed.

FJM: There's generally much more irony and bite in the play—and much more humor, too. Johan and Marianne take themselves much less seriously than before.

LLM: And they now step in and out of character at will. In what you call the interludes, the transitions between the scenes, they chat freely with the audience. That makes it a very open kind of play. We're reminded all the time that what we are watching is life, but at the same time what we are watching is also theatre. The screens at the back of the stage open, and stage hands come in to shift the furniture. At every juncture we're kept from getting lost in realistic details and considerations.

IB: I hope so, yes!

LLM: All the overt violence in the film has been translated into suggestion. Johan's beating of Marianne in the scene with the divorce papers becomes much more terrifying because it isn't shown. They simply disappear—and we wonder what he has done to her. Perhaps he has killed her, we think.

IB: Yes, that's the idea. Their fight is terrifying because it's a matter of life and death, you know—they have tried to hold it down for such a long time, and now it suddenly explodes.

FJM: What about all the realistic detail in Ibsen and in Strindberg? How much of that can be eliminated?

IB: Today, I think, you ought never to cut Strindberg—but you should always cut Ibsen.

FJM: Why do you think so?

IB: Because Ibsen has such enormous difficulties with himself. It's always said that Ibsen was a marvelous architect of the drama—but in *A Doll's House* he still has immense difficulties with the building, the construction of the drama. So if you make cuts, you make it easier for him, you make it easier for the actors, and you make it easier for the audience to grasp what he means.

FJM: You've told us before that you enjoy cutting your own films. Do you think the process of cutting a film is similar in some ways to the process of cutting a play like *A Doll's House*?

IB: Maybe. Yes—maybe.

FJM: A scene can be shot in only one way, you once said—the trick is to find the right way. Is something similar at work when you direct a play? By cutting this play as you have done—stripping it down, isolating each scene and giving it a sharp, undivided focus—you lay bare the real essense of Nora's struggle, it seems to me.

IB: Ibsen had such problems knitting his scenes together. If you read his letters, you find he always had great problems—

FJM: With the connections?

IB: Yes. Strindberg never had that kind of difficulty—and I think you must take that difficulty away.

LLM: Ibsen was very preoccupied with all that, wasn't he—motivating the entrances of characters, excusing their absences, providing realistic explanations for everything that happens on the stage.

IB: Terrible, terrible. (*laughter*) Because by doing that Ibsen allows for so many ways around things. You can get lost in all those details. Suddenly you find the wrong ways. There are always so many *things* lying around everywhere—sofas and chairs and Christmas trees and pianos. The actress playing Nora is tempted just to be nice and to tease the audience—so she can get all the compassion.

LLM: At the beginning, for instance, when Ibsen has Nora come in munching her macaroons, being charming—?

IB: Yes, yes, yes—oh, good heavens!

FJM: That's naturalism, though, isn't it—the depiction of character within an environment—and, as you say, the multiplicity of ways into and out of a situation that goes with it. By isolating the characters and the scenes, you close off those possibilities.

LLM: As a result, the transitions between the scenes became completely dream-like in your production. The other characters simply came before Nora as though bidden. It became virtually a dreamplay.

IB: Yes. In a way, you know, it was the same device as in *Hedda Gabler*. Nora is on the stage throughout. Time has stopped—it doesn't exist anymore. Everyone is there from the outset, surrounding her—and she reacts.

LLM: The audience got its first shock as soon as the curtain went up— with your new beginning. Nora just sits there on the sofa. She seems discouraged, tired. No macaroons in sight!

IB: Yes, she's bored and tired and unhappy. Of course. We must *know*, from the very beginning, that this woman is under terrible stress—that she's filled with the sense of being unsatisfied, unfulfilled.

FJM: And with a sense of anger, too?

IB: Oh, yes—my Nora [Rita Russek] is very aggressive.

LLM: Nora's desperate struggle is watched all the time in your version by the other characters—by those four isolated, impassive figures seated around the central platform. What led you to that remarkable device of having all the characters remain present on the stage throughout?

IB: I've always liked the idea of keeping all the actors on the stage from the beginning to the end of a performance. It helps concentration—their concentration and the concentration of the audience. But this time I think we had a good reason—it was absolutely logical to have them there. It grew out of our decision—the decision by Gunilla [the designer, Gunilla Palmstierna-Weiss] and me—to have only a wall enclosing the characters. To make a prison.

FJM: With dark wooden panels that made it look like a courtroom, too?

IB: Yes, exactly. The courtroom effect was Gunilla's idea. At first I disliked it—at first I wanted something more subtle and not so obvious and direct. But now I've come to like her wall very much. She was right.

FJM: The setting looked just a little bit like an old-fashioned Victorian dining-room, too. In Helmer's house. With the characters sitting around on old-fashioned dining room chairs.

IB: Oh, yes. And we arranged it so that we had two different banks of lights—one for the small stage in the middle, and the other for the wall area around the perimeter. That way we could continually regulate and change the relationship between wall and stage.

LLM: What did you tell the actors. Although they don't react, they remain in character while they're sitting there, don't they?

IB: Yes, yes.

LLM: Are they listening to what is being said?

IB: It isn't necessary for them to listen. They're involved in the play and in the atmosphere. We didn't discuss that very much. We just talked about being careful, about being very quiet—because even if the audience is very concentrated on what is happening on the stage, the slightest movement will snap their concentration. And it's very difficult for an actor to sit motionless like that, you know. (*chuckles*) The chairs were very uncomfortable, I think.

LLM: Each one sat in a different way. Completely isolated, completely self-absorbed. Krogstad, for instance, never once took his hands out of his pockets.

IB: No. Exactly.

LLM: In this production he became almost a tragic figure.

IB: Yes. I've always *liked* that Krogstad, and I think that every performance I have ever seen has misinterpreted him—

FJM: As a villain, you mean?

IB: Yes. In hell, you know, the damned are condemned to torture one another. Krogstad is in hell, and he knows it—he's condemned to torture Nora. All of them are in hell—Rank and Mrs. Linde, too. Mrs. Linde is a very strange woman.

LLM: If there *is* a villain in your interpretation of the play, isn't it Mrs. Linde?

IB: Exactly—and the actress [Annemarie Wernicke] disliked that enormously in rehearsal.

LLM: We see her turn against Nora deliberately—

IB: Yes—oh, yes.

LLM: —and she seems so envious and so terribly unattractive.

IB: Yes, but she has to be—because, of course, she's condemned to hell, too. Just think what she has experienced in her life! And now she's filled with a terrible resentment and aggression; she's aggressive toward Nora from the very first moment. Ibsen's perception of the humiliation Mrs. Linde feels in that relationship is brilliant, I think.

LLM: Usually Mrs. Linde is seen as merely the stock confidante—a dull sort of character with hardly any stage life at all.

IB: No, Ibsen's perception of her is fantastic. There are those small moments, in the first encounter between Nora and Mrs. Linde, when she bites. You can see them in the play. There is poison in her—she's venomous. And later, of course, she causes the catastrophe.

LLM: By making her rather spiteful decision to expose Nora, you mean?

IB: Yes, yes.

LLM: That entire scene between her and Krogstad remained very dark and subdued in your production, I thought. That's hardly a very happy reconciliation between them, is it?

IB: No. What would happen to the two of them afterward is terrible, when you stop to think about it.

FJM: Is it?

IB: Oh, yes. Because she hates everyone. And she's strong—he's not. So she will take over everything. Mrs. Linde is a parasite.

LLM: Your Doctor Rank [Horst Sachtleben] provided a kind of lyrical antithesis to her spitefulness.

IB: When I first began thinking about cuts for this play, you know, the character that puzzled me most was Rank—I found him very strange. At first I asked myself what would happen if you simply took him out. Why is Rank there? And then I realized that Ibsen has played a very sophisticated game here. When I began to think about *why* he had written *A Doll's House*, I saw that this is a play about love—Ibsen's love for a woman he himself had created. Can you understand what I mean? Nora is one of the most wonderful of Ibsen's women—and Rank is Ibsen. In love, as you know, Ibsen was always reluctant. He was extremely fearful of touching others, of coming into contact with them. I think he had extreme difficulty with physical intimacy. So he creates Rank, who is syphilitic—

a man who is dying and has no possibility of making intimate contact with anyone else. And yet he could have been the right man, the only man for Nora. That is the way Ibsen planned it—he created the wonderful character of Nora because he had fallen in love with her, and then he wrote himself in as Rank just to say goodbye to Nora. You remember what he says when he goes away at the end, don't you? "Goodnight, and thanks for the light"—"*Und Dank für das Feuer*"—because she has held the match for his cigar.

LLM: Literally, thanks for the fire—it's such a wonderful line, and it loses all its flavor in English translation.

IB: But it tells us everything about Nora. She is full of life—and she is full of the devil. She's lived her whole life with a lie. The best thing, the thing she prizes most in the whole world is the fact that she has saved Helmer—with a lie, by means of a lie. And when that achievement is taken from her, her immense aggression against Helmer and against her father pours out. It's very strange, very interesting. In that last scene, in the third act, her aggression and brutality are enormous. And she crushes Helmer completely.

LLM: Has Nora had any idea beforehand that Helmer is going to react as unsympathetically as he does when he learns the contents of Krogstad's letter?

IB: No, I see Helmer as a very nice guy, very responsible. . . . Haven't you read what Strindberg wrote about *A Doll's House*? He hated the play. He wrote a wonderful analysis of it in his preface to *Married*. Some of what he says is very perceptive.

LLM: You'd agree with Strindberg, then, that Helmer ought to be defended?

IB: *A Doll's House* is really the tragedy of Helmer. It really is. And it must be made clear that Helmer's tragedy is fully as interesting as the development of Nora. He's a decent man who is trapped in his role of being the man, the husband. He tries to play his role as well as he can— because it is the only one he knows and understands.

LLM: Strindberg says that she treats *him* like a doll.

IB: Yes, of course. And then suddenly Nora stands there in front of him with her coat on and her bag in her hand, intending to go away. In my production, Helmer has gone to bed and he's undressed, you see. Then he wakes up, completely naked, and sits there—and *everything* pours out from Nora, who is fully clothed, over Helmer, who is sitting there naked in his bed. And when she goes away, with her enormous aggression and her incredible brutality, he collapses completely. Ibsen gives Helmer the last line, you know—something about "the most wonderful thing." Well, I've taken that out. He simply lies down on the bed and cries like a very small child.

FJM: What motivates Nora's decision to leave Helmer? A desire for self-fulfillment?

IB: I think the reason Nora goes away is because she feels that her former life has been so . . . dirty. Because she has been living a lie—and she has loved her lie. She obtained this money, you know—four thousand eight hundred crowns from Krogstad—and she says to Mrs. Linde: "We went to the south, and *I enjoyed it tremendously.*" And yes, of course, she did enjoy it tremendously. She got the money, she falsified her father's signature, she has really behaved very badly—but then, you see, she's an anarchist. All of Ibsen's women are real anarchists. I think that's splendid! You can see it everywhere, in almost every play by Ibsen.

FJM: So often in other performances of *A Doll's House*, it seems hard to reconcile the Nora of the first act—the doll wife, the squirrel, the lark—with the strong Nora who emerges at the end, two days or so afterward.

IB: I know.

FJM: But you have seen her as being strong from the outset, haven't you?

IB: The one great mistake—and I've seen it committed time after time in productions of *A Doll's House*—is to forget that, with this play, you must always start at the end. Then you can go forward from there. But most directors and most actresses begin at the beginning, in the first act, and then they are naturally very astonished when they come to the last act and don't know exactly what to do with it. Generally they just let Nora cry all the time. (*laughter*) That's a very strange *tour de force*—or *pièce de résistance*, I don't know which it is—but in any case the end collapses completely. No, you must always start with the last scene—with an understanding of what happens in the last scene. Once you have understood that, then you can go back and begin at the beginning. In that last scene you have the whole solution to the rest of the play.

LLM: And for whom is the audience meant to feel sympathy at the end—for Helmer?

IB: For both of them. I really do hope that they feel sympathy for both of them. *Miss Julie* is a play that's like that, too, you know. You almost always see Julie played as very beautiful, delicate, fragile—a creature of Meissen porcelain. And Jean as the big, brutal, insensitive one. I've

seen productions of *Julie* all my life, and it's always done that way. And that's all wrong—because Julie is the one who's big and clumsy, you see, and it's Jean who is the aristocrat.

FJM: And Strindberg, unlike Ibsen, must be played uncut?

IB: Completely. I took out just one small speech near the end of the play. Did you notice that in the script?

LLM: Yes—Julie's hypnotic trance. "The whole room is like smoke around me—and you look like an iron stove—one that's like a man in black clothing and a high hat—and your eyes glow like coals in a dying fire—and your face is a white spot—like ashes."

IB: Strindberg was very fascinated by the idea of hypnotism. It's a little bit ridiculous, I think. So I took that out.

FJM: But the change you made goes much farther than that, doesn't it? Jean doesn't hand Julie the "broom"—the razor—and then whisper a command in her ear. In your production, Julie holds the razor in her own hand all the time—and that puts her in a very powerful position.

IB: Yes, she *is* powerful. She forces *him*. From the moment she decides, she becomes stronger than anyone else.

FJM: I think you and Peter Weiss [as the translator] made some other additions as well, didn't you?

IB: In Strindberg's original handwritten manuscript, we found something very strange. After Julie has made her fiancé jump over her riding whip, he strikes her on the cheek with the whip before he goes away. Because of that she has this horrible scar. That passage has always been cut before. It was originally cut by Strindberg, I think, or by Bonnier— no, Bonnier didn't publish it . . .

FJM: No, he rejected *Miss Julie*—that that has become the firm's historic mistake . . .

IB: Exactly—one of them. (*Boisterous laughter*) Well, at the beginning of the play Jean tells Christine about the blow with the whip, and Christine replies that this is the reason Julie has painted her face white. Then in the second part, after the seduction, her makeup starts to come off and the scar becomes visible and red. That is also the reason she hasn't gone with her father to the party—she has stayed at home because she's ashamed of it. Then, you see, when Jean deflowers her and she is bleeding, the scar on her cheek starts to bleed, too. When Jean gives her this second "wound"—her second physical humiliation at the hands of a man—it destroys her. If you look closely at the play, you'll find that poor Miss Julie's physical suffering is terrible. She has convulsions as well. As you can see in the text, her mother suffered from convulsions and paralysis— some kind of epilepsy—and Julie has inherited this sickness from her mother. Suddenly she has the same sort of epileptic seizure.—It's a very strange play. And it stinks, in a fantastic physical sense. There's a fantastically brutal, cruel eroticism that runs beneath the surface of it. Miss Julie wants to dominate Jean, and she humiliates him when she first comes down into the kitchen. Then they act out a terrible struggle that rages back and forth all the time. And she wins it.

LLM: Anne-Marie Kuster has created an immensely forceful, authoritative Julie for you. That became especially apparent in the way her monologues were made to dominate the rhythm of the performance. Because they *are* really monologues, aren't they? You let Jean remain completely frozen while she talks. Isn't that a very unusual way of directing *Miss Julie*?

IB: I don't know. Perhaps it is.

FJM: Those long speeches were, in fact, like musical arias in your production. Did you have a conscious sense of sustained musical phrasing in the dialogue?

IB: It's never difficult. With Strindberg you never run into difficulties, because you can hear his way of breathing—you can feel his pulse rate—

you know *exactly* how it's meant to work. Then all you have to do is recreate that rhythm.

FJM: I can't help wondering, though, whether any other director has heard the Strindberg rhythm as clearly as you hear it.

IB: Yes, but I've lived with his lines, with his words, all my life—ever since I was eleven. So it isn't difficult for me. It's a kind of security—I feel at home. You can always see it in the score. Michael Degen [Jean] noticed that, too. He was talking about Jean's eating, while he's sitting there at the table. You know how actors hate to eat on the stage—it's very hard to do. Jean has a very long story to tell. But, Degen said, it isn't difficult because Strindberg has pointed out exactly where I can eat, where I can chew. It's perfectly timed.—The rehearsal period for *Miss Julie* was very, very exciting—I found it *very* stimulating. I was happy with that experiment.

LLM: A certain amount of realistic detail is indispensable to a production of *Miss Julie*, isn't it? You need things like the food Jean eats, the wine he drinks, the beer he gives Julie to drink. But you recreated the Count's kitchen complete to the smallest detail. You could even smell the kidneys Christine was frying! It came as a surprise, after the very simple, fragmentary settings you used for *A Doll's House* and *Scenes from a Marriage*.

IB: (*laughs*) Yes. It's Midsummer Night. Midsummer plays a very important part in this play, you see—in terms of the light—and in terms of obsession. I wanted to show the Munich audience that this is a Swedish Midsummer Night in a Swedish kitchen in a small Swedish castle. That was very important to me. If I had staged the play in Stockholm, I might have done it differently. But in Munich I wanted to—I made it as a kind of protest, too—against the production by Mr. Wendt.* Ibsen said somewhere that people who don't know my country cannot know my plays. Well, you can say the same thing about Strindberg.

LLM: The ballet of peasants that Strindberg describes is related to the Midsummer atmosphere, too, isn't it—though your version of it is more brutal and ominous?

IB: I think the people *are* a threat.—In my production there's no ballet—just some peasants who come in and sing this little song, a very, very obscene little song. People looking around for something to drink, looking around for Jean, sit around in the kitchen doing obscene things. Then Christine comes and throws them out—and because of that she knows that something is going on in there, in the next room. So she sits there

* Ernst Wendt's production of *Miss Julie* had been seen earlier in the year at the Munich Kammerspiele.

waiting for them, and when they come back she runs away. But when she returns in the second part of the play, she already *knows* what has happened.

FJM: Christine watches all the time, doesn't she. She sees and watches and knows everything.

IB: Oh, yes. I have a young, extremely strong girl [Gundi Ellert] playing Christine. And a young Christine is very fascinating, I think. She rules not only her kitchen, but also Jean. *She* is the reason why Jean is a winner—because Christine is the strongest of them all. She knows that one day she will sit in this house with Jean—one day they will rule this house together. They're absolutely certain of that, both of them—certain that the future belongs to them.

FJM: So Christine is a winner, too?

IB: Yes, she's a winner. It's fantastically cruel, you know, the way they kill Miss Julie. She's like a big, white, clumsy bird who is already wounded and who fights for her life in a very, very hopeless kind of way—hopeless because she wants only to die.

FJM: The winners and the losers—a strong Jean, a weak Julie . . .

IB: Except, you know, at the final moment when Julie makes up her mind to die, when she takes death for her companion, then she becomes the stronger of the two. And Jean collapses. Throughout the play you can watch Jean and Julie exchanging masks—all the time. I think Jean is strong because he's realistic. He's an actor, that Jean, and he plays his part to perfection. From the very first moment, he thinks out his own play and then acts his part in it. Julie is only a stepping stone for him on his way up.—He's a winner in much the same way that Marianne is one, too. You remember when Johan says to Marianne as a joke at the end of *Scenes from a Marriage*: "You should be a politician." "Yes, perhaps," she answers! I think she will make a new career for herself later on, you know. Johan, on the other hand, breaks under the strain. He is forced to accept his own limitations

LLM: How, then, would you describe the nature of the relationship between the three women in this triad of plays?

IB: Nora and Julie are, in a way, sisters. Nora is the anarchist, she is immensely strong. She breaks out of her social milieu. Julie, on the other hand, is crushed by hers. By her upbringing and her circumstances. Then, a hundred years later, Nora and Julie have another sister in Marianne—and Marianne sits there trying to figure out what Nora has already told us a hundred years before. A change has only begun to set in—just the beginnings of a change. We have taken a step, but only a very small one. The standard roles, the set patterns change very slowly. Marianne hasn't come much further. She searches for a new role and begins to find her own identity. She is in a very precarious situation. How will the future work out for her? We really don't know.

LLM: No final conclusions can be drawn, you mean?

IB: I haven't intended to use this Project to make any specific statements or draw any conclusions—on the contrary. The important thing to me is the tension that arises when men and women are brought together. Out of that tension, something positive can arise—but also something totally disasterous. Besides, I don't believe that complications and tension of this kind exist only between men and women. It has to do with something larger—with our incredible inability to understand each other as human beings, with something incredibly primitive and barbaric that exists not only in relations between the sexes, but in our relations with all human beings. And if we could ever resolve these tensions between human beings—then the problems between man and woman would naturally also be resolved. I think we're slowly making progress with this, too—even the most extreme feminist is beginning to recognize that we are two sexes, that men and women really do have an immense need for each other, and that a solitary woman isn't complete, that a solitary man isn't complete, and that this solitude—or freedom, as the feminists often like to call it—is crippling. Emotionally crippling.

LOVE WITHOUT LOVERS
A Commentary on the Bergman Project

Nora, the first production in the seven-hour cycle of works that the Residenztheater and the German critics christened the Bergman Project, was, at one and the same time, a boldly transformed theatrical paraphrase and a penetrating clarification of Ibsen's *A Doll's House*. Bergman's terse, starkly simplified stage version of the play is perhaps the freest and most experimental of the three texts that he brought together to form his Project. In it, the photographic surface accuracy and literalistic details that associate *A Doll's House* with the audience's tastes and problem-play conventions of another era have been resolutely swept away. Instead, with the precision of a surgeon, Bergman lays bare the inner essence of Ibsen's modern tragedy. His production exposed and explored, with unbroken and hypnotic concentration, the spiritual and psychological landscape that underlies the play's realistic superstructure.

The title of this version clearly reveals its focus. Its undivided concern is with Nora's existential struggle to free herself, by breaking out of the stifling atmostphere of a moribund world of masks and roles in which she finds herself a prisoner. Throughout her ordeal, she remained surrounded in the production by the silent, dream-like presences of the figures who populate and define her world. Nothing was permitted to distract us from the director's controlling concept of the play as a drama of destiny and entrapment, in which Nora is conscious from the outset of her frustration and longing to escape from a narrow, constrictive existence that is gradually suffocating her.

Bergman and his stage designer, Gunilla Palmstierna-Weiss, employed strongly expressive visual means to communicate his perception of the inner rhythm and hidden tensions of the play. The deceptively "natural" and idyllic framework that surrounds the characters in Ibsen's stagnant bourgeois universe was methodically dismantled. The heavy mosaic of realistic details that fill up the "tastefully but not expensively furnished living room" described in the original stage directions was condensed into an entirely suggestive—and hence all the more effectively evocative—theatrical image of oppressiveness and joylessness. The entire stage space was a limbo cut off from any contact with the world of reality—a void encompassed by an immense, non-representational box that was uniformly lined with a dark-red, velvetlike fabric. Within this vast, closed space, a smaller enclosure was defined by high, dark walls that suggested both the panelled interior of a courtroom and the wainscoting of a polite mid-Victorian parlor. Neither windows nor doors existed to alleviate the impression of solemnity and constrictive solidity conveyed by this maximum-security coffin-prison. "Neither air nor light nor sound from the outside could penetrate this closed, hermetically sealed realm of fixed social values and conventions," one critic (for *Rheinischer Merkur*) observed.

At the geometrical center of the stage, a low, quadrilateral platform stood like an island in the midst of this forbidding framework of wall-screens. This was the acting area proper—the "magical point of magnetic energy" that Bergman believes must always be located and defined in every stage space. A succession of deliberately fragmentary settings, each consisting of a bare minimum of indispensable furniture and significant objects, appeared on the platform to delineate the distinct developmental movements into which his *Nora* divides itself. At first, a heavy, darkly upholstered sofa and chair took up the center of the stage; the background was dominated by an elaborately trimmed Christmas tree, mountains of presents heaped beneath it. Scattered across the front of the small platform-stage were more wrapped and unwrapped presents and toys—a helmet, a sword, a decorative brass doll-bed, and, most striking of all, two large dolls with pale and oddly human porcelain faces. Together, these objects made a silent but eloquent comment on the Helmer world as a playpen, a doll's house of eternal childhood. Then, as the alien forces that shatter this fragile world of gameplaying and make-believe gradually took over, the playpen was discarded and the sole physical delineation of the arena of conflict became a large, round dining table and four stiffly old-fashioned chairs placed around it. For the final bitter and disillusioned settling of accounts between Nora and Helmer, however, the focal physical object was not, as it is in Ibsen, the dining table but a more intimate item of domestic furniture—a large brass bed that was an unmistakable replica of the miniature doll-bed seen among the toys at the beginning.

Here as elsewhere in his theatre work, meanwhile, Bergman's preoccupation is only with human figure compositions and never with inert scenery. "The important thing is what happens to the bodies," he likes to insist. "No furnishings that overshadow the action, nothing that stands around anywhere unless it contributes to a choreographic pattern that must be able to move in complete freedom in relation to space and scenery.

Nothing must get in the way." His method of direction exerts a pressure from the stage toward the auditorium that eliminates all distance. The direct and unimpeded contact between the audience and the living actor that results from this is, in turn, dictated by his reiterated conviction that any drama must always be played in two locations at once—on the stage among the actors and in the consciousness of every spectator in the audience. "A performance is not a performance until it encounters its audience," he maintains. "The audience is the most important part of it." In his *Nora*, his radical dematerialization of the physical setting was accompanied by a choreographic strategy that served, in an even more startlingly direct way, to thrust the action forward and thereby engage the spectator's active and conscious participation in it. There are literally no "entrances" or "exits" as such in Bergman's playing script, for the actors never left the audience's sight. Each in turn, the four characters who precipitate Nora's desperate struggle for survival simply stepped forward, as though bidden, to confront her—and then returned again to one of the six old-fashioned dining-room chairs that stood marched up, with severe symmetry, along two walls of the "courtroom." Seated there, they were once again actors, awaiting their cues in a drama in which the very concept of role-playing and masquerade is, Bergman emphasizes, the central metaphor. Yet, at the same time, these watchers were still characters, confined together with Nora in the claustrophobic hell of Ibsen's domestic wasteland. Seated in the subdued, softly diffused light of the stage, these four isolated, impassive presences appeared like half-real figures in a dream landscape. Each was dressed in a dark, subdued shade of unrelieved monochrome that ranged from pale gray (Helmer) to spider black (Mrs. Linde). Only Nora's brighter clothing offset the uniform colorlessness of their traditional period costumes—perhaps, as one reviewer suggested, as a sign of her vitality and her consequent ability to break out of the unbreakable pattern.

The source of this ability on Nora's part is, in the last analysis, the most crucial problem that Bergman's interpretation has to address. To circumvent the totally unsatisfactory impression that her final repudiation of her shadow-life with Helmer is somehow a transformation or a result of some unexpected infusion of new-found courage, any director of *A Doll's House* must, Bergman argues, "always start with the last scene—with an understanding of what happens in the last scene. Once you have understood that, you can then go back and begin at the beginning." The nature of the firm and organic relationship he himself established between the beginning of the play and its ending is epitomized in the graphic but unpretentious theatrical metaphor of the waiting, watching characters who surrounded Nora from start to finish. Their very presence signified that a predetermined and ineluctable process was taking its course—a process during the course of which Nora would eventually have to summon and come to terms with each of "her" characters in turn. For, without a trace of expressionism or hallucinatory distortion in the production, Nora was made the controlling consciousness in the play. Alone, in the midst of a setting that was hardly a stage setting at all, she acted out a dream of life, from which she was struggling to awaken. And, as we know from so many other examples of Bergman's art, the insistent, inescapable reality of the dream is far stronger than the reality of life itself. "I like to think of these dreams as an extension of reality," he says in an apposite statement that refers to his television film *Face to Face*. "This is therefore a series of *real* events which strike the leading character during an important moment of her life."

The compositional logic of Bergman's version of *A Doll's House* is therefore very like the associational, mutational logic of a Strindbergian dreamplay. In this version, the play is no longer governed or even remotely influenced by rigid realistic considerations of time and place. Indeed, of the nearly thirty percent of the original text that Bergman has pared away, the deepest and most penetrating of his cuts are aimed at the punctilious exposition and naturalistic "small talk" with which Ibsen invariably seeks to explain when and how and why characters behave or think as they do. The basic plot of the play has remained unchanged, but its meticulously constructed logic of cause and effect—which, in Bergman's view, serves only to dissipate its potential imaginative impact on a contemporary audience by "closing doors, leaving no other alternatives"—has been displaced by an intuitive logic of feeling, sustained by means of associations and contrasts.

Any truly living work of art—be it cinematic or theatrical—functions, in Bergman's poetics, solely through its appeal to the imaginative faculty; it must reach the spectator directly through the medium of the senses, without any intermediary landing in the conscious intellect. Art, as he has often argued, is not a rational phenomenon to be comprehended by logical analysis; rather, it is "a matter between the imagination and the feelings." The fifteen brief scenes into which his *Nora* is divided are emotional units that are linked together by the master filmmaker's apprehension of contrasting moods and juxtaposed emotions. Characters come and go freely, in neutral space, with no need for parlormaids or ringing doorbells or carefully established "motivations" to aid (or impede) them. Fluid, often unexplained transitions from one episode to another create what Strindberg calls "the inconsequent but transparently logical shape of a dream." In such a composition the sole unifying factor remains the dreamer—in this case Nora herself.

In Bergman's production, a sense of incipient rage and frustration within Nora was emphasized from the outset, in an emotionally charged mime sequence with which he prefaced and defined the play. Ibsen's Nora makes her entrance in high spirits, humming contentedly to herself as she struggles with an armful of presents for the children. By contrast, Bergman's version revealed her already seated, utterly immobile, in the midst of a wilderness of toys, dolls, and other suggestive relics of childhood. Leaning back against the pillows of the plush sofa, she stared out into empty space—virtually the picture of a human doll waiting to be taken up and played with. The very distant and faintly audible sound of an old-fashioned music-box tune added to the strongly oneiric mood of nostalgia and suppressed melancholy that was created by this silent image of her motionless, oddly dejected figure. Then, as she stood up and quickly pushed off her shoes, the feeling of latent tension and restlessness within her exploded into action. Impatiently, she tore the wrapping off several of the children's presents, and then promptly stuffed the paper out of sight beneath the sofa. A visible and forcible effort to regain control of herself was required before she called out to her husband to come and admire her purchases.

As Helmer stepped forward from the chair where, less than fifteen feet away, he waited for her summons, the mood of the scene changed perceptibly. Nora—always the consummate and resourceful actress in Rita Russek's impressive performance—became at once the charming, ingratiating doll-wife who takes an essentially naive delight in exploiting her beauty and sexual appeal to gain her own ends. Helmer, too, obligingly took on his prescribed role as the eagerly affectionate but overbearing husband who showers his attractive wife with kisses and affection. As they knelt together on the floor, grasping each other's hands and engaging in laughing, semi-erotic horseplay, they became children playing a treasured and familiar game. Overshadowing their game from the beginning, however, was the clear sense that *both* of them were trapped within the fixed limits of roles that had been assigned to them. The fact that only Nora was consciously, if dimly, aware of the masquerade defined the perceptional gulf between them. This ostensibly light and playful scene ended with a final kiss—which Russek surreptitiously wiped from her mouth with a quick, automatic gesture.

Hence, beneath the facade of charming, childlike submissiveness that this Nora so readily and engagingly adopted at will, a deep and angry impatience with life's pattern festered—a gnawing, even a romantic longing to transcend this narrow, confining existence of hers. ("To be carefree," is how she defines her longing at first. "Without a care, not having a care in the world.") The forces of disruption that break loose over Nora and shatter her ostensible domestic security were thus, in Bergman's interpretation, more than merely external forces; they arose just as certainly from within her, from her own consciousness of isolation and spiritual alienation. Once established, this mood of disillusionment and spiritual malaise continued to grow and spread until it colored every feature of the dramatic action.

Its first tangible manifestation was Mrs. Linde's sudden, startling intrusion into Nora's world. Heavily veiled and dressed entirely in black (in mourning for a husband who had been dead three years!), she appeared like some spectral omen of disaster. The palpable sensation of foreboding created by this pale, dispirited figure from Nora's past was transmitted—as is inevitably the case in any Bergman production—by means of a concrete semiotic pattern of movements and gestures. This Mrs. Linde bore little resemblance to the innocuous, quietly pathetic friend and stock confidante we know from countless productions of *A Doll's House*. Bergman's penetrating psychological portrait of the character conveyed a different and much harsher image—of a woman filled with futility and resentment after her long years of deadening self-sacrifice, corroded in her very being by a bitterness that has consumed her warmth and her humanity and left only an empty shell. Throughout the performance, the inert, cramped figure portrayed by Annemarie Wernicke provided an emphatic contrast to Nora's vivacious mobility and lively, impulsive gestures. Every physical detail, from her tightly drawn lips and oddly flat, emotionless manner of speech to her reluctant, angular movements, proclaimed with graphic clarity the spiritual prison house, built of rancor and perceived humiliation, in which Mrs. Linde found herself confined.

Above all, her insistent determination to pry into Nora's past and force from her a confession of the complete "truth" gave her actions the noxious, parasitical quality of a moral fanatic—"the sort of person who runs around sniffing out moral illness and then maneuvers the subject into a convenient position where he can be kept under close observation." This line from the play (which has been cut in Bergman's version) is, in fact, a description by Doctor Rank of the moral turpitude of Krogstad. However, in the densely interwoven fabric of character relationships that Bergman's interpretation developed, the description could apply with even greater validity to Mrs. Linde, the self-appointed and vindictive apostle of truth. She precipitated the conclusive confrontation between Helmer and Nora deliberately, insisting, in a virtual paroxysm of self-righteous evangelical rage, that "this wretched secrecy" must be exposed and "all this lying and concealment must come to an end," in order that judgment might be passed on Nora and punishment meted out.

Hence, this approach to the play placed Nora under the oppressive influence of not one but two malicious emotional cripples—of whom Mrs. Linde was by far the more venomous and dangerous. Both she and Krogstad shared the same hell where, as Bergman says, "the damned are condemned to torment one another." Each of them was dominated and deformed by the same sense of entrapment in a menacing world, a hostile social order that conspired to humiliate and annihilate them. Seen through the prism of this director's dark and uncompromising vision of Ibsen's drama, even the scene in which these two former lovers are finally brought face to face was exposed as one more facet of a bleak pattern forged by the life-denying forces that hemmed Nora in and sought to dictate her destiny. Most productions—and most critics—have tended to idealize this encounter between Krogstad and Mrs. Linde, seeing in it a (more or less contrived) sentimental reconciliation between two ship-wrecked people who will now begin life again on a fresh basis of under-standing. Not so Bergman. ("What would happen to the two of them afterward is terrible, when you stop to think about it," he remarks.) The terse stage direction contained in his playing script—"It is night, snowy and cold"—is a perfectly apt and bone-chilling evocation of the moribund atmosphere that gripped this scene until, at last, it exploded into the shrill hostility of Mrs. Linde's destructive outburst against Nora. An in-novative visual effect also added an expressive double focus to this crucial episode. Throughout the loveless reunion of these two grotesque and wretched lovers, Nora herself could be seen, in full view of the audience, standing in the shadows beside the low stage-platform. At first she stood, as motionless as a mannequin in her flame-red dancing costume, staring straight ahead into the darkness of the auditorium. Then, drawing her dark shawl around her as if to protect herself from a chill wind, she turned away to await the foregone conclusion of Mrs. Linde's pent-up rancor to be reached.

Krogstad himself, however, was Bergman's most striking and pro-vocative innovation. As played by Gerd Anthoff, the character of the hole-and-corner lawyer who tries to exploit Nora's forged promissory note be-came a far more complex and contradictory figure than the simple moral degenerate that Rank describes (at greater length in Ibsen than in Berg-man's version)—and also a far more interesting one than the deep-dyed theatre villain perpetuated by generations of stage tradition. In contrast to the deliberately sudden shock created by Mrs. Linde's first appearance, each of Krogstad's entrances signaled a change of mood that was prepared for with emphatic slowness. A few moments before he was to step forward to take part in the action, this pale, black-clad figure could be seen each time rising from his chair and hovering silently beside the stage-plat-form—or even slowly circling behind it. Perceived by the audience in a kind of theatrical slow motion, his movements projected a strong visual suggestion of a threat to Nora that was far more insidious and more universal than simple blackmail. Yet, from the moment Krogstad first rose, isolated in a lacerating, chalk-white shaft of light, his hands buried in the pockets of a heavy overcoat that enveloped him like a straitjacket, his figure also clearly bespoke the tormentor who is in turn the sufferer, tormented by the same condition of anguish and dread he seeks to instill in his victim. Even as he made his first brief appearance, scuttling sideways across the stage like an obsequious crab, everything about this fantastic, shadowy figure conveyed the impression of a man who was dangerous and even brutal because he was trapped, isolated in a hostile world where he had discovered that "suddenly all roads were closed."

More than any other character, then, Krogstad was the embodiment of the palpable atmosphere of coldness and darkness—the undercurrent of "freezing, coal-black water"—that was, in Bergman's interpretation, never very far beneath the surface of Ibsen's drama. As such, his struggle to retain "a modest position in the bank," conducted by him with almost apologetic but dogged brutality, became a fierce and utterly desperate existential struggle for survival. In their first confrontation, Nora's reaction to this bitter, melancholy anti-villain was one of cold contempt. In their second and crucial encounter, however, the mood changed and the tension between them became tinged by a curious irony. In this oddly compassionate scene, Krogstad seemed to have come not merely to coerce Nora but also to commiserate with her as a fellow sufferer—someone locked together with him in a hell (or a nightmare) where everything moves in circles and events are doomed to be repeated over and over again. Condemned to suffer for a crime no different from Nora's, he now watched the fixed pattern repeat itself. In a series of spasmodic (and circular!) movements, he tried awkwardly to reach out to her, in order to persuade her of the ultimate futility and meaninglessness of the desperate action that "is the first thing most of us think of." But, as Bergman warns, "between oppressor and oppressed there can be no relationship." Nora's stubborn resistance rekindled the resentment and the sense of humiliation that permeated this dark figure's every shaky gesture and every outburst of hollow laughter. After a moment's hesitation, he dropped his letter exposing the lie Nora has been living into a barred, locked mailbox that hung, without any realistic "excuse" for its being there, on the panelled wall beside the watching characters. Once Nora's vain efforts to break the lock with a hairpin had convinced her that the catastophe was now inevitable, she sat quietly on the edge of the table and covered her face with her hands, in a gesture of terror that a child might make.

The intensified emotional texture of a scene such as this one—Krogstad's effort to communicate with Nora juxtaposed with her accumulating sensation of isolation and panic—lifted it decisively above the level of a contrived plot turn (the arrival of the incriminating letter that Helmer must under no circumstances be allowed to read). Krogstad's thwarted, self-contradictory attempt to reach out to Nora was a deformed image of the countless attempts made by all the characters in the play—indeed,

by the characters in all three of the plays that Bergman presented together—to reach out to one another, without success. The aftermath of
the confrontation between Nora and Krogstad—the famous tarantella
scene—became the one last effort of this kind on Nora's part to reach
Helmer, to communicate her anguish to this amiable but hopelessly hand-
icapped emotional illiterate who understood nothing of her pain. In Bergman's radically altered version of this episode, Nora's tarantella was not
really a dance at all—at least not the frantic and increasingly more con-
fused and pathetic dance that generations of Noras have performed, to
the tuneful accompaniment of Doctor Rank at the upright, in order to
distract her husband's attention from the fateful letterbox. Instead, Rita
Russek's defiant, whirling tarantella, danced on top of the table to the
rebellious pounding of her tambourine, was not a coy maneuver designed
to divert Helmer's attention but a hieroglyph of desperation intended to
attract it. This passionate choreographic outburst, watched thoughtfully
by Rank and with incomprehension by Helmer, was virtually a mute,
conscious outcry for help in a situation that Nora herself now knew to
be beyond help. The dance was brief; the clattering tambourine she let
fall to the floor signified its finality, as the last game in a played-out
masquerade.

If Nora's life with Helmer is a well-meant but utterly hollow fiction,
constructed of roles to be played and poses to be adopted, her relationship
with Rank was transformed by Bergman's interpretation into the sole
breathing space in which a spirit of understanding and happiness, as
opposed to assumed gaiety, prevailed. In terms of the emotional rhythm
of this version, their scenes together were brief moments of rest that
punctuated the rising tension of the drama and thrust it into heightened
relief. The nature of the unusual bond of communication and understanding Bergman sought to establish between them is amplified by his pro-
vocative statement that "Rank is Ibsen" in a play that is charged with
the spirit of "Ibsen's love for a woman he himself has created." Obviously,
this remark is intended less as a literal statement of fact than as a suggestive, creative metaphor that served, among other things, to inspire Horst
Sachtleben, who played the role, to achieve a fresh and extraordinarily
moving approach to one of Ibsen's most puzzling physician-observers.
Death-marked from the beginning, Rank is (as surely as the playwright
is) set apart as an outsider, an onlooker rather than a participant in the
emotional life of the drama (or the emotional drama of life, as the case
may be). Yet in this "play about love," Bergman's interpretation made
it plain that only Rank's manifest love for Nora had any genuine meaning—although it was only a fleetingly perceived dream-image of love, as
wistful and nostalgic as the old music-box melody (*Träumerei*, from Robert Schumann's *Scenes from Childhood*) that attached itself to this figure

throughout the production. His profound compassion for Nora was built on his love and his sympathetic understanding of her ("with Doctor Rank I can talk about *everything*," she tells Mrs. Linde proudly). It in turn evoked a reciprocal warmth and compassion on her part that figured as prominently as her strength and her rebelliousness in the complex portrait of Nora that Bergman drew—as "one of the most wonderful of Ibsen's women."

Rank first appeared behind her, in the unannounced and yet perfectly expected way a figure in a dream might materialize, in direct response, as it were, to her need—her passionate longing "to be alive and to be happy." The shadow that had been cast by Krogstad's brief, ominous appearance was instantly banished by Rank's presence, and Nora's sense of unease evaporated. The eager and unaffected way in which she grasped both his hands, their laughing, conspiratorial sharing of the forbidden macaroons, and his amused encouragement of her anarchistic urge to say something "bad" for once ("Kiss my arse," proclaimed by her as she stood on the sofa) were very simple but powerfully expressive visual signs of a deeper, unspoken relationship that stood in marked contrast to the fragile artificiality of the Helmer's playpen-marriage.

Nora, Bergman reminds us, is to Rank the light that illuminates his otherwise gloomy and solitary passage into the encroaching darkness. Inherent in this suggestion is this director's deep concern with the significance of compassion as the wellspring of human contact—"a kind of mercy" that is "the enormous chance of looking after each other, of helping each other, of showing affection" (Eva's letter in *Autumn Sonata*). With all the visual poignancy that we so readily associate with a Bergman film, he gave full and profound expression to this concern in the one crucial scene of the play in which Rank and Nora are seen alone with each other.

Bergman's version of this scene resolutely strips away every detail of naturalistic clutter—Nora's dilatory and rather inane chatter about the pernicious effects of truffles, oysters, and champagne, the distracting references to Mrs. Linde's presence in the next room, the interruptions of the maid—and in the process the "realistic" but emotionally diffused impression of characters talking at cross-purposes disappears as well. As Sachtleben's Rank knelt to her, his hand on his heart in a wryly theatrical gesture of supplication, the real purpose of his visit was perfectly transparent—his need to find a way to leave with her some memory or some expression of his love that would survive him. Also Nora's purpose, as she in turn knelt before his chair and later stood behind him to cradle his head against her bosom, was equally plain—to comfort him by somehow assuaging the anguish and despair that now overcame him in the face of death. Nothing in this unit of action was permitted by the director to matter more than its emotional texture—least of all its function as a plot reversal in which Nora, having conceived the idea of asking Rank for money with which to pay off her debt, is prevented from doing so by his unexpected declaration of love. Many critics of this play—and generations of directors along with them—have toiled with the almost unredeemable vulgarity that Nora displays when she prepares to solicit Rank's aid by flirtatiously dangling a pair of "flesh-colored" silk stockings before his eyes. ("As far as I understand it," wrote Strindberg with unconcealed disgust in his preface to *Married*, "Nora offers herself for sale—to be paid for in cash.") In Bergman's hands, meanwhile, this moment of perilously quaint Victorian eroticism underwent an extraordinary transformation. Slowly, in a virtually hypnotic manner, Nora helped Rank to push back the horror of death. As he began to relax, he leaned his head against her; slowly she covered his eyes with her hands. Then, with dreamlike slowness, she drew a silk stocking (*not* "flesh-colored"!) across his closed lids, as though somehow conjuring up a consoling vision of loveliness for him—a dream of Nora dancing only for him ("and for Torvald, too, of course—that goes without saying"). Thus transformed, the moment became a living icon of compassion asked for and bestowed—the pivotal image in a truly oneiric scene that shone with warmth and humanity in the midst of the cheerless and rapidly darkening world of the play.

When Rank appears for the last time, following the costume ball at the Stenborgs, to pay his touching farewell to "these cherished and familiar surroundings" and, above all, to Nora, his brief visit marks the beginning of the play's final movement. Bergman required no symbolic calling cards marked with black crosses to convey the fact—obvious by now to all but Helmer—that this character's departure from the drama signaled the end of masquerades and "amusing disguises," not only for Rank but also for Nora. A crucial irony in Bergman's interpretation is contained in his observation that this play is fully as much "Helmer's tragedy" as it is a drama about Nora's development. As played by Robert Atzorn, this disarmingly sincere and boyishly self-centered Helmer perceived nothing of the reckoning that was nearly upon him. Intoxicated by the charming fable of romantic secrecy that he weaves around their erotic life—and more than a little drunk from quantities of the Stenborgs' excellent champagne—he remained egoistically oblivious not only to Rank's suffering but also to the mood of icy disillusionment in which Nora now prepared to face the reality of their imminent confrontation. Even the shock of Krogstad's revelations passed quickly over him. Once he had torn up the incriminating documents and had taken another glass of champagne to reassure himself that he would not "sink miserably to the bottom and be ruined" after all, he resumed his determined efforts to make love to his wife. Such crises had been met in this way before, he might have reasoned—when her vain attempt to dissuade him from sending Krogstad his dismissal had failed, he had cradled her in his arms and dried her bitter, helpless tears. This time, however, neither tears nor hope were left in Nora as, hardly noticing his lovemaking, she thanked him coldly for his forgiveness.

This is, of course, the point in Ibsen's play at which, Bernard Shaw declares, the heroine "very unexpectedly stops her emotional acting" and demands instead that they sit down at the table for a discussion. In Bergman's *Nora*, no such "unexpected" point occurs (he would argue that it does not occur in Ibsen either). His Nora has begun long ago to be conscious of the futility of the roles they play at. Her wish is for an emotional "accounting," not an intellectual discussion around a table; and any feeling of "unexpectedness" generated by her demand is confined entirely to Helmer ("You're making me uneasy, Nora. I don't understand you.").

Naked and asleep in their decorative brass doll-bed, his sexual desire presumably satisfied, Atzorn's Helmer awakened suddenly to find himself face to face with a woman in a black traveling dress, a packed overnight bag in her hand. The utter vulnerability of his nakedness, accentuated by a single, piercing shaft of light that turned his figure and the bedclothes into a blaze of white, was confronted by what Bergman's script describes as Nora's "complete ruthlessness and brutality." As he listened uncomprehendingly and the other characters watched silently from the shadowy darkness behind his bed, she reviewed the wreckage that he and her father had made of her life. The climax of vehement physical anger with which she met his uncertain attempt to reassert the ritual of domination ("Oh, you think and talk like a naive child") subsided at last into the deep sorrow that shattered her aggressiveness. But the locked pattern was now conclusively broken, as in a bad dream from which one finally awakens. Without a sound, as if by magic, a hidden aperture in the apparently solid wall swung open, and Nora stepped through it to freedom—an escape artist who left the captors of her dream behind.

The uncompromising emotional honesty of Bergman's innovative interpretation of *A Doll's House* leaves no room for the drawing of easy conclusions about the play (Nora achieves redemptive self-realization) or even comfortably "open" ones (perhaps, given the grace of human understanding, "the most wonderful thing of all" is ultimately attainable). His vision of the play is both dark and complex. Nora has been described by him as "a winner"—yet in his production the victory she achieves was rent by grief and an intense sense of loss. The anguished conclusion of her bitter indictment of Helmer—"I've got to do it by myself. And that's why I'm leaving you"—is underscored in the director's script as "absolutely the central line in the entire play"—and this Nora found it the

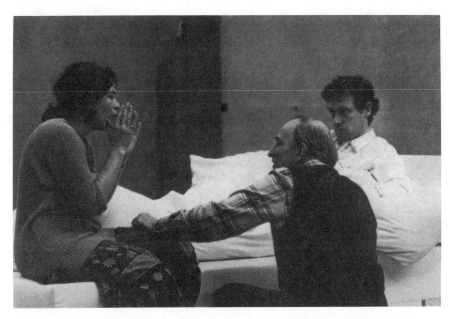

Bergman with Rita Russek and Robert Atzorn, rehearsing the final scene of *Nora*.

most difficult and painful statement she had to make. Torvald Helmer, on the other hand, the "loser" in this confrontation, is perhaps in part the victim of his entrapment in the socially imposed role of being the man, the husband. "And he collapses under it," Bergman has suggested. But this Helmer was even more obviously crippled and trapped by a deep inner malaise—a kind of ignorance of others and of himself that a Bergman character like Johan in *Scenes from a Marriage* would later come to define, with bitter self-irony, as emotional illiteracy. Groping in the dark, stricken by the inability to reach others and be reached by them in return, "we're left without a chance, ignorant and remorseful among the ruins of our ambitions."

*   *   *   *

"Love Without Lovers" was the expressive title that Bergman gave to a film he once began and later abandoned. But in itself the title might well be invoked as a concise and apposite phrase to describe all three of the dramas of sexual warfare and marital strife that he brought together to create the Bergman Project. Above all, perhaps, the phrase fits *Miss Julie*, with its remorseless and destructive encounter between the Count's daughter and her father's valet. The hallmark of Bergman's Munich production of it (which later played to a tumultuous reception at the Royal Dramatic Theatre in Stockholm as well) was the clarity and decisiveness of the theatrical rhythm that he imparted to this loveless, life-and-death struggle between the sexual combatants in Strindberg's complex play.

Although in some respects (and particularly in terms of the dialogue itself) Bergman's playing script for *Julie* might seem to be the most "faithful" of his three stage versions, it has by no means remained unaffected by his customary and outspoken impatience with what he calls the "trumpery" of mere pedantic "word fidelity." A text—even a text by his favorite author, Strindberg—is, he has repeatedly insisted, neither more nor less than "a hidden path into the writer's consciousness." It is then the task of the director to translate the explicit or implicit choices and values he discovers there into the language of the theatre—which is, in the last analysis, the only language in which a playwright *can* be heard by a living, contemporary audience. "In my case," Bergman reminds us, "it has always been a matter of reading closely. And interpreting in the same way a conductor interprets a score."

The first fundamental change affecting his reinterpretation of this particular dramatic score found its inspiration in small but crucial hints that were provided by deletions made by Strindberg in the original holograph manuscript of the play. Beneath her white, mask-like makeup, Bergman's Julie bore an ugly scar on her face—inflicted, as Jean informs Christine with satisfaction, when the angry and mutinous fiancé Julie has been trying to subjugate rebels and hits back. This humiliating injury became the outward sign of a deep, inner wound in her being. Beneath the commanding and haughty presence that Anne-Marie Kuster conveyed in the role, there festered a thinly concealed anguish and despair that foretold her ultimate destruction. Hence, in a very physical sense, this Julie was marked by her destiny from the outset—and, what is equally important, both Jean and Christine *knew* the meaning of her scar and recognized, with a sure predatory instinct, the vulnerability it signified. An informal note made by the director in his copy of the play crystallizes the dominant image of Miss Julie that his production projected: "She is a big, helpless animal who is done to death by smoothly functioning beasts of prey. Who is still bound by conventions. Defeated by her own kind, destroyed by the others. The moral is simple: 'Julie has no finesse.'" The "simple moral" is, of course, Jean's, spoken by Michael Degen with infinite vulgarity as he chewed his kidney dinner and sipped contentedly on his master's burgundy.

A second and yet more radical change in Strindberg's text counterbalances the fact that in Bergman's interpretation Julie is so manifestly doomed from the beginning. In this version, she also becomes, unambiguously and decisively, the mistress of her own fate rather than simply the victim of Jean's hypnotic (perhaps even diabolical) influence. The entire final movement of the production was shaped by Bergman's observation that "from the moment she decides, she becomes stronger than anyone else. She forces *him*." The two sharp rings of the bell, announcing the Count's return, instantly transformed Degen's impudent and cocksure Jean into the cringing valet again, rendered impotent by the burden of "this damned servant boy sitting on my back." Even as Julie pleaded, with profound weariness, for his help, she herself already held the razor firmly in her hand. As she stood motionless in the middle of the room, bathed in the sunlight that filled the kitchen with a white, brilliant radiance, she seemed to be intently engaged in her own inner struggle, rather than caught in the hypnotic "trance" that Bergman has almost completely eliminated in the play. The fragment of a command that she does at last wring from Jean in this version ("Go now—go out to the barn and—") was hardly a command at all, spoken as it was, virtually in tears, from the chair beside the stove where he crouched. Only an instinct for self-preservation appeared to propel the panic-stricken valet into action. As Julie prepared to leave, he hastily scooped up handfuls of the money that she had taken from her father's desk and—lest he should bear the blame for the theft—callously crammed them into the pockets of her dress. Unheeding and completely absorbed in her own decision to die, Julie walked calmly and without hesitation into the bright sunlight outside. Jean, for whom the taking of such a decision was incomprehensible, snatched up his master's boots and breakfast with an air of relief. During one or two of the rehearsals, Degen was even heard to whistle as he hurried away!

Julie's rejection of the world of "reality"—which in Bergman's interpretation is the very tangible world represented by Jean and the wine he steals from the cellar, by Christine and the noisome food she fries on her cast-iron stove, and by the six other watching, leering servants who bear witness to Julie's humiliation and destruction—was a process of gradual disillusionment and steadily growing revulsion. Bergman orchestrated the progressive stages of this process, almost in a musical way, to form an ironic and insistent counterpoint to her erotic encounter with Jean.

Very early in that encounter, the prattle of her childishly explicit erotic challenges was snapped, abruptly and unexpectedly, by the intrusion of a completely different tone. Her utterly dreamlike meditation on the "strangeness" of everything in life—"all of it scum drifting on the water, drifting along, until it sinks, sinks down!"—was conceived as a monologue that gazed inward, at something that Jean would never be able to see or comprehend. However, the Jean that Degen drew was, above all, an able and quick-witted actor, and he was swift to pick up his cue, following her lead with his own animated, improvised "dream" of ambitiousness. When more tangible physical advances failed, he resorted again to his reliable histrionic skills. At first, Julie's sense of revulsion and incipient self-disgust rose dangerously at his colorfully embellished but loathsome tale of his coprolitic adventures in the Count's outdoor "Turkish pavilion." But his subsequent sobbing recital of the deprivations of "a poor farmer's child" driven from Paradise—which reached its peak of exaggeration when Degen casually mopped his tear-stained face with a handy kitchen towel!—gave him a fresh hold on his naive and illusion-prone listener. With the approach of the servants singing their ribald song (which is much more explicitly malicious in this version than in Strindberg's text), he had the pretext he needed to hurry Julie into his own room. He took the opportunity with cynical composure, without a trace of erotic passion.

The unseen seduction is the turning point in the play. Following it, their masks now laid aside, Julie and Jean sit through the rest of the brief Midsummer Night discussing alternatives. With the rising of the sun that at last dispels the darkness (and "the spooks"), Julie realizes that she has neither any illusions nor any alternatives left.

Bergman's version introduces a new choreographic interlude that makes a far harsher and more decisively ironic comment on the seduction than does the rather idyllic Midsummer folk dancing described by Strindberg in his text.* The grotesque and obscene actions of the drunken, copulating servants who invaded the kitchen underscored the true, sordid nature of Jean's easy conquest; it became the rough equivalent of the rutting of Diana, Julie's wayward lap dog, by the porter's mutt. At the same time, the presence of the sneering intruders and of Christine turned the sexual act into a ritual of humiliation for Julie. In Strindberg's play, she takes out a powder puff and nervously powders her face after reappearing from Jean's bedroom; Anne-Marie Kuster's Julie emerged in extreme physical pain, retching and bleeding visibly from her scar and from her ruptured hymen. The strong emphasis on a more overt and intense physical suffering on Julie's part that pervaded Bergman's production was no shock tactic, however, but a concrete means of exteriorizing the self-destructive anguish and despair within her.

At first, the emotional nausea and revulsion that overwhelmed her following the seduction made no impression whatever on Jean, who devoted himself to his train schedule, his cigar, and his schemes for acquiring a hotel ("with first-class accommodations for first-class customers") and perhaps even a Rumanian count's title. Once Julie's

---

* Bergman's interlude is described in detail in the stage directions which, in this case and elsewhere throughout his playing script, have been substituted for Strindberg's own.

revelation that she has no money of her own had effectively closed off that alternative, however, his manner toward her shifted abruptly from callous indifference to open hostility. Not, Jean insists, that he has no pity for her—following the first of her two panic-induced convulsions, he smugly consoled her with a glass of the wine he had pilfered from her father's cellar; then, as she lay huddled on the floor after her second seizure, he patted her sympathetically on the back, his cigar still in his hand, as he told her the truth about his concocted fable of the servant boy's tragic romance. This Jean gradually became, in his own way, as visibly consumed by the bitterness of his disillusionment with false ideals as Julie herself was. Seated in his and Christine's favorite corner chair beside the stove, Degen's class-conscious lackey-aristocrat shook with a mixture of fury and chagrin as he pondered his "discovery" that he had been duped by the false glitter of cat's gold—"that the hawk's back was as gray as the rest of it, that the whiteness of the cheeks was nothing but powder, that polished fingernails could have black edges, and that the handkerchief was dirty, even if it did smell of perfume."

Julie, meanwhile, was already far away. She struggled for her life, as Bergman observes, "in a very, very hopeless kind of way—hopeless because she wants to die." She had barely enough resistance to fight off Jean's sudden and explosively violent attempt to force her to have sex with him again. The introspective, dreamlike tone in her voice became steadily more insistent, until it completely suffused her long, exhausted monologue about her ingrained family heritage of sexual strife and man-hatred. Jean, however, barely listened. The alternatives—to stay, to run away together and die or torment one another to death, to live by renting sleazy villas to the "loving couples" who visit the rainy shores of Lake Como—were not encouraging, and they dwindled rapidly in the rose-colored dawn that preceded the sunrise.

Julie's reminder of "the consequences" that might result from their affair was cleansed of its faintly melodramatic air in this production, where it became instead an idea that Jean seized upon as an unlooked-for solution to his problem—the means of convincing Julie that she must run away alone. When she came back to the kitchen dressed for travel, however, she had stolen enough of her father's money to cause Jean to reconsider his plan. All through the elegiac dream-monologue in which she describes her "childhood memories of midsummer days," he sat at the kitchen table frantically counting the cash. The amount was sufficient to persuade him to go with her—but his brutally indifferent destruction of the irksome greenfinch released in Julie the final eruption of a self-abhorrence and a despair that she could no longer keep down. "*Here Julie goes to pieces*" is the simple, emphatic notation marked in the director's copy at this point.

The arrival of Christine, dressed for church in funereal black, put an end to Jean's plan of escape, but Julie's awareness of the utter futility of further struggle had already overtaken her. Kneeling before this implacable agent of self-righteous moral indignation, Julie pleaded with her for a compromise in which she herself no longer believed. The tempo of her appeal increased to a lightning speed; then it faltered, came to a halt, and died away. When it was finished, she collapsed at the kitchen table and sank her head down between her arms.

Christine, the cook, is developed in Bergman's *Julie* into something very different than the supporting character that Strindberg describes in his famous Preface as "a female slave, filled with a sense of dependence and apathy, bound to her stove, brutishly ignorant in her hypocrisy, stuffed full of morality and religion as her excuse and pretext for everything." The essence of Bergman's decisively altered approach to Christine is contained in his remark that "she rules not only her kitchen, but also Jean. *She* is the reason why Jean is a winner—because Christine is the strongest of them all." His version amplifies her strength and the control she exercises in a variety of ways.

In the Munich performance, the young, strongly sensual Christine created by Gundi Ellert was Julie's antithesis. She embraced and fondled Jean with a laughing, possessive animality that stood in marked contrast to the shy, awkward behavior of her mistress—who, moreover, inadvertently walked in on their passionate lovemaking on two occasions. Almost from the outset, in the mimed sequence that replaced the "Pantomime" in Strindberg's text, she communicated both her awareness of her lover's propensity for philandering—as readily with household rivals like Clara or Sofie as with their mistress—and also her intention of maintaining a tight surveillance on his activities. "*Is it possible?*" she demands, with an angry clatter of dishes and pots, the next morning—but her vigil in the darkened kitchen during the seduction left no doubt that she already knew the answer to her question. Her knowledge fueled the self-righteous wrath of the hieratic denunciation she pronounced, like a high priestess before the altar of her cast-iron stove, over Julie—unmindful, to be sure, that her text, from Matthew 19, is immediately preceded in the Bible by the parable of the unmerciful servant who is damned for his failure to show compassion for his fellow man. As she left for church, the glance of mutual understanding and conspiracy that she exchanged with Jean spoke eloquently enough of the attitude shared by these two "smoothly functioning beasts of prey" toward their exhausted quarry.

Christine is rooted, in a very tangible sense, in the midst of the "real" world that both repudiates and is repudiated by Julie. The six non-speaking servant figures that Bergman's version introduced—again on the basis of hints found in Strindberg's text—were a further means of

Ingmar Bergman (right) rehearsing *Julie* with Gundi Ellert (Christine) and Michael Degen (Jean).

strengthening the atmosphere of concrete reality to which the ferocious cook belonged (although she would doubtless consider herself a notch above these lower types). In his notes, the director assigns each member of this mocking chorus of prying onlookers to a particular position in the socio-sexual hierarchy of the place. Thus, Clara "considers Jean her personal property"; Sofie is pregnant from her affair with Johan, the stable foreman; Anna goes out with Lars, the self-important coachman, but she is otherwise "everybody's property." One result of this largely unseen but deftly suggested dimension of sexual entanglements—perceived on a plane somewhere between Christine's affair with Jean and Diana's brush with the porter's mutt—was to deepen the sense of what Bergman calls "the fantastically brutal, cruel eroticism that runs beneath the surface of the play." In addition, the presence of this servant chorus of malicious eavesdroppers amplified the felt hostility of a society that participates willingly in the exorcism of its enemy, the outsider. ("No, Miss Julie, they don't love you," Jean warns her. "They take your food—but they spit at you afterward.")

Christine's kitchen kingdom, around which the watchers prowled and down into which Julie quite literally descended in Bergman's production, likewise became a manifestation of the "real" world to which everyone in sight belongs, except the rootless and self-dispossessed Julie. As such, it was a place where realistic specificity (down to the smell of food cooking and coffee brewing on the stove) existed at maximum intensity. The realism of the kitchen setting was thus virtually magical—a picture of sharp focus and precise representation, outside which, beyond the windows that looked out on the park (but which Bergman had made increasingly opaque as rehearsals went on), no other reality existed. Magic realism is a term that is sometimes applied to the work of painters who, by using an exceedingly exact realistic technique, try to persuade us that extraordinary and dreamlike things are possible simply by painting them as if they existed. In very much this same manner, and with a completeness of detail that took many by surprise, Bergman's production delineated with a cool, camera-sharp surface fidelity the prison world of the spirit in which Julie acts out her dreamlike and hopeless struggle to exist.

Nora—and in particular Bergman's Nora—is the center and therefore, as it were, the creator of her stage world; when she leaves, she takes that world away with her. The kitchen world of Christine and the others possessed an objective and remorseless permanence of its own, and Julie's departure from it was a thing that would make very little discernible difference. The only small, pathetic reminders of her passage through it were the empty birdcage and the light traveling shawl that was carelessly draped over the back of a kitchen chair.

*   *   *   *

Scenes from a Marriage, the last and longest of the plays comprising Bergman's theatrical trilogy, is much more than just an effective stage adaptation of his popular 1973 film of the same name. It is an original work, put together by the author-director and his actors on the basis of selected episodes and characters from the filmscript, but arranged in such a way that a new and tightly dramatic concentration on the psychological struggle of the married couple, Johan and Marianne, is achieved. Everything outside the married life of these two characters has been eliminated. The result became what Bergman calls "a distillation of life," which in performance generated a sense of audience involvement so intense that several of the German reviewers were inclined to pronounce this production the most effective of the three.

"Involvement" is a word that requires careful modification when applied to Bergman's art. As different as the three productions in the trilogy were in other ways, they shared a common emphasis upon conscious and

purposeful theatricality. "The real theatre always reminds—the real theatrical creation always must remind the audience that it is watching a
performance," Bergman insists. A rhythmic oscillation between emotional engagement and detachment is, in his view, the true key to the
nature of the audience's involvement in the mimetic experience. "From
being completely involved at one instant," he continues, "the spectator
is at the very next instant aware of being in the theatre. The next second
he is involved again, completely involved; then after three seconds he is
back in the theatre. And that is a part—and a very, very important part—
of his being a participant in the ritual. Because that word *verfremdung*
[alienation] is a complete misunderstanding. The spectator is always involved and he is always outside, at one and the same time."*

Familiar examples of how this attitude has spilled over into his films
(for it is a case of his theatre work having influenced his filmmaking in
this respect) are plentiful. The security-shattering moment when the film
breaks in *Persona*, the sound of Bergman's own voice instructing his film
crew in *Hour of the Wolf*, the four "interludes" in which the actors come
forward to comment on their roles in *A Passion*, or the inclusion of the
audience as a "character" in *The Magic Flute*—these and other compa-
rable "meta-filmic" strategies are intended, as Bergman says, "to awaken
people for a moment, in order to send them back into the drama afterward." He disagrees vigorously with critics who persist in referring to
such breaks in the action as "alienating" devices, however. "I believe that
if you pull the audience out of the action for a time and then lead them
back into it, you will increase emotional sensibility and receptivity instead of diminishing it," he maintained in an interview published more
than a dozen years ago.

In his new stage version of *Scenes from a Marriage*, the interludes
(*Zwischentexte* is the word used in the German prompt copy) that occur
between the scenes and sometimes during them reflect his stated intention perfectly. In these passages—which were developed during rehearsals and which find no equivalent in the screenplay—Johan and Marianne
address the audience directly, and the trenchant irony of their comments
on the action fosters, in turn, a deeper involvement that reaches beyond
irony. In this and other ways, the audience seated in the intimate, 123-
seat miniature theatre that Bergman constructed within the cavernous
open space of the Theater im Marstall was made an aware and active
collaborator in the creative process.

All physical signs of a barrier between stage and auditorium were
erased, The house lights remained on for several minutes after the play
had begun, and they were never entirely extinguished. Mrs. Palm, the

* From an interview in *Ingmar Bergman: Four Decades in the Theater*, by Lise-
Lone Marker and Frederick J. Marker (London and New York, 1982), p. 231.

caricature of a journalist who interviews the couple for a women's magazine, took her seat in the front row of the audience and conducted a large
part of her interview from there. Scenery as such did not exist. Within
a framework of low screens that never changed, a small collection of
simple, contemporary (demonstrably Swedish!) furniture was moved into
different constellations by four stagehands who appeared at the end of
each scene. These reminders of the intrinsic theatricality of the dramatic
event came through sliding doors at the rear, and Johan and Marianne
mingled freely with them. The actors themselves wore clothing that was
virtually indistinguishable from the ordinary street clothes they had
worn during rehearsals. Even for the scenes that are played in a large
double bed, no concession was made to realism by resorting to changes
of costume. In a word, Bergman's method—here as so often in the past—
was to strip away everything that could "de-theatricalize" the hypnotic
presence of the living actor and thereby dissipate his power to influence
and ultimately control the audience's emotional involvement. "The theatre calls for nothing," he has said. "T.V. includes everything, film includes everything, there everything is shown. Threatre ought to be the
encounter of human beings with human beings and nothing more. All
else is distracting." The conviction summarized in this remark accounted
for one of the most important differences between Bergman's treatment
of the drama of Johan and Marianne on the screen and in the living
theatre.

In structural terms as well, many differences separate the stage text
of *Scenes from a Marriage* from the much more loosely knit screenplay—
differences that must be ascribed to a deliberate change in dramatic emphasis rather than merely to a need to satisfy the practical requirements
of another medium. Immediately after the prologue, with its wry taste
of what Bergman calls "the pseudo-reality we all consume every day,"
the play takes a very different direction than the film. The first episode
of the screenplay gave us what its director calls "a pretty picture of an
almost ideal marriage." Confronted by the terrifying hatred that their
friends Peter and Katarina display toward one another, the complacent
Marianne and Johan of the film are inclined to look on them as lunatics
to be pitied. "Don't you think the danger of loneliness and estrangement
is just as great in the life we live?" she inquires of her husband. "Definitely
not," he replies self-confidently. In the play, the territory where the struggle rages is internal, and nearly all such external referents have been
systematically eliminated. This Marianne and Johan now seem suspended and trapped in the same void occupied by later Bergman characters like Peter and Katarina and their fellow puppets in *From the Life
of the Marionettes*. In Gaby Dohm's physically expressive performance,
Marianne's sense of frustration and incipient panic was evident from the

outset, even in the way she lay in bed watching her sleeping husband. She needed no meeting with Mrs. Jacobi (as fine as that scene was in the film) to amplify her rising sensation of the dread of emotional bankruptcy. Nor did the Johan of Erich Hallhuber, younger and far more vulnerable than the character drawn by Erland Josephson, require a laboratory colleague's cold response to his poetry to fuel his gnawing discontent. Time and place have in general been radically telescoped in the play, to great dramatic advantage. The troubled questions raised by Johan in the very first of the marriage scenes—"Can the scheme of things be so treacherous that life suddenly goes wrong?" "Is it a matter of choosing, and making the wrong choice?"—have now become a point of departure, rather than, as in the film, a stage to which the action gradually develops.

In the next scene, entitled "Nora"—Johan and Marianne have been to see (what else?) a production of *A Doll's House*—the unanswered questions multiply and swiftly escalate into a weary, late-night quarrel. At the real heart of their discord is the disillusionment and loss of hopefulness that Marianne tries to speak of, but its immediate cause is Johan's expression of dissatisfaction with his wife's diminished sexual responsiveness. This scene ends—in a sequence that bore, in performance, a strong and perhaps conscious resemblance to Nora's rebuff of Torvald's advances—with Marianne's rejection of her husband's mild attempt at lovemaking. This brief show of resistance (or frigidity, depending on one's point of view) is undercut almost at once in the screenplay, when, after a solicitous visit to her daughters' room, Marianne tries to sweep the crisis under the rug by offering to let Johan have his way. He thanks her for the favor, but begs off—and the aftermath of this episode is his abrupt revelation of the existence of Paula, his mistress. In the play, however, the sequence of events and the dramatic logic that links them have been drastically altered. Marianne makes no such offer to appease Johan. Instead, "a few months later, or maybe only a few days later, on a completely ordinary evening," she breaks the news that she is pregnant. Their botched and painfully dishonest discussion of the "problem" represented by the child occurs much earlier in the film, as a reaction to the appalling quarrel they have witnessed between Peter and Katarina. In the play the scene is used, in a more dramatic way, as the outcome of their *own* marital crisis. The abortion they ostensibly agree should not be performed became the subject of a separate and deeply moving scene in the film, fraught with Marianne's remorse and despair. The full impact of that scene is compressed in the play into the one bleak, ironic sentence with which Marianne announces to the audience the choice imposed on her: "Two weeks later, Marianne underwent a small operation." And the aftermath of *that* line in the play is her crushing humiliation at Johan's hands, when he reveals his infidelity.

"Paula," the episode in which John ("oxidized by the cheerful self-ishness of the new infatuation," Bergman writes) tells her, with casual brutality, that he is going away with another woman, remains as much of a turning point in the play as in the television film and the subsequent motion picture of *Scenes from a Marriage*. The persistently concealed discontent that has infected the marriage from the beginning is at last brought out in the open. In the stage production, however, the entire scene was played in or around the big double bed which, together with a single chair, now "represented" the summer house of Johan and Marianne. Almost every trace of a photographic "reality"—real changes of clothing, the actual passage of time during the long night, the couple's lovemaking, the "ingrained routine" of their final breakfast together—had been resolutely trimmed from the scene, leaving only the intensified emotional reality of the human confrontation as its focus. Marianne and Johan each appeared to be defined by a single, overriding objective—she by her determination to keep him from leaving, he by his need to summon the courage to make a final break. The "real" world outside no longer had any bearing on their lonely and isolated struggle. Even the figure of Paula had become, through heavy and repeated cutting in Johan's lengthy descriptions of her and her sexual powers, only the shadowy occasion for the confrontation, rather than its true cause.

After Johan has left, Marianne makes a distraught telephone call to someone she believes to be a friend. This is the second and the last time in the play (apart from a brief call for a taxi that never arrives) when we actually see her attempt to communicate with the world outside—the other occasion is her faint-hearted telephone call to her mother in the first scene. In both cases the result is exactly the same—a demonstration of the folly of ever expecting to be able to communicate openly and truthfully with other people. Fredrik, the friend who has betrayed her trust, tries in the film to call back after she has slammed the receiver down in a rage. In the play, even this does not happen.

The second half of the drama consists of three scenes in which the characters wander through the wreckage of their broken marriage. They wander entirely alone, moreover, without encountering any of the figures who populate this section of the film version—David, the unseen lover who calls Marianne while Johan is visiting her, the night watchman who nearly catches them making love in Johan's office, Marianne's newly widowed mother, and Eva, the mistress Johan throws over in order to pursue his new affair with Marianne. Trapped instead in an essential aloneness, the pair seems consigned to a hell of the sort that Johan describes (in the filmscript but *not* in the play, from which a great many such "Bergmanesque" reflections have been excised)—"a place where no one believes in solutions any more." The conclusion toward which the drama moves is accordingly much more ambiguous and much darker than it appeared to be in the work's earlier cinematic form.

"The Reunion" is hardly a reunion at all. Bergman has described this painful and clumsy meeting of the estranged couple as a mixture of reconciliation and aggressiveness. "For brief moments they reach one another through isolation and aloofness," he writes. "Everything is fragile, infected, ragged." The stage production added the ironic touch that, despite all their talk about new haircuts and hairdos and Marianne's new red dress, absolutely nothing about either of them had changed visibly. The furniture, too, was the same, arranged in yet another configuration. The atmosphere of strain and distrust in the scene was accentuated by the fact that even the superficial sense of contact provided in the film by their eating of a meal together was now denied them. The passionate attempt that Johan makes to achieve sexual contact with Marianne was, under these painful circumstances, doomed to fail. In turn, her eager, intellectual effort to reach him by reading aloud from her diary was inevitably destined to put Hallhuber's perpetually weary and boyishly bewildered Johan soundly to sleep, both in a literal and a metaphoric sense. Finally they agree that he should stay the night—but there this inconclusive encounter ends, stripped of the conciliatory bedroom scene that is one of the many incidents in the film that makes it, as Bergman himself remarks, ultimately "weaker, in a way, much more tender" than the play.

In Johan's dreary, inhospitable office at the Psychotechnical Institute (same furniture, placed in a new pattern) the divorce papers are at last signed by Johan and Marianne—but not before they make a savage and nearly successful effort to destroy one another, physically and mentally. In this climactic scene of unmasking, the two "emotional illiterates" suddenly find themselves engulfed by "all the aggressions, all the hate, all the mutual boredom and rage they have been suppressing for years." The unsettling revelation of just how short the distance is from banal normality to utter chaos is perhaps Bergman's most forceful dramatic coup, both in the play and in the film.

In the stage production, the illusion of physical reality was again attenuated in several different ways by an interposed sense of critical distance that, paradoxically, drew the inner emotional turmoil of the characters that much closer to the audience. The contestants in this life-and-death struggle were seen almost always in deliberately horizontal, two-dimensional figure compositions, and this caused their subtly choreographed moves of approach and withdrawal to stand out in heightened relief, etched against a depthless background. Marianne's dispassionate seduction of Johan crackled with brittle irony; she simply got down on the floor and straddled him for a moment, as he dryly announced to the audience, "For the first time in Johan and Marianne's small, furiously

discussed sex life, they did it on the rug." The unseen beating that Johan
inflicts on her later was likewise able—as Bergman well realized—to
convey a far more vicious and frightening impression of reality than any
conventional stage fight could possibly have done.

The reality of the scene was thus a psychological and emotional one,
fueled in this performance by Gaby Dohm's fiercely aggressive mental
counterattack on her lover-adversary. After their interlude of "lovemaking" had reassured her, as it were, that she no longer had anything to
fear from her emotions on that count, the tables turned. She took over
Johan's place at the desk—and, by implication, the dominant position in
the conflict as well. His pessimistic recital of the setbacks life had dealt
him was met by her with angry contempt: "Do you know what I think,
Johan? I'm in the process of becoming free from you." His attempt to
regain ground through an open declaration of his own suppressed hatred
of her elicited a savage outburst of the rage that had been pent up within
her virtually from the beginning: "When I think of what I endured and
what I've at last broken free from, I could scream. *Never again, never
again, never again.*" The final and decisive humiliation of her opponent
followed swiftly, with her accusation that Johan had in reality never
wanted a divorce at all, and her charge was borne out by his baffled and
tearful admission: "Is it a crime? I confess I'm beaten. Is *that* what you
want to hear?" This moment of utter humiliation seemed to mirror other
similar moments in the trilogy—the ignominious collapse of Jean, the
lackey with no last name, in the face of Julie's contemptuous attack; the
capitulation of Torvald Helmer, the husband whose supposed moral superiority had turned to dust in his hands, before Nora's furious onslaught.

As so often happens in the Bergman scheme of things, the victor very
quickly became the victim. The battering of Marianne came as a desperate reaction on Johan's part, a tormented and futile gesture of reprisal.
After it, the divorce papers were rapidly signed, in bitter silence. Marianne's often-quoted concluding remark—"We should have started fighting long ago. It would have been much better"—was ultimately cut from
the play, lest it convey a false impression that something definitive (even
cathartic) has finally been achieved. It has not been. The conclusion of
this scene in the play is as open and suspended as the ending of the last
movement of *A Doll's House*—a scene that it resembles in many respects.

"In reality, these scenes from a marriage could end here, with the
signing of the divorce papers," Johan tells the audience in the last of the
interludes. "But we would like to perform an epilogue." There is much
literal truth in this statement. The play could indeed have ended following the brutal confrontation in Johan's office—and, shortly before the
opening, Bergman had actually made up his mind to let it do just that,
until the pleas of his actors persuaded him to retain the conciliatory final

scene. The anecdote helps to illustrate the degree to which the artistic vision that underlies the new stage version of the work has darkened.

The play's brief epilogue goes some distance toward dispelling the darkness, it is true—but it does not go nearly as far in that direction as the corresponding episode in the film, from which its essence was extracted. In that episode, which Bergman gave the evocative title "In the Middle of the Night in a Dark House Somewhere in the World," Johan and Marianne had begun to change and to become what their creator calls "citizens of the world of reality in quite a different way than before." They are shown coping in a mature, adult way with life and people around them; their new love affair together is thus presumed to rest on the much firmer basis of their newly acquired self-knowledge. Nothing of the kind is seen in the rewritten epilogue, however, where the pair, glimpsed for one muted and poignant moment together, seem very much alone in their dark house. On the stage a bright spotlight picked the double bed, in which the entire scene was played, out of the shadowy darkness that surrounded it. Johan tells Marianne that he has now come to terms with his limitations and his weakness: "This makes me kind and a bit mournful." She (the would-be politician!) tells him of her newly found ability to regard the vicissitudes and even the meaninglessness of life with equanimity: "Unlike you, I endure it all. And enjoy doing it." But beneath all their brave talk lurks an anxiety that is manifested in Marianne's terrifying nightmare of sinking in soft sand, without hands, unable to reach those dearest to her—an anxiety bred of the nagging suspicion that utter confusion ("Fear, uncertainty, folly. I mean confusion") may, after all, be the inescapable condition of all human existence.

Perhaps these sufferers have come through the worst and survived it—though only barely. But perhaps there is worse yet to come. At any rate Marianne, the stronger of the two, is still, as Bergman reminds us, "trying to figure out what Nora has already told us a hundred years ago" about standard roles and set patterns. "A change has only begun to set in—just the beginnings of a change. We have taken a step, but only a very small one."

Henrik Ibsen

NORA

Stage version of *A Doll's House* by Ingmar Bergman
Stage design by Gunilla Palmstierna-Weiss
Musical arrangement by Rudolf G. Knabl
Costumes by Charlotte Flemming

Torvald Helmer, *a lawyer*.....................................Robert Atzorn

Nora, *his wife* .... Rita Russek

Mrs. Linde... Annemarie Wernicke

Nils Krogstad, *a lawyer*...Gerd Anthoff

Doctor Rank .... Horst Sachtleben

Directed by Ingmar Bergman
Premiere 30 April 1981

CHARACTERS

Torvald Helmer, *a lawyer*

Nora, *his wife*

Mrs. Linde

Nils Krogstad, *a lawyer*

Doctor Rank

The action takes place in Helmer's home.

(A sofa, an armchair, a decorated Christmas tree in the background. Scattered on the floor are packages and toys—a helmet and sword, two large dolls, a locomotive.)

Scene 1

NORA: Come here, Torvald, and I'll show you all the things I've bought.

HELMER: Don't disturb me! (*Enters.*) Bought, did you say? All this?

NORA: But, Torvald, surely this year we can be a little extravagant. This is the first Christmas when we haven't had to skimp and save.

HELMER: We can't begin squandering money, you know.

NORA: Oh yes, Torvald, surely we can squander a little bit now. Can't we? Just a tiny little bit? You're going to get a big salary now and make lots and lots of money.

HELMER: Yes, but not until the New Year. And there'll be three whole months before the first paycheck comes in.

NORA: Never mind. We'll borrow in the meantime.

HELMER: Nora! Just suppose I went out and borrowed a thousand kroner, and you spent all of it during Christmas week, and then on New Year's Eve a roof tile fell and hit me on the head, and there I lay . . .

NORA: If a horrible thing like that ever did happen, I wouldn't care whether I had debts or not.

HELMER: And what about the people I had borrowed from?

NORA: Them? Who cares about them? They're just strangers.

HELMER: Nora, Nora, now be serious, Nora. You know how I feel about that sort of thing. No debts! Never borrow! There's always something oppressive, something ugly too, about a home that's built on credit and borrowed money. The two of us have held up bravely until now, and we'll go on doing it for the short while we still have to.

NORA: Yes, yes, whatever you say, Torvald.

HELMER: (*Takes out his wallet.*) Nora, what do you suppose I have here?

NORA: Money!

HELMER: There, you see. Good heavens, of course I realize it costs a lot to run a house at Christmastime.

NORA: (*Counting the bills.*) Ten—twenty—thirty—forty. Oh thank you, Torvald, thank you. I'll make this go a long way.

HELMER: And now, tell me what my little spendthrift has thought of for herself.

NORA: What, for me? I don't want anything.

HELMER: Of course you do. Come on, tell me. Name something within reason that you'd like to have.

NORA: No, I really don't. But listen, Torvald . . .

HELMER: Yes?

NORA: If you want to give me something, you could—you could . . .

HELMER: Come on, let's have it.

NORA: You could give me money, Torvald. Only as much as you think you can spare. Then I could buy something for it one of these days.

HELMER: But, Nora . . .

NORA: Oh yes, Torvald, please do. Please. Then I'll wrap the money in pretty gold paper and hang it on the Christmas tree. Wouldn't that be fun? And then I'll have time to decide what I need most. That makes good sense, doesn't it?

HELMER: Yes, certainly it does. Provided you really could hold on to the money I give you and really did buy something for yourself with it. But it just gets used for housekeeping and for all sorts of useless things, and then I have to fork out all over again.

NORA: But, Torvald . . .

HELMER: No good denying it, my sweet little Nora. My little songbird is adorable, but it uses up unbelievable amounts of money. Incredible how expensive it is for a man to keep a little songbird like that.

NORA: How can you say a thing like that? I save everyplace I possibly can.

HELMER: Truer words were never spoken. Everyplace you *can*. The problem is, you can't. (*Laughs, wants to leave.*)

NORA: You haven't forgotten to invite Doctor Rank, have you?

HELMER: No need. It's taken for granted he'll be having dinner with us. I've ordered a good wine. Nora, you have no idea how much I'm looking forward to this evening.

NORA: So am I. And the children will be so happy, Torvald!

HELMER: Oh, what a marvelous feeling it is to have gotten a safe, solid position. With a comfortable income. It's nice to think about, isn't it?

NORA: Oh, it's wonderful!

(*A final kiss.*)

Scene 2

(*As* NORA *arranges packages around the Christmas tree,* MRS. LINDE *enters, like a shadow, veiled and dressed in black.*)

MRS. LINDE: Hello, Nora.

NORA: Hello . . .

MRS. LINDE: You don't recognize me.

NORA: No—I'm not sure . . . but wait—of course—why, Christine! Is it really you?

MRS. LINDE: Yes, it's me.

NORA: Christine! To think I didn't recognize you at once! But then how could I—you've changed so much, Christine!

MRS. LINDE: Yes, I suppose I have. In nine, ten long years—

NORA: Has it been that long since we've seen one another? Yes, you're right.

MRS. LINDE: (*Pause.*) I arrived this morning by steamer.

NORA: Oh, please take off your things. Or are you cold? (*Takes her hands.*) Yes, now you seem like your old self again. It was just that first moment. But you are a little paler, Christine—and maybe a little thinner.

MRS. LINDE: And much, much older, Nora.

NORA: Yes, perhaps a little bit older; just a tiny, little bit; not very much at all. Dear, sweet Christine, can you forgive me?

MRS. LINDE: What do you mean, Nora?

NORA: Poor Christine, you've become a widow.

MRS. LINDE: Yes, three years ago.

NORA: Oh, I knew it; I saw it in the paper. Oh, Christine, you must believe me, I often wanted to write to you at the time, but I always kept postponing it, and something always interfered.

MRS. LINDE: Nora dear, I understand very well.

NORA: No, it was dreadful of me. Poor Christine, what you must have gone through. And he left you nothing to live on?

MRS. LINDE: No.

NORA: And no children?

MRS. LINDE: No.

NORA: Nothing at all, then?

"Yes, now you seem like your old self again." Annemarie Wernicke as Mrs. Linde and Rita Russek as Nora.

MRS. LINDE: Not even a sense of grief or loss to sustain me.

NORA: But, Christine, how can that be?

MRS. LINDE: Oh, it happens sometimes, Nora.

NORA: All alone like that. How terribly hard that must be for you. I have three wonderful children. You can't see them right now, because they're out with the maid. But now you must tell me everything—

MRS. LINDE: No, no, no. Tell me about yourself instead.

NORA: No, you begin. Today I'm not going to be selfish. Today I want to think only about you. There is *one* thing I must tell you, though. Have you heard about the great stroke of good luck we've just had?

MRS. LINDE: No. What is it?

NORA: Can you imagine, my husband has been made manager of the Cooperative Bank!

MRS. LINDE: Oh . . .

52

NORA: Oh, you can believe we're happy! He takes over at the bank right after New Year's, and then he'll draw a huge salary and plenty of commission. Our life will be completely different from now on—we can do just as we please. How nice it will be to have lots of money and not have to worry about things. Won't it?

MRS. LINDE: At least it must be nice to have enough for the necessities.

NORA: No, not just for necessities, but really and truly lots of money.

MRS. LINDE: Nora, Nora, have you still not learned to be sensible? At school you always were the great spendthrift.

NORA: Yes, that's what Torvald keeps saying. (*Wagging her finger in imitation.*) But "Nora, Nora" isn't as foolish as all of you think. Why, we certainly haven't any money that I could squander. We've both had to work.

MRS. LINDE: You, too?

NORA: Yes, needlework, crocheting, embroidery, and things like that— (*Casually.*) and other things, too. I suppose you know that Torvald left the civil service when we got married. There was no opening for a promotion in his department, and obviously he needed to earn more money than before. But during that first year he exhausted himself completely. Worked day and night at all kinds of extra jobs. He couldn't stand the strain, and in the end he became dangerously ill. The doctors said it was essential for him to travel south.

MRS. LINDE: Yes, you spent a whole year in Italy.

NORA: That's right. But it was no easy matter to get away, believe me. Ivar had just been born. But naturally we had to go. Oh, it was an absolutely wonderful trip. And it saved Torvald's life. But it cost an awful lot of money, Christine.

MRS. LINDE: I can well imagine.

NORA: Four thousand eight hundred kroner. That's a very great deal of money, let me tell you.

MRS. LINDE: Well, at least in a situation like that, it's a lucky thing you had it.

NORA: Well, we got it from Papa, you see.

MRS. LINDE: I see. That must have been just before his death.

NORA: Yes, Christine. And just to think, I couldn't even go to him and take care of him. Here I was, expecting Ivar any day. And I had to look after my poor, deathly ill Torvald besides.

MRS. LINDE: I know how much you loved your father. So after that you left for Italy?

NORA: Yes, then we had the money, you see, and the doctors kept insisting. So we left about a month later.

MRS. LINDE: And your husband came back completely cured?

NORA: Sound as a bell! Oh God, oh God, isn't it a glorious thing to be alive and to be happy, Christine!—Oh, but how horrid of me—here I go on talking only about myself. Please don't be angry with me! Tell me, is it really true that you didn't love your husband? Why did you agree to marry him, then?

MRS. LINDE: My mother was still alive at the time; she was bedridden and helpless. Besides that, I had my two younger brothers to look after. I felt I had no right to refuse his offer.

NORA: No, no, you were right—. I suppose he was wealthy at the time?

MRS. LINDE: He was fairly well off, I think. But his business dealings were risky, Nora. When he died, everything collapsed and I was left with nothing.

NORA: And then—?

MRS. LINDE: Well, then I had to make ends meet with a small shop and a little teaching and whatever else I could think of. These past three years have been like one endless and wearisome workday for me. Now it's all over, Nora. Mother doesn't need me any longer, she passed away. And the boys don't either—they both have jobs now and can take care of themselves.

NORA: What a relief you must feel—

MRS. LINDE: No, only an unspeakable emptiness. No one to take care of anymore. That's the reason I couldn't stand it any longer, up there in that little backwater. At least here it must be easier to find something to keep me busy and fill my thoughts. If only I were lucky enough to find a steady job, some office work—

NORA: Oh, but Christine, that's so terribly strenuous and you already look so exhausted as it is. You'd be better off going to some health spa for a rest.

MRS. LINDE: I have no father to give me money for the trip, Nora.

NORA: Oh, please don't be angry with me.

MRS. LINDE: Dear Nora, don't *you* be angry with me. The worst thing about my kind of situation is the sense of bitterness it brings with it. There's no one left to work for, and yet you can't just sit around with your hands in your lap. You have to live, and so you grow selfish. When you were telling me the good news about your own change of fortune— would you believe it?—I was less happy for your sake than for my own.

NORA: What do you mean? Oh, I understand. Because you think Torvald might be able to do something for you.

MRS. LINDE: Yes, that's what I was thinking.

NORA: And so he will. Just leave it to me. Oh, I do so much want to help you.

MRS. LINDE: How kind of you to take such trouble for my sake, Nora—doubly kind because you yourself know so little of the hardships and sorrows life can bring.

NORA: You're just like the others. You all think I'm incapable of anything serious—that I haven't faced any of life's difficulties.

MRS. LINDE: Nora dear, you told me just now about all your troubles.

NORA: Oh, well—I haven't told you the main thing.

MRS. LINDE: Which main thing? What are you talking about?

NORA: I told you about the trip to Italy. Torvald wouldn't have gotten over his illness if he hadn't gone there.

MRS. LINDE: And your father gave you the money you needed.

NORA: Yes, that's what Torvald thinks, and what everyone else thinks, too; but—

MRS. LINDE: But—?

   (*Pause.*)

NORA: Papa didn't give us a penny. I raised the money myself.

MRS. LINDE: You? The entire sum?

NORA: Four thousand eight hundred kroner. What do you have to say to that?

MRS. LINDE: But how, Nora, how could you? Did you win in the lottery?

NORA: In the lottery? *That* wouldn't take any skill.

MRS. LINDE: You couldn't have borrowed it.

NORA: Really? Why not?

MRS. LINDE: Because a wife can't borrow without her husband's consent.

NORA: Oh, when the wife has a little business sense—and knows what's what.

MRS. LINDE: But Nora, I don't understand a word of this—

NORA: And you don't have to either. Besides, who says I borrowed the money. Perhaps I got it from some admirer or other. When somebody's as good-looking as I am—

MRS. LINDE: You're crazy.

NORA: (*Laughing.*) And now you're dying of curiosity, Christine.

MRS. LINDE: Now listen to me, Nora dear—you haven't done anything foolish, have you?

NORA: Is it foolish to save your husband's life?

MRS. LINDE: I think it's foolish of you to act without his knowledge—

NORA: But the whole idea was for him not to know! My God, don't you understand that? He couldn't even be told how dangerously ill he really was.

MRS. LINDE: And didn't your husband find out from your father that the money hadn't come from him?

NORA: No, no. Papa died just at that time.

MRS. LINDE: And you never told your husband the truth afterward?

NORA: No, for God's sake, what gives you that idea? He's terribly strict about things like that. And besides—Torvald with his manly pride—how hurt and humiliated he'd be to find out he owed me anything.

MRS. LINDE: Won't you ever tell him, then?

NORA: Yes—perhaps someday—many years from now, when I'm no longer so attractive. (MRS. LINDE *laughs.*) You needn't laugh at that! I mean of course, when I'm not so much fun for him any more. Then perhaps it's a good idea to have something in reserve. (*Pause.*) Silly nonsense! That time will never come.—Now, what do you think of my great secret, Christine? Aren't I good for something after all? Believe me, this whole thing has caused me plenty of worry. It hasn't by any means been easy for me to meet my payments on time. In the business world, you see, they have something called quarterly interest and then something called—(*Searches for the word,* MRS. LINDE *supplies it simultaneously.*) amortization. And the money is always terribly hard to raise. I've had to economize everywhere I could. Every time Torvald gave me money for clothes and things, I never used more than half of it. I always bought the simplest and least expensive outfits. But it was often hard on me, Christine. After all, it is nice to be well-dressed. Don't you think so?

MRS. LINDE: Oh, yes.

NORA: Well, I found other sources of income, too. Last winter I was lucky enough to get a lot of copying work to do. So every night I shut myself in and sat copying till all hours. Oh, I often felt so tired, so tired. But it was great fun all the same—working like that and making money. It was almost like being a man. (*Emphatic laughter.*)

MRS. LINDE: But how much have you been able to pay off like that?

NORA: Oh, I don't really know exactly. Accounts like that are hard to keep track of, you see. All I do know is that I've paid out everything I can scrape together. Many a time I had no idea which way to turn. (*Smiles.*) Then I'd sit here pretending to myself that a rich old gentleman had fallen in love with me—and now he was dead. And when his will was opened, they found written there in big letters: "All my money is to be paid at once, in cash, to the charming Mrs. Nora Helmer." —>Oh God, isn't it marvelous, Christine! To be carefree! Without a care, not having a care in the world. And soon spring will come with its big, blue sky. And then maybe we can travel a little. Maybe I'll be able to see the ocean once more. Oh yes, oh yes, it's truly wonderful to be alive and to be happy.

Scene 3

(KROGSTAD *appears on the stage. Strong reaction on the part of* MRS. LINDE, *who sees him first.*)

NORA: You? What is it?

KROGSTAD: Bank business—of a sort. I have a small position in the Co-operative Bank, and your husband is to be our new manager, I hear—

NORA: So it's . . .

KROGSTAD: Strictly cut-and-dried business, Mrs. Helmer, nothing more.

NORA: Well, then please be good enough to go into his office.

   (KROGSTAD *scuttles across the stage and exits.*)

NORA: Do you know that man?

MRS. LINDE: I knew him once—years ago. He was a clerk in a law office in our town for a while.

NORA: Yes, that's right.

MRS. LINDE: How he's changed.

NORA: He was very unhappily married, I understand.

MRS. LINDE: And now he's a widower?

NORA: With several children.

MRS. LINDE: They say he's involved in all kinds of business, don't they?

NORA: Oh? Could well be, I don't know. But let's not talk about business. That's so boring.

   (RANK *appears.*)

RANK: Oh, forgive me. Am I intruding?

NORA: No, not in the least. Doctor Rank. Mrs. Linde.

(*As the others talk,* NORA *quickly removes her apron, adjusts her dress, and smooths her hair.*)

RANK: A name often heard in this house. I believe I passed you on the stairs.

MRS. LINDE: Yes, the stairs are difficult for me. I have to take them slowly.

RANK: Oh, a small internal defect.

MRS. LINDE: More a matter of overexertion, really.

RANK: Nothing else? And so I presume you've come here to recuperate in a whirlwind of parties.

MRS. LINDE: I've come here to look for work.

RANK: Is that an approved remedy for overexertion?

MRS. LINDE: One has to live, Doctor.

RANK: Yes, it appears to be the common opinion that one must.

NORA: Now, Doctor Rank.—You're eager to keep on living, too.

(*She leads him to the armchair, where he sits.*)

RANK: Naturally. No matter how miserable I feel, I want to go on suffering as long as possible. My patients are no different. And with the morally ill, it's just the same. There's a moral cripple like that in with Helmer at this very moment.

MRS. LINDE: Ah!

NORA: Whom do you mean?

RANK: A certain lawyer called Krogstad. You wouldn't know him. Someone whose character is rotten to the core, dear lady. But even he began by talking about how utterly essential it was for him to *live.*

NORA: Oh? What does he want with Torvald?

RANK: I really don't know, except that I heard something said about the Cooperative Bank.

NORA: I had no idea that Krog—that this lawyer named Krogstad had anything to do with the bank.

RANK: Yes, he's got some kind of job there.

(NORA, *lost in thought, laughs quietly and claps her hands.*)

RANK: What are you laughing at?

NORA: Tell me this, Doctor Rank. Will all the people employed in the bank be dependent on Torvald now?

RANK: Is that what you find so immensely comical?

NORA: Yes, I really do find it immensely amusing that we—that Torvald
has so much power now over so many people. (*Takes a bag of macaroons
from behind a sofa pillow.*) Doctor Rank, what about a little macaroon?

RANK: Just look at that. Macaroons. I thought they were outlawed here.

NORA: True, but Christine bought me these.

MRS. LINDE: What? I—?

NORA: Now now, you had no way of knowing that Torvald had forbidden
them. It's because he's afraid they will ruin my teeth. Never mind—
just this once. Doctor Rank? There! (*Pops a macaroon into his mouth.*)
And you too, Christine. And I'll have one, too—just a small one—or
two at the most. There, now I really am fabulously happy. Now there's
only one thing in the world I have an awful desire to do.

RANK: And what's that?

NORA: I have an awful desire to say something—so Torvald could hear
it, too.

RANK: And why can't you say it?

NORA: I don't dare, because it's bad.

MRS. LINDE: Bad?

"What about a little macaroon?" Rita Russek (Nora) with Horst Sachtleben (Doctor Rank).

RANK: In front of us it's all right, though. What is it you have such a desire to say so Torvald hears it?

NORA: I have an awful desire to say—(*Jumps up on the sofa for her declaration.*)—Kiss my arse!

RANK: (*Laughing.*) Why Nora!

MRS. LINDE: (*Laughing.*) Say it. Here he comes.

(HELMER *appears.*)

NORA: Shhh, shhh, shhh! (*Hands the bag of macaroons to* RANK, *who hides it in his pocket.*) Now, Torvald dear, did you finally get rid of him?

HELMER: Yes, he's gone now.

NORA: May I introduce you—this is Christine, who's just arrived.

HELMER: Christine—? Forgive me, I don't think I know—

NORA: Mrs. Linde, Torvald dear. Mrs. Christine Linde.

HELMER: Ah yes. Presumably a childhood friend of my wife's?

MRS. LINDE: Yes, we knew each other back in the old days.

NORA: And just think, now she's made the long trip here especially to talk to you.

HELMER: I'm not sure I understand.

MRS. LINDE: Well, actually . . .

NORA: The point is, Christine is exceptionally clever at office work, and so she's been very eager to come under the direction of a capable man who can teach her more than what she already knows.

HELMER: Very sensible, Mrs. Linde.

NORA: And when she heard you had been named bank manager—it was in all the papers—then she hurried here as fast as she could and . . . You will, Torvald, won't you? Do something for Christine, for my sake?

HELMER: Yes, that's not at all inconceivable. I presume you're a widow, Mrs. Linde?

MRS. LINDE: Yes.

HELMER: And you have experience in office work.

MRS. LINDE: Yes, quite a lot.

HELMER: Very well, then it's highly probable I can find a place for you—

NORA: You see, you see!

HELMER: You come at an opportune moment, Mrs. Linde.

MRS. LINDE: Oh, how can I thank you—?

HELMER: No need to. (*Puts on his overcoat.*) But today I must ask you to excuse me—

"You will, Torvald, won't you?" Nora asks Helmer (Robert Atzorn), as Mrs. Linde (Wernicke) and Doctor Rank (Sachtleben) look on.

RANK: I'll come with you.

NORA: Don't be long, Torvald dear.

HELMER: An hour at the most.

(*As the two men leave,* RANK *gestures to* NORA *and quickly passes her the bag of macaroons.*)

NORA: Must you go too, Christine?

MRS. LINDE: Yes, now I must get out and look for a room for myself.

NORA: What a shame we're so cramped here, but it just isn't possible for us to . . .

MRS. LINDE: Please don't give it another thought! Good-bye, Nora dear, and thank you for everything.

NORA: Good-bye for now. Of course you'll join us this evening.

(MRS. LINDE *leaves.*)

Scene 4

(*Faint, distant music.* NORA, *left alone, sits dejectedly on the sofa. The music stops, and she is startled to find* KROGSTAD *standing before her.*)

KROGSTAD: Excuse me, Mrs. Helmer.

NORA: My husband is not at home, Mr. Krogstad.

KROGSTAD: I know.

NORA: Then—what do you want here?

KROGSTAD: I want a word with you.

NORA: You want a word with me?

KROGSTAD: That's right.

NORA: Today? But it's not the first of the month yet—

KROGSTAD: No, it's Christmas Eve. And it's up to you how merry your Christmas will be.

NORA: What is it you want? Today I couldn't possibly . . .

KROGSTAD: Let's leave that aside for the moment. This concerns something else. You have a few moments to spare, I hope?

NORA: Oh yes, of course, I suppose so, although—
   (*Pause.*)

KROGSTAD: Mrs. Helmer, will you be good enough to use your influence on my behalf?

NORA: (*Sits in the armchair.*) But how? What do you mean?

KROGSTAD: Will you be good enough to see to it that I keep my modest position at the bank?

NORA: What are you talking about? Who wants to take away your position?

KROGSTAD: Oh, with me you don't have to pretend innocence. I'm well aware that your friend would find it unpleasant to encounter me at the bank. And now I realize, too, whom I have to thank for my dismissal.

NORA: But I assure you . . .

KROGSTAD: Yes, yes, yes, the point is this: there's still time, and I advise you to use your influence to prevent it.

NORA: (*Sits up, coldly.*) But I *have* no influence, Mr. Krogstad.

KROGSTAD: I don't think our new bank manager is any less susceptible than most husbands.

NORA: Speak disparagingly about my husband and I'll show you the door.

(*Pause.*)

KROGSTAD: The good lady has courage.

NORA: I'm not afraid of you any longer. Come the New Year, I'll soon be done with this whole thing.

KROGSTAD: Now listen to me, Mrs. Helmer! If need be, I'm prepared to fight for my little job at the bank the same way I'd fight for my life. Not just for the sake of the salary; that concerns me least. It has to do with something else.—You see, like everybody else you know that some years ago I was guilty of an indiscretion.

NORA: I believe I've heard something of the kind.

KROGSTAD: The case never came to court, but suddenly all roads were closed to me. So I turned to the kind of business transactions you know about. But now there has to be an end to all that. My sons are growing up. Now I must try to regain my good name—for their sakes. My job at the bank was the first step up the ladder, as it were. And now your husband wants to kick me back down into the mud.

NORA: For God's sake, Krogstad, there's absolutely nothing I'm able to do to help you.

KROGSTAD: No, because you don't want to. But I have the means to compel you.

NORA: You wouldn't tell my husband I owe you money, would you?

KROGSTAD: Hmm—and what if I did tell him?

NORA: That would be a disgraceful thing to do. To have my secret—the source of my joy and my pride—to have it revealed to him in such a crude and ugly way—by *you*. You'd expose me to the most terrible unpleasantness—

KROGSTAD: Merely unpleasantness?

NORA: But go right ahead. You'll get the worst of it, because then my husband will recognize you for the sort of man you really are, and then you'll never get your job back.

KROGSTAD: I asked you if it was only domestic unpleasantness you feared?

NORA: If my husband finds out, naturally he'll pay back the rest of the loan at once—and then we'll have nothing more to do with you.

KROGSTAD: Listen to me, Mrs. Helmer! I see I'd better explain the matter to you a little more carefully.

NORA: In what way?

KROGSTAD: When your husband became ill, you came to me and borrowed four thousand eight hundred kroner.

NORA: I had no other choice.

KROGSTAD: I promised to get the money for you—

NORA: And you got it.

KROGSTAD: I promised to get the money for you on the strength of a promissory note I drew up.

NORA: Yes, and I signed it.

KROGSTAD: Fine. But I added a clause in which your father guaranteed the loan. This clause was to be signed by your father.

NORA: He did sign it.

KROGSTAD: I left the date blank. In other words, your father was supposed to insert the date on which he signed the paper. Do you remember that, Mrs. Helmer?

NORA: Yes, I think so—

KROGSTAD: Then I gave you the promissory note so you could mail it to your father. Correct?

NORA: Yes.

KROGSTAD: And naturally you did so at once. Because after only five or six days, you brought this document back to me with your father's signature. And then you got the money.

NORA: Yes, yes—and haven't I made my payments promptly?

KROGSTAD: By and large, yes. (*Pause.*) But—to return to the topic of our conversation—that was a very difficult time for you, wasn't it?

NORA: Yes.

KROGSTAD: Your father was seriously ill, I believe.

NORA: He was dying.

KROGSTAD: And he passed away shortly afterward?

NORA: Yes.

KROGSTAD: Tell me, Mrs. Helmer, do you happen to recall the date of your father's death?

NORA: Papa died on the twenty-ninth of September.

KROGSTAD: Quite right. I've checked on it myself. And that's why I'm left with this curious circumstance I simply can't explain. (*Pause. He takes a paper from his pocket.*)

NORA: What circumstance? I don't know what—

(*Pause.*)

KROGSTAD: The fact, Mrs. Helmer, that your father signed this paper three days after his death.

(*Pause.*)

NORA: How? I don't understand—

KROGSTAD: Your father died on the twenty-ninth of September. But look here. Here your father has dated his signature the second of October. Isn't that strange, Mrs. Helmer? (NORA *remains silent.*) Can you explain it? (NORA *remains silent.*) Remarkable, too, that the words "October second" and the year are not written in your father's handwriting, but in another handwriting that I seem to recognize. Well, that could be explained. There's nothing seriously wrong in that. The signature itself is what matters. And that is genuine, isn't it, Mrs. Helmer? It really was your father who signed his name here?

NORA: (*Defiantly.*) No. *I* signed Papa's name.

(*Pause.*)

KROGSTAD: Listen to me, Mrs. Helmer—do you realize that's a dangerous admission to make?

NORA: Why? You'll soon have your money.

KROGSTAD: Answer me one question—why didn't you send the paper to your father?

NORA: That was impossible.

KROGSTAD: Then it would have been better if you had given up your trip abroad.

NORA: My husband's life depended on that trip. I couldn't give it up.

KROGSTAD: And you never took into consideration that you were swindling me?

NORA: I couldn't possibly consider that.

KROGSTAD: Mrs. Helmer, obviously you have no clear conception of what it is you're actually guilty of. But I can assure you that it was neither a greater nor a worse thing that I once did—and paid for with the loss of my reputation.

NORA: Are you trying to tell me that what you did was an act of courage to save your wife's life?

KROGSTAD: Laws aren't concerned with motives.

NORA: Then they must be very unfair laws.

KROGSTAD: Unfair or not—if I produce this paper in court, you'll be judged according to those laws.

NORA: (*Seated in the chair, very angry.*) You mean a daughter has no right to save her old, dying father from worry and anxiety? A wife has no right to save her husband's life? I don't know very much about laws, but I'm certain of this—somewhere in them it must say that such things are allowed. And you, who pretend to be a lawyer, don't know that? You must be a very inept lawyer, Mr. Krogstad.

KROGSTAD: Be that as it may. But business—the kind of business the two of us have had together—that I do understand. Or don't you think so? Very well. Do as you wish. But I'll tell you this much: If I go under a second time, you're going to keep me company.

   (KROGSTAD *leaves, and* NORA *is left alone.*)

Scene 5

(HELMER *enters, carrying papers. He draws* NORA *over to the sofa, where she sits on his lap.*)

HELMER: Has anyone been here?

NORA: Here? No.

HELMER: Strange. I saw Krogstad going out the front 'door.

NORA: Did you. Oh yes, that's true. Krogstad was here for a moment.

HELMER: Nora, I can see by looking at you that he's been here, pleading with you to put in a good word for him.

NORA: Yes.

HELMER: And you were supposed to pretend it was all your own idea? You weren't supposed to let on to me that he'd been here. Wasn't that what he asked you to do?

NORA: Yes, Torvald, but—

HELMER: Nora, Nora, how could you agree to such a thing? To talk to such a man in the first place, and promise him anything. And then, on top of it all, to tell me a lie!

NORA: A lie?

HELMER: You told me no one had been here. (*His arm around her waist.*) Isn't that so? Well, I knew anyway. (*Releases her.*) And now no more about that. (*Pats her on the behind, and leaves the stage with his papers. Pause.*)

NORA: (*Calls.*) Torvald!

HELMER: (*Calls back.*) Yes?

NORA: I'm really looking forward to the costume ball at the Stenborgs, the day after tomorrow.

HELMER: And I'm really curious to see what you're going to surprise me with.

NORA: I can't think of a thing that will do. Everything seems so foolish, so silly.

HELMER: Has my little Nora now come to *that* conclusion?

NORA: Are you very busy, Torvald?

HELMER: Umm.

NORA: What are those papers?

HELMER: Bank matters.

NORA: So soon?

HELMER: The retiring management has authorized me to make some necessary changes in staff and policy. I'll need Christmas week to finish it. I want everything to be in order by the first of the year.

NORA: So that's the reason this poor Krogstad—

HELMER: Hmm.

NORA: Torvald! If you weren't so busy, Torvald, I'd ask you to do me a terribly big favor.

HELMER: (*Comes back.*) Let's hear. What is it?

NORA: Nobody else has such good taste. And I do so much want to look pretty at the costume ball. Torvald, couldn't you take charge of me and decide what I should be and which costume I should come in?

HELMER: Ah, so now my little egoist is looking for a rescuer, is she?

NORA: Yes, Torvald, without your help I can't get anywhere.

HELMER: Very well, very well. I'll give the matter some thought. We'll come up with something.

NORA: Oh, how sweet of you. (*Pause.*) Tell me, was the crime this man Krogstad committed really so bad?

HELMER: He forged signatures. Have you any idea what that means?

NORA: Couldn't it have been because he was in need?

HELMER: Oh yes, or else because he was reckless, like so many others. I'm not so heartless that I'd condemn a man on account of one single act like that.

NORA: No, of course you wouldn't, Torvald!

HELMER: Plenty of men are able to regain their integrity, once they confess their crime and take the punishment.—But that wasn't the route Krogstad chose. He wriggled out of it by hook and by crook, and that's what's caused his moral downfall.

NORA: Do you really think that would—?

HELMER: (*Interrupts.*) Just imagine how a guilt-ridden individual like that has to lie and deceive and put on a false front for everyone, even for those closest to him, even for his own wife and children. And it's them, the children, who always suffer most, Nora.

NORA: Why?

HELMER: Because the stench of lies like that infects and poisons the very life of a family. Every breath the children take in such a house is tainted by the germs of something foul. (*Stretches out his hands to her.*) And so, my sweet little Nora must promise me not to plead for him. Your hand on it. Come, come, what's this? Give me your hand. There now. So that's settled. I assure you that I couldn't possibly have worked side by side with him. Just being near such a person literally makes me feel ill. (*He kisses her and starts to fondle her.*)

NORA: (*Quickly.*) It's so hot in here. And I have so much to do.

HELMER: Yes, that's right, and I must get some of this read before dinner. Besides, I also have to give some thought to your costume. And something to hang on the tree in gold paper—I may even take care of that, too.

(HELMER *strokes her cheek and departs with his papers.* NORA *is left alone, seated on the sofa.*)

A short pause in the action.

A round table and chairs are now on the stage.

Scene 6

(NORA, *standing in half light, bangs once or twice on a tambourine as she tries a dance step, then impatiently flings the tambourine aside. The lights come up, and* MRS. LINDE *appears.*)

MRS. LINDE: They said you were looking for me.

NORA: You simply must help me! You see, tomorrow evening the Stenborgs are holding a costume ball upstairs, and Torvald wants me to go as a Neapolitan peasant girl and dance the tarantella I learned on Capri.

MRS. LINDE: Oh, so you're going to give a real performance?

NORA: Yes, Torvald says I should. Look, here's the costume. Torvald had it made for me down there. But now it's so torn everywhere that I really don't know—

MRS. LINDE: That's easy to fix. It's just the trim that's come loose here and there. A needle and thread? Fine, here's just what we need.

NORA: It's very sweet of you.

MRS. LINDE: (*Sewing.*) Well, Nora, so you'll be in disguise tomorrow?— By the way, I've completely forgotten to thank you for yesterday evening.

NORA: Oh, I didn't think it was a cozy as usual last night.

MRS. LINDE: Tell me, is Doctor Rank always as depressed as he was yesterday?

NORA: No, it was especially noticeable last night. He has a very serious illness. His father, you see, was a pretty disgusting person who kept mistresses and all that. As a result, the son was sickly from birth. You understand. (*Pause.*)

MRS. LINDE: Does Doctor Rank come here every day?

NORA: Every single day. He's Torvald's oldest and best friend, you know. And he's *my* friend, too. Doctor Rank is almost one of the family.

   (*Pause.*)

MRS. LINDE: But tell me this—can that man really be trusted? I mean, he likes to flatter people, doesn't he?

NORA: Quite the contrary. What put that into your head?

MRS. LINDE: Yesterday when you introduced me to him, he declared that he'd often heard my name in this house; but afterward I noticed that your husband hadn't even the slightest idea who I was. So how could Doctor Rank . . . ?

NORA: But it's perfectly clear, Christine. Torvald is so terribly in love with me that, as he says, he wants me all to himself. When we were first married, he'd almost get jealous if I even mentioned any of my old friends from back home. So naturally I stopped doing it. But with Doctor Rank I can talk about *everything*.

MRS. LINDE: I'm going to tell you something: You ought to put a stop to all of this with Doctor Rank.

NORA: Put a stop to all of what?

MRS. LINDE: Both the one thing and the other, it seems to me. Yesterday you were talking about a rich admirer who'd give you money—

NORA: One who doesn't exist, more's the pity. So what?

MRS. LINDE: Is Doctor Rank wealthy?

NORA: Yes, he is.

MRS. LINDE: And has no one to look after?

NORA: No, no one, but—?

MRS. LINDE: And he comes here every day?

NORA: I've already told you that once.

MRS. LINDE: But how can someone so cultivated make such a nuisance of himself?

NORA: I don't understand you.

MRS. LINDE: Now don't pretend, Nora! Do you imagine I haven't guessed who loaned you the four thousand eight hundred kroner?

NORA: Where could you have gotten such an idea! A friend of ours, who visits us every day! What a horribly embarrassing situation that would be!

MRS. LINDE: It really wasn't him, then?

NORA: No, absolutely not. It never even occurred to me.—Besides, he had no money to lend at the time. He inherited it later.

MRS. LINDE: Well, Nora dear, I think that was a lucky thing for you.

NORA: No, it would never have occurred to me to ask Doctor Rank— although I'm certain that if I did ask him . . .

MRS. LINDE: But of course you won't?

NORA: No, of course I won't. I can't imagine why it would be necessary. But I'm absolutely sure that if I did speak to Doctor Rank—

MRS. LINDE: Behind your husband's back?

NORA: (*Direct.*) When you pay off everything you owe, you get your promissory note back, don't you?

(*Pause.*)

MRS. LINDE: That goes without saying. Nora, you're hiding something from me.

NORA: Can you see that by looking at me?

MRS. LINDE: Something's happened since yesterday morning. Nora, what is it?

NORA: Christine! Shhh! Torvald's coming. Please go into the children's room for a little while. Let Anne-Marie give you a hand with that.

MRS. LINDE: All right, but I'm not leaving here before we've had an honest talk together.

(MRS. LINDE *leaves, taking the dress with her. The box containing the rest of the outfit is left on the table.*)

Scene 7

(HELMER *enters, carrying a portfolio.*)

NORA: Oh, how I've been *waiting* for you, Torvald dear!

HELMER: Was that the seamstress?

NORA: No, it's Christine—she's helping me get the costume ready. I'll make quite a splash with it, believe me.

HELMER: Yes, wasn't that a good idea I had?

NORA: Fabulous! But wasn't it nice of me, too, to let you have your way?

HELMER: Nice—that you let your husband have his way?—Never mind, I won't disturb you. You probably want to try things on.

NORA: And you've got work to do?

HELMER: Yes. (*Shows her a sheaf of papers.*) Just look. I've been down to the bank. (*Prepares to leave.*)

NORA: Torvald.

HELMER: Nora—is it that business from yesterday morning again?

NORA: Yes, Torvald. I'm begging you!

HELMER: And you actually have the nerve to bring that up once more?

NORA: Yes, yes, you *must* listen to me! You *must* let Krogstad keep his job at the bank!

HELMER: My dear Nora, his job is the one I'm giving to Mrs. Linde.

NORA: Yes, and that's terribly sweet of you. But you could just let someone else go instead of Krogstad. Just so long as it isn't Krogstad!

HELMER: What incredible obstinacy! You go and make a rash promise, and then I'm expected to . . .

NORA: That isn't why, Torvald. It's for your own sake. That man writes for the very worst kind of newspapers. He said so himself. He can cause you immense harm. I'm terrified to death of him—

HELMER: Ah, now I understand. You're frightened by old memories.

NORA: What do you mean by that?

HELMER: Of course, you're thinking about your father.

NORA: Yes. That's it. Just remember how those malicious people slandered Papa in the newspapers.

HELMER: My dear little Nora, there's a considerable difference between your father and me. Your father wasn't by any means above reproach in his work. But I am; and I hope I'll continue to be, for the rest of my career.

NORA: Oh, there's no way of knowing what evil minds may think of next. Now everything could be so perfect for us now. We could be so peaceful and contented in our quiet, carefree home—you and I and the children, Torvald! That's why I'm begging you like this—

HELMER: And the more you plead for him, the more impossible you make it for me to keep him. People at the bank already know that I'm getting rid of Krogstad. If word now gets around that the new manager has let his wife talk him out of it—

NORA: Yes, what of it—?

HELMER: You want me to make a fool of myself in front of the entire staff—give people the impression I'm swayed by every sort of outside influence? You can bet I'd soon be made to feel the consequences of that! Besides—there's something else that makes Krogstad's presence in the bank unthinkable as long as I'm its manager.

NORA: And what's that?

HELMER: His moral failings I could overlook, if need be—

NORA: Oh yes, couldn't you, Torvald?

HELMER: In fact he's quite capable, I've been told. (*Sits at the table across from Nora.*) But I've known him before. One of those rash friendships that one so often comes to regret later on in life. Well, I may as well come straight out and tell you—we're on first names with one another. And this tactless individual makes no effort whatsoever to conceal the fact when others are present. On the contrary—he seems to believe that it entitles him to a tone of continual familiarity, with his "Torvald this" and "Torvald that" the whole time. It's extremely embarrassing for me, let me tell you. He'd make my position in the bank intolerable.

NORA: Torvald, you can't be serious about all this.

HELMER: Oh no? Why not?

NORA: Surely those are only petty considerations.

HELMER: What did you say? Petty? So you find me petty!

NORA: No, quite the contrary, Torvald, and that's exactly why . . .

HELMER: No matter. You called my motives petty, so that must apply to me as well. Petty! Very well! (*Angrily, as he takes a letter from his portfolio, signs it, and places it in an envelope.*) Now I'll soon put an end to all this!

NORA: Torvald, what is that letter?

HELMER: Krogstad's dismisal. (*He seals the envelope.*)

NORA: You don't know what this can bring down on all of us.

HELMER: Nora dearest, I forgive you for this terror of yours, even though basically it's an insult to me. Oh yes, it is! Or maybe you think it isn't insulting to suggest that *I* should be afraid of a worn-out hack lawyer's revenge? But I forgive you all the same, because it's such a beautiful demonstration of your deep love for me. (*Holds her and rocks her gently as she cries helplessly.*) That's the way things ought to be, my own dearest Nora. Whatever may happen, I have courage and strength enough to face it when the time comes, believe me. I'm man enough to take it all upon myself, you'll see.

NORA: What do you mean?

HELMER: Everything, I tell you—

NORA: That's something you shall never, never do!

HELMER: (*Kisses her.*) Then we'll share it, Nora, as man and wife. That's how it should be. (*Pause.*) Happy, now? (*Drying her tears with his handkerchief.*) There, there, there—now you ought to rehearse your tarantella and practice the tambourine. I'll sit in my study with both doors closed, so I won't hear a thing. You can make as much noise as you please.

(HELMER *leaves.* NORA *remains seated at the table, absently fingering a string of beads from her costume.*)

Scene 8

(DOCTOR RANK *enters and, as he catches Nora's eye, kneels to her, his hand on his heart.* NORA *smiles at his courtly gesture.*)

NORA: Hello, Doctor Rank. Please, don't go into Torvald just yet. I think he's busy with something.

RANK: And you?

NORA: Oh, I always have time for you—you know that.

RANK: Many thanks. I'll take advantage of that as long as I can.

NORA: What do you mean by that? As long as you can?

RANK: Does that alarm you?

NORA: Yes, it's a strange thing to say. Is something about to happen?

RANK: Something I've long been prepared for. But I really never thought it would come so soon.

NORA: What is it? You must tell me, Doctor Rank!

RANK: These past few days I've taken a general audit of my internal accounts. Bankrupt!

NORA: What a horrible thing to say!

RANK: The thing itself is damned horrible, too. But the worst of it is all the other ugliness before it's over. I have one more test left to run; when that's finished, I'll know roughly how soon the disintegration will begin. (*Pause.*) There's something I want to say to you. Helmer has such a profound distaste for anything ugly. I don't want him at my bedside—

NORA: But Doctor Rank—

RANK: I won't have him there. That's final. I'll lock my door to him.

NORA: (*Kneeling in front of his chair.*) Dearest, dearest Doctor Rank, you mustn't die and leave us—Torvald and me.

RANK: Oh, that's a loss you'll soon get over. What's gone is quickly forgotten.

NORA: You think so?

RANK: People form new attachments, and then—

NORA: Who forms new attachments?

RANK: You yourself have already made a start, I'd say. Why else was this Mrs. Linde here last evening?

NORA: (*Laughing and crying.*) Aha—you don't mean to tell me you're jealous of poor Christine?

RANK: Of course I am! She'll be my successor in this house.

NORA: Good heavens, how impossible you are. (*Pause. She moves behind his chair and places her hands on his shoulders. Slowly he relaxes, closes his eyes, and rests his head against her.*) Now just be nice, Doctor Rank. Tomorrow you'll see how beautifully I'll dance; and then you must imagine that I'm dancing only for you—and for Torvald, too, of course— that goes without saying. Doctor Rank, I want to show you something.

RANK: What?

NORA: (*Covers his eyes with her hands, then runs a stocking across his closed eyelids.*) Silk stockings. (*Sits on the table edge.*) Aren't *they* lovely? It's so dark in here now, but tomorrow—(*Pause.* RANK *looks at her.*) Why are you looking so critical? Is it because you don't think they'll fit?

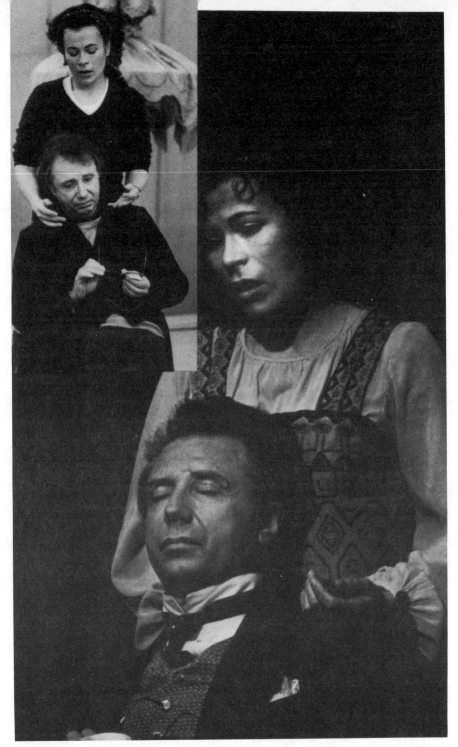

The same scene in rehearsal and performance. Nora (Russek) and Doctor Rank (Sachtleben). ". . . then you must imagine that I'm dancing only for you."

RANK: I couldn't possibly have an informed opinion about that.

NORA: Shame on you! (*A playful slap.*)

RANK: And now what other delights am I to be shown?

NORA: You won't be shown another thing, because you're indecent.

(*Long pause.*)

RANK: As we sit here together like this, talking so intimately, I can't imagine—no, I simply cannot conceive—what would have become of me if I'd never come into this house.

NORA: Yes, I really do think you like being here with us.

RANK: And now I have to leave it all—

NORA: You aren't going to leave.

RANK: —without being able to have left even the poorest token of gratitude behind.

(*Pause.*)

NORA: And if I were to ask you now—? No . . .

RANK: For what?

NORA: For a great proof of your friendship—

RANK: Yes?

NORA: No, I mean—for a terribly great favor—

RANK: Would you really, this once, give me that happiness?

NORA: Oh, you don't even know what it is.

RANK: All right, then tell me.

NORA: No, I can't, Doctor Rank—it's much too much to ask—advice and help and a favor—

RANK: The more the better. I haven't the slightest idea what you mean. So tell me. You trust me, don't you?

NORA: Of course I do, more than anyone else. You're my truest and best friend, I realize that. That's the reason I'm telling you this. All right, then, Doctor Rank: there's something you must help me to prevent. You know how deeply, how passionately Torvald loves me. He wouldn't hesitate for a moment to give up his life for my sake.

RANK: Nora—do you think he's the only one—who'd gladly give up his life for your sake?

(*Pause.*)

NORA: I see.

RANK: I promised myself you should know that before I'm gone. I'll never find a better opportunity.—Yes, Nora, now you know. And now you also know you can confide in me as in no one else.

NORA: Oh, dear Doctor Rank, that was really horrible of you.

RANK: That I've loved you as passionately as anyone? Was that horrible?

NORA: No, but that you had to blurt out and tell me. That was totally unnecessary.

RANK: What do you mean? Have you known—? Nora!

NORA: Oh, how can I say whether I knew or didn't know? I honestly can't tell you.—But for you to have been so clumsy, Doctor Rank! Just when everything was so good.

RANK: Well, at any rate you're now assured that I'm at your service, body and soul. So please, won't you tell me?

NORA: After this?

RANK: I'm begging you to tell me what it is!

NORA: You can't be told anything now.

RANK: You must. You must. You can't punish me this way. Let me do whatever is humanly possible for you.

NORA: Now there's nothing you can do for me.—Besides, I'm sure I won't need help anyway! It's all pure imagination—wait and see. Of course it is! Nothing else.—And what a fine gentleman you turned out to be, Doctor Rank. I hope you're ashamed of yourself?

RANK: No, not really. But maybe I ought to go—for good?

NORA: No, you mustn't do that. Naturally you must continue to visit us as always. Torvald can't do without you. You know that.

RANK: Yes, but you?

NORA: Oh, I always enjoy it immensely when you're here.

RANK: Many times I've had the feeling that you're fully as happy being with me as with Helmer.

NORA: Well, you see, there are those people you love most, and those people you most of all love to be with.

(RANK *strokes her cheek, then goes off to join Helmer.*)

Scene 9

NORA: (*Finds herself face to face with* KROGSTAD.) My husband is home.

KROGSTAD: What of it.

NORA: What do you want from me?

KROGSTAD: A little information.

NORA: Then be quick. What is it?

KROGSTAD: I assume you know I've received my dismissal?

NORA: I couldn't prevent it, Krogstad. I did everything in my power to help you. To no avail.

KROGSTAD: Does your husband love you so little? He knows what I can put you through, yet even so he . . .

NORA: What gives you the idea that he knows?

KROGSTAD: Oh no, I really didn't think so either. It wouldn't be like our old friend Torvald Helmer to show such courage—

NORA: Mr. Krogstad, I demand respect for my husband.

KROGSTAD: Why, of course, all due respect. But since you're now so anxious to keep it a secret, Mrs. Helmer, I dare say you know somewhat more than you did yesterday about what you've actually done?

NORA: More than *you* could ever teach me.

KROGSTAD: No doubt—a lawyer as inept as I am—

NORA: What is it you want with me?

KROGSTAD: Just to see how you're getting along, Mrs. Helmer. I've gone around all day thinking of you. Even a money lender, a crooked lawyer, a—even a man like me isn't entirely heartless, you know.

NORA: Then prove it—think of my small children.

KROGSTAD: Did you and your husband think of mine? But never mind that. I just came to tell you not to take this thing all too seriously. In the first place, I don't intend to prosecute.

NORA: No, you won't, will you! Oh, I knew it.

KROGSTAD: The whole affair can be settled quite amicably. No need to make it public. It won't go beyond the three of us.

NORA: My husband must never hear a word about this.

KROGSTAD: How can you prevent it? Are you by any chance able to repay the rest of the loan?

NORA: No, not right away.

KROGSTAD: Then perhaps you have some way of raising the money within the next few days?

NORA: No way I'd want to make use of.

KROGSTAD: It wouldn't have done you any good anyway. Even if you stood there with all the money and more in your hands, you still wouldn't be able to get your note back from me.

NORA: Then will you explain what you intend to do with it?

KROGSTAD: I'll just hold on to it—for safekeeping. No one else will know about it. So if you've been thinking of doing something desperate—

NORA: I have.

KROGSTAD: —if you should decide to leave your home and family—

NORA: I will!

KROGSTAD: —or if you should think of doing something worse—

NORA: How did you know that?

KROGSTAD: —then put it out of your mind.

NORA: How did you know I was thinking of *that*?

KROGSTAD: *That* is the first thing most of us think of. I thought of it, too. Though God knows I didn't have the courage—

NORA: I don't either.

KROGSTAD: No, of course not, you haven't the courage either. Have you?

NORA: I haven't. I haven't.

KROGSTAD: It would also be a great mistake. Once the first domestic hurricane passes—. I have a letter here in my pocket, for your husband—

NORA: Revealing everything?

KROGSTAD: As delicately as possible.

NORA: That letter must not reach him. Tear it up. I'll find some way to raise the money after all.

KROGSTAD: Pardon me, Mrs. Helmer, but I think I just told you—

NORA: Oh, I'm not talking about the money I owe you. Tell me how much you're demanding from my husband. I'll find enough to pay you.

KROGSTAD: I'm not demanding any money from your husband.

NORA: Then what is it you want?

KROGSTAD: I'll tell you. I want your husband to create a position for me—

NORA: He won't do it!

KROGSTAD: He'll do it. I know him. And once I'm there beside him, then you'll see! Within a year I'll be the manager's righthand man. And then it'll be Nils Krogstad and not Torvald Helmer who runs the bank.

NORA: You'll never see that day.

KROGSTAD: You mean you might—?

NORA: Now I have the courage for it. ←

"And remember this, your husband himself is the one who forced me." Gerd Anthoff as Korgstad and Rita Russek as Nora.

KROGSTAD: Under the ice, perhaps? Down in the freezing, coal-black
water? And then float up again in the spring, ghastly, unrecognizable,
without hair—

NORA: You don't frighten me.

KROGSTAD: Are you forgetting that whatever reputation you leave behind is still in my hands? (NORA *holds her hands over her mouth, speech-
less.*) Well, now you see the way things stand. Don't do anything foolish!
When Helmer gets my letter, I'll be expecting to hear from him. And
remember this, your husband himself is the one who forced me to take
this route again. I'll never forgive him for that. And so good-bye, Mrs.
Helmer.

(KROGSTAD *leaves. A letter is dropped into the mailbox.*)

Scene 10

NORA: (*Quiet, motionless.*) Torvald—now we're beyond help!

(MRS. LINDE *enters with the dress, and carries it to the table.*)

MRS. LINDE: There, now it's all fixed. Want to try it on—?

NORA: Christine, come here.

MRS. LINDE: What's wrong? You look so upset.

NORA: Come over here. Do you see that letter there? *There*—through the window in the mailbox.

MRS. LINDE: Yes, yes, I see it.

NORA: That letter is from Krogstad.

MRS. LINDE: Nora—Krogstad's the one you borrowed money from!

NORA: Yes, and now Torvald will find out everything.

MRS. LINDE: Believe me, Nora, that's the best thing for both of you.

NORA: I forged a signature—

MRS. LINDE: In God's name—?

NORA: There's just one thing I have to tell you now, Christine—you must be my witness.

MRS. LINDE: Witness to what? What should I—?

NORA: If I should lose my mind—and that could well happen—

MRS. LINDE: Nora!

NORA: —or if something else happened to me—so I wasn't here any longer—

MRS. LINDE: Nora, Nora, you're completely beside yourself!

NORA: If anyone tries to take on everything, assume the full responsibility, you understand—

MRS. LINDE: Yes, yes, but what makes you think—?

NORA: Then you must bear witness that it isn't true, Christine. No one else has known about this. I have done it all myself.

MRS. LINDE: I don't understand a word of this.

NORA: Oh, how could you possibly understand it? Now the wonderful thing is about to happen.

MRS. LINDE: Wonderful thing?

NORA: Yes, the wonderful thing. But it's so terrible, Christine—it *mustn't* happen, not for anything in this world.

MRS. LINDE: I'll go to Krogstad at once and talk to him.

NORA: Don't go near him. He'll harm you.

MRS. LINDE: There was once a time when he's have done anything for my sake.

NORA: Him?

MRS. LINDE: Where does he live?

NORA: He lives just around the corner. But it won't help. The letter is there in the box.

MRS. LINDE: And your husband has the key with him?

NORA: Yes, always.

(NORA *makes a frantic attempt to force the lock with a hairpin, without success.*)

MRS. LINDE: Krogstad must demand his letter back unopened, he must find an excuse. Stall for time. I'll come back as fast as I can.

(MRS. LINDE *leaves.*)

Scene 11

(NORA *sits motionless on the edge of the table, covering her eyes with her hands. A long pause.*)

NORA: (*In a whisper.*) Torvald!

(HELMER *and* RANK *come in together.*)

HELMER: What's this now? Rank had prepared me for a brilliant masquerade scene—

RANK: So I thought, but I must have been mistaken.

NORA: That's right, no one gets to admire me in costume before tomorrow night.

HELMER: Nora dear, you look so overstrained. Have you been practicing too hard?

NORA: No, I haven't practiced at all yet.

HELMER: But you must, you know—

NORA: Oh yes, it's very necessary, Torvald. But I can't get anywhere without your help. I've forgotten the whole thing completely.

HELMER: Well, we'll soon refresh your memory.

NORA: Yes, Torvald, please take care of me. Will you promise me that? This evening you've got to devote yourself entirely to me. Promise me that, Torvald dear?

HELMER: I promise. Tonight I'm totally at your service.

NORA: I can't dance tomorrow if I don't practice with you! Let's start right away. Correct me, guide me the way you always do.

(NORA *sweeps everything off the table and climbs on top of it. Laughter.*

NORA *dances.* RANK *stands behind the table in the background, watching.*)

HELMER: Stop! Stop, I tell you! It's true, you've forgotten everything I taught you.

NORA: There, you see.

HELMER: This is going to require some careful instruction, no doubt about that.

(RANK *withdraws quietly.*)

NORA: Yes, now you see how necessary it is. You've got to instruct me right up until the last minute. Will you promise to do that, Torvald?

A short pause in the action.

Same furniture as before.

Nora's tarantella in performance.

Scene 12

(*It is night, snowy and cold.* KROGSTAD *and* MRS. LINDE *are on the stage.*)

MRS. LINDE: Krogstad, let's talk.

KROGSTAD: Have the two of us anything left to say to each other?

MRS. LINDE: We have a great deal to talk about.

KROGSTAD: I wouldn't have thought so.

MRS. LINDE: Because you've never really understood me.

KROGSTAD: What more is there to understand, except that it's the commonest thing in the world? A woman throws a man over as soon as a better offer comes along.

MRS. LINDE: Do you think it was easy for me to break it off? (KROGSTAD *is silent.*) Krogstad, is that what you actually thought?

KROGSTAD: If not, then why did you write me the kind of letter you did?

MRS. LINDE: There was nothing else I could do. When I had to break up with you, I felt it was my duty to destroy any feeling you might still have left for me.

KROGSTAD: And all that—all that just for money!

MRS. LINDE: You have to remember, I had a helpless mother and two young brothers. We couldn't wait for you, Krogstad.

   (*Pause.*)

KROGSTAD: When I lost you, it seemed as though the ground slipped away from under my feet.

MRS. LINDE: I didn't know until today that it's you I'm replacing at the bank.

   (*Pause.*)

KROGSTAD: I believe you. But now that you know, will you resign?

MRS. LINDE: No, because you'd have nothing whatsoever to gain by that.

KROGSTAD: Oh, gain!

MRS. LINDE: I've learned to act sensibly. Life and bitter necessity have taught me that.

KROGSTAD: And life has taught me not to believe everything people say.

MRS. LINDE: Then life has taught you a very sound lesson. But you do believe in actions, don't you? Why else do you suppose I came here to this town?

   (*Pause.*)

KROGSTAD: Had you really been thinking of me?

MRS. LINDE: All my life, so as long as I can remember, I've had to work, and that's been my greatest and only joy. But now I'm all alone in the world, deserted and empty. Working for yourself—there's no joy in that. Nils, I need someone and something I can work for.

KROGSTAD: You know about my past?

MRS. LINDE: Yes.

KROGSTAD: And you know the kind of reputation I have?

MRS. LINDE: You said before that with me you could have been a different man.

KROGSTAD: I'm certain of it.

MRS. LINDE: Couldn't it still happen?

KROGSTAD: Christine—!

MRS. LINDE: I need someone to take care of; and your children need a mother. We need each other.

(*They turn to face one another. Pause.*)

KROGSTAD: (*Rises.*) No, it's no use anyway. You don't know about the step I've taken against the Helmers.

MRS. LINDE: I know everything.

KROGSTAD: Oh, if only I could undo what I've done.

MRS. LINDE: You can. Your letter's still there in the mailbox.

KROGSTAD: Are you sure of that?

MRS. LINDE: Quite sure, but—

KROGSTAD: Oh, so that's it? You're willing to pay any price to save your friend. You may as well tell me honestly. Isn't that so?

MRS. LINDE: Anyone who sold herself *once* for somebody else's sake isn't about to do it again.

KROGSTAD: (*Takes her hands.*) I'll ask for my letter back.

MRS. LINDE: No!

KROGSTAD: Of course I will. I'll wait here until Helmer comes home. I'll tell him he's got to return my letter—that it's just something about my dismissal—that he shouldn't read it—

MRS. LINDE: *No*—you mustn't take your letter back. Helmer has to find out everything. This wretched secrecy must be exposed to the light of day. A complete understanding has to be reached by those two. All this lying and concealment must come to an end.

(*She indicates that* KROGSTAD *should leave, and he disappears silently. She takes up her knitting.*)

Scene 13

(HELMER, *slightly drunk, brings* NORA *in. Over her dance costume she wears a dark shawl.*)

HELMER:　Still here, so late?

MRS. LINDE:　Yes, I'm sorry, but I wanted so much to see Nora in her costume.

HELMER:　(*Removes the shawl.*) Well, have a good look. She's worth looking at, I'd say. Isn't she lovely?

MRS. LINDE: Yes, I should say so—

HELMER:　Isn't she remarkably lovely? Everyone at the ball thought so, too. But she's terribly stubborn! What shall we do about that? Believe it or not, I nearly had to use force to get her to leave.

NORA:　Oh, Torvald!

HELMER:　She danced her tarantella—had a tumultuous success—which she deserved—even if the performance was a shade too undisciplined; I mean, more so than the rules of art strictly permit. No matter! The point is, she was a success, a tumultuous success. I couldn't let her stay there after that, could I? And ruin the effect? Naturally not. So I took my lovely little Capri maiden—my capricious little Capri maiden, I should say—by the arm. One quick whirl around the room; bows to all sides; and then—as they say in novels—the beautiful vision vanished. An exit always has to be effective, Mrs. Linde, but *that's* what I can't get Nora to grasp.—Phew, it's hot in here! Excuse me—

(HELMER *leaves to shed his domino and dress coat.* NORA *looks at* MRS. LINDE.)

MRS. LINDE:　I talked to him.—Nora, you must tell your husband everything.

NORA:　I knew it.

MRS. LINDE:　You've got nothing to fear from Krogstad, but now you must speak.

NORA:　I won't do it.

MRS. LINDE:　Then the letter will do it for you.

NORA:　Thank you, Christine—now I know what has to be done.

HELMER:　(*Returns, bearing a champagne bottle and a glass.*) Well now, Mrs. Linde, have you admired her?

MRS. LINDE:　Yes, and now I must say good night.

HELMER:　Oh, so soon? Does this knitting here belong to you?

MRS. LINDE: Yes, thanks. I almost forgot it.

HELMER: So you knit, do you?

MRS. LINDE: Oh, yes.

HELMER: You really should embroider, you know.

MRS. LINDE: Why?

HELMER: Because it's much more graceful, that's why. Look here—you hold the embroidery in your left hand, like that—and you guide the needle with your right hand—like this—in an easy, flowing curve—see?

MRS. LINDE: Yes, I suppose so . . .

HELMER: Whereas knitting now—that can never be anything but ugly. Look here—with the arms all cramped—the knitting needles going up and down all the time—there's something oriental about it.—Ah, the champagne they served upstairs was superb.

MRS. LINDE: Well, good night, Nora—and don't be stubborn any longer.

HELMER: Bravo, Mrs. Linde!

MRS. LINDE: Good night, Mr. Helmer

HELMER: (*As he rushes her off the stage.*) Good night, good night, hope you get home safely. I'd be glad to—but you haven't got far to go. Good night, good night.—There! We got rid of her at last. What a frightfully tedious woman she is. (*Kisses* NORA *long and passionately.*)

NORA: I'm so tired.

HELMER: There, you see! I was right when I said we shouldn't stay.

NORA: What you do is always right.

HELMER: And now my little lark is talking like a real grown-up. By the way, did you notice how full of life Rank was tonight?

NORA: Oh? Was he? I didn't get a chance to talk to him.

HELMER: I scarcely did either, but it's been a long time since I've seen him in such a good mood. Hmm—it's nice to be home again, all alone with you! (NORA *is silent.*) Oh, you know—when I'm at a party like that with you—do you know why I say so little to you, and keep so far away from you, and just steal a quick glance at you now and then—do you know why I do that? Because I make believe that you're my secret love, and no one else has any idea what's going on between us. (NORA *is silent.*) And when we have to go, and I place the shawl around your shoulders—then I make believe you're my young bride, we've just been married, and I'm bringing you home with me for the very first time—for the first time I'm going to be alone with you, completely alone with you.—All this evening I longed for nothing else but you. When I watched you dance the tarantella, I couldn't stand it any longer—and that's the reason I wanted to bring you down here so early—

NORA: (*Resisting his embrace.*) Get away from me, Torvald! I don't want any of this.

HELMER: What's that supposed to mean? You must be making fun of me, little Nora! Don't want; don't want? I'm your husband, aren't I?

(RANK *appears in the background.*)

RANK: Dare I come in for a moment?

HELMER: What does he want now? (*Aloud, as he leads him in.*) How nice of you not to pass by our door!

RANK: I thought I heard your voice, and I just wanted to look in. Ah yes, these cherished and familiar surroundings. Things are so cosy and pleasant in here for you two.

HELMER: You looked like you were having a pleasant enough time yourself this evening, upstairs at the party.

RANK: Splendid. Why shouldn't I? Why not enjoy all that the world has to offer? (*Takes a glass.*) As much as we can, at least, for as long as we can. The wine was first rate—

HELMER: Especially the champagne.

RANK: You noticed that too, did you?

NORA: Torvald drank lots of champagne this evening.

RANK: Oh?

NORA: Yes, and then he's always so amusing afterward.

RANK: Well, why shouldn't we deserve a merry evening after a day well spent.

HELMER: Well spent? I'm afraid I can't claim that much.

RANK: But I can, you see.

NORA: Doctor Rank, you must have finished a scientific experiment.

RANK: Quite right.

HELMER: Listen to that, will you! Our little Nora talking about scientific experiments!

NORA: And may I congratulate you on the results?

RANK: You most certainly may.

NORA: They were good, then?

RANK: The best possible, for physician and patient alike— (*Laughs.*) certainty.

NORA: Certainty?

RANK: Absolute certainty. So don't I deserve to celebrate a little after that?

NORA: Yes, that you do, Doctor Rank.

HELMER: That's what I say, too. Just hope you don't have to pay for it in the morning.

RANK: Nothing is free in this life.

NORA: Doctor Rank—you're very fond of masquerades, aren't you?

RANK: Yes, provided there are plenty of amusing disguises.

NORA: Tell me—what are the two of us going to be at the next masquerade?

HELMER: Don't tell me you're thinking about the next one already!

RANK: We two? Yes, I can tell you that. You shall go as Fortune's favorite—

HELMER: But where do you find a costume to indicate *that*?

RANK: Just let your wife appear exactly the way she looks every single day.

HELMER: Very well said. But what about you? Don't you know what you're going to be?

RANK: Oh yes, my friend, I have no doubt whatsoever about that.

HELMER: Well?

RANK: At the next masquerade, my friend, I shall be invisible.

HELMER: A witty idea.

RANK: (*Pulls his own cape over his head.*) A big, black cape—have you never heard tell of the cape of invisibility? Once you pull it over you, nobody sees you're there.

HELMER: Quite right.

(RANK *pulls the cape off, hits on an excuse to get away.*)

RANK: But I'm forgetting completely what I came for. Helmer, give me a cigar, one of your dark Havanas.

HELMER: With the greatest pleasure.

RANK: Thank you. (*Tries to light it.*)

NORA: Let me give you a light. (*She strikes a match and holds it for him.*)

RANK: Many thanks. And now, good-bye.

HELMER: Good-bye, good-bye, dear friend!

NORA: Sleep well, Doctor Rank.

RANK: Thanks for that wish.

NORA: Wish me the same.

RANK: You? All right, if you like—sleep well. And thank you for the light.

(*Exit* DOCTOR RANK.)

Scene 14

HELMER: He's been drinking heavily.

NORA: Perhaps. Torvald—what are you doing now?

HELMER: I have to empty the mailbox. It's almost full; no room for the morning papers.

NORA: Are you going to work tonight?

HELMER: You know very well I'm not.—What's this, now? Somebody's been at the lock.

NORA: At the lock—?

HELMER: Yes, no question about it. How can that be? I can't imagine that one of the maids—? Here's a broken hairpin. Nora, it's one of yours—

NORA: Then it must be the children.

HELMER: You'd better get them out of that habit. Hmm, hmm—there, I got it open after all. Just look at how much has piled up! (*Sorting.*) What's this one, I wonder?

(HELMER *glances at Krogstad's letter, tosses it aside, then changes his mind. He reads the letter.*)

Nora! What is this? Do you know what's in this letter?

NORA: Yes, I know. Let me go! You can't save me!

HELMER: Is it true what he writes?

NORA: It *is* true. I've loved you above everything else in the world.

HELMER: Spare me your foolish evasions.

NORA: Torvald—!

HELMER: What have you done!

NORA: You're not to take it upon yourself for my sake. You're not to bear my guilt.

HELMER: Do you understand what you've done? (*Pause.*) Answer me! Do you understand?

NORA: Yes, now I'm beginning to understand—fully.

HELMER: For these past eight years—the woman who was my joy and my pride—a hypocrite, a liar—worse, much worse—a criminal! (NORA *is silent and watches him closely.*) I should have known something like this would happen. I should have foreseen it. All your father's crazy ideas—you've inherited them. No religion, no morals, no sense of responsibility. (NORA *nods.*) Now I'm at the mercy of a totally ruthless individual. He can do what he likes with me, demand anything he wants from me, order me around however he pleases—I don't dare say a word. And so I'm to sink miserably to the bottom and be ruined, all on account of a frivolous woman!

NORA: Once I'm out of the way, you'll be free.

HELMER: Oh, stop pretending! What good would it do me even if you were out of the way, as you put it? It wouldn't help me one bit. He can still make the whole thing public; and if he does, I'll come under suspicion as an accessory to your crime. They might even think I was behind it—that I was the one who put you up to it! And I have you to thank for all this—you, to whom I gave everything and for whom I did everything since the day we were married. Now do you realize what you've done to me?

NORA: Yes.

HELMER: It's so incredible I can hardly grasp it. But now we have to start sorting things out. Take off that shawl. Take it off, I say! (*Pause.*) Somehow or other I've got to satisfy him. The matter has to be hushed up, whatever the price.—And as far as you and I are concerned, everything between us must seem exactly as before. But only in the eyes of the world, naturally. So you'll go on living here in the house—that's obvious. But you'll have nothing to do with my children's upbringing. I wouldn't trust you for that.

(MRS. LINDE *steps forward and hands* HELMER *a letter.*)

What's this?—A letter for you! From him. No, you don't get it. I'll read it myself. (*Reads.*) Nora! (NORA *looks at him inquiringly.*) Nora!—No, I must read it once more. (*Reads.*) Yes, yes, it's true. I'm saved! Nora, I'm saved!

NORA: What about me?

HELMER: You, too, of course. He's sent back your promissory note. He writes that he's sorry and regrets what's happened—he says a happy change in his life—oh, what difference does it make what he says. We're saved, Nora! (*Tears up both letters and the note.*) Oh, these must have been terrible days for you, Nora.—No, we won't think about all that ugliness any more. It's over; it's over! (*Gets himself a glass of cham-*

"Nora, I swear it; I have forgiven you everything," Helmer tells his wife, who still wears her masquerade costume.

pagne.) Do you hear that, Nora? You don't seem to grasp it—it's all over. (*Lifts her face.*) Oh, my dear, little Nora, I understand now—you're thinking you can't believe that I've forgiven you. But I have, Nora, I swear it; I've forgiven you everything. I realize you did what you did out of love for me.

NORA: That's true.

HELMER: You have loved me the way a wife should love her husband. It was just that you were incapable of judging the means. But do you imagine you're any less dear to me just because you're not able to manage all by yourself? No, no. Forget my harsh words to you—they were spoken in the first moments of shock, when I thought everything was falling apart around me. (*Begins to kiss her passionately.*) I've forgiven you, Nora; I swear I've forgiven you.

NORA: And I thank you for your forgiveness.

   (HELMER *embraces her passionately and starts to unbutton her dress.*)

A short pause in the action.

Scene 15

(*Silence. A dark stage.* NORA *is dressed in a dark coat. She carries a small traveling bag.* HELMER *is lying in a double bed, naked.*)

HELMER: (*Awakens.*) You've gotten dressed?

NORA: Yes, Torvald, I've changed my clothes.

HELMER: But why, now, so late?

NORA: I won't sleep tonight.

HELMER: But, Nora dear—

NORA: It's not that late yet. We have a lot of things to talk about.

HELMER: Nora—what is all this?

NORA: I have a great deal to say to you.

HELMER: You're making my uneasy, Nora. I don't understand you.

NORA: That's exactly the point. You don't understand me. And I've never understood you, either—until tonight. No, don't interrupt me. Hear me out. (*Sits on the far corner of the bed, controlling her anger.*) I want an accounting, Torvald.

HELMER: What do you mean?

NORA: We've been married eight years now. Doesn't it occur to you that this is the first time that we, you and I, husband and wife, have had a serious talk together?

HELMER: What do you mean by that?

NORA: In eight whole years—no, longer than that—right from the first time we met, we've never exchanged one serious word about serious things.

HELMER: What was I to do? Involve you day in and day out in problems you couldn't help me to handle anyway?

NORA: I'm not talking about problems. I'm saying we've never sat down together and tried in a serious way to get to the bottom of anything.

HELMER: But Nora dearest . . .

(*Pause.*)

NORA: I've been greatly wronged, Torvald. First by Papa and then by you.

HELMER: What! By us—by the two people who have loved you more than anyone else?

NORA: Neither of you has ever loved me. You thought it was fun to be in love with me, that's all.

HELMER: But Nora, how can you say such a thing?

NORA: Because it's true, Torvald. When I lived at home with Papa, he used to tell me his opinions, and then I held the same opinions, too; or if I had other ideas, I had to conceal them, because he would have disliked that. He called me his doll child, and he played with me the same way I played with my own dolls. Then I came here to live with you—

HELMER: Is that the way you'd describe our marriage?

NORA: I simply mean that I passed from Papa's hands into your hands. You arranged everything according to your own taste, and so I acquired the same taste as you; or else I just pretended I did—I really don't know which it was. A little of both, I suppose, first one way, then the other. When I look back on it now, it seems to me I've lived here like a beggar—from hand to mouth. I lived by doing tricks for you, Torvald. But you wanted it that way. You've done me a great injury, you and Papa. It's your fault that I never amounted to anything.

HELMER: Nora, you're being unreasonable and ungrateful. Haven't you been happy here?

NORA: No, never. I thought I was; but I never have been—

HELMER: Not—not happy!

NORA: No—only gay. You've always been very nice to me. But our home has been nothing but a playroom. I've been your doll wife here, just as I was Papa's doll child at home. And so our children became my dolls. I thought it was fun when you played with me, just as they thought it was fun when I played with them. That's been our marriage, Torvald.

HELMER: (*Pulls on his nightshirt and sits up in bed.*) There's some truth in what you say—exaggerated and hysterical though it sounds. But from now on, everything will be different. The games are over. Now comes the time for instruction.

NORA: Whose instruction? Mine or the children's?*

HELMER: Yours and the children's alike, Nora darling.

NORA: (*Brutally.*) Oh, Torvald, you're not the man to teach me how to be a proper wife for you.

HELMER: How can you say that?

NORA: And I—how am I prepared to bring up the children?

HELMER: Nora!

---

* Now comes Nora's complete ruthlessness and brutality.—IB

NORA: (*Bitterly.*) You said so yourself a while ago—you wouldn't trust me for that.

HELMER: (*Indignant.*) In a moment of anger! Are you going to take that seriously?

NORA: Yes, I am. You were right. It's a task I'm not up to. There's another task I must accomplish first. (*With long pauses between each sentence.*) I've got to educate myself. *You're* not the man to help me. I've got to do it by myself. and that's the reason I'm leaving you.

HELMER: (*Pause.*) What did you say?

NORA: If I ever hope to learn anything about myself and the things around me, I've got to stand completely on my own. That's why I can't stay here with you any longer.

HELMER: Nora, Nora!

NORA: I'm leaving at once.

HELMER: You're crazy! I won't let you! I forbid it!

NORA: From now on, you can't forbid me anything. I'm taking only those things that belong to me. I want nothing from you, either now or later.

HELMER: But this is insanity!

NORA: I'm going home—I mean back home where I came from. There I'll find something to do more easily.

HELMER: Leave your home, your husband and your children! And without even a thought about what other people will say.

NORA: I can't concern myself with that. I only know what's necessary for me.

HELMER: And so you turn your back on your true responsibilities, just like that.

NORA: What do you consider my true responsibilities?

HELMER: You need me to tell you that? You have responsibilities toward your husband and your children, haven't you?

NORA: I have other responsibilities that are equally important.

HELMER: No, you don't. What responsibilities might *they* be?

NORA: Responsibilities toward myself.

HELMER: Above all else you are a wife and a mother.

NORA: I no longer believe that. I believe that, above all else, I'm a human being, just as you are—or at least I have to try to become one. Oh, I know most people would agree with you, Torvald, and I know it's the kind of argument that's found in books. But I can't let myself be satisfied anymore with what most people say and with what's found in books. I have to think these things through for myself and try to make sense of them.

HELMER: You talk like a child. You understand nothing of the society you live in.

NORA: No. But now I'll learn about it. I've got to find out which view is the right one, society's or mine.

HELMER: You're sick, Nora; you must have a fever. I really believe you've lost your reason.

NORA: I've never felt more clearheaded and confident in my life.

HELMER: And so—clearheaded and confident—you're going to desert your husband and your children?

NORA: Yes, I am.

HELMER: Then there's only *one* possible explanation.

NORA: What?

HELMER: You no longer love me.

NORA: No. That's quite true.

HELMER: Nora!

NORA: It hurts me so much, Torvald, because you've always been so good to me. But I can't help it. I don't love you anymore, Torvald.

HELMER: And that's a clearheaded and confident conclusion, too?

NORA: Yes, completely. That's why I don't want to stay here any longer.
   (*Pause.*)

HELMER: And can you explain to me, then, what I did to lose your love?

NORA: While Krogstad's letter was lying there in the box—I never for one moment supposed you'd be willing to submit to such a person's demands. I was absolutely convinced that you'd say to him: Tell the whole world about it. And when that happened—

HELMER: Yes, then what? After I'd left my own wife open to disgrace and scandal . . .

NORA: When that happened, I was convinced beyond any doubt that you'd step forward and take everything upon yourself and say: I am the guilty one.

HELMER: (*Angrily.*) Nora, my joy has been to work day and night for you—endure hardships and troubles for your sake. But no one is willing to offer up his honor for the one he loves.

NORA: Hundreds of thousands of women have done it.

HELMER: Oh, you think and talk like a naive child.

"There's some truth in what you say," Helmar admits in this performance shot of the final scene. "I could tear myself to pieces," laments Nora during rehearsal of the same scene.

NORA: (*Punching him repeatedly with all the force she can muster.*) And you neither think nor talk like the man I could live my life with! Once you'd gotten over your fear—not fear of what threatened *me*, but only of what you yourself might risk—once the danger had passed, you acted just as if nothing had happened. I was your little doll again, a doll that you'd have to look after twice as carefully as before, now that it had turned out to be so fragile and frail. (*Her fury abates.*) Torvald—at that moment I realized that for eight years I'd been living with a stranger, and I'd had three children with him.—Oh, I can't stand thinking about it! I could tear myself to pieces.

(*Pause.*)

HELMER: I see it; I do see it. A great gulf has opened between us.—But Nora, couldn't we try to reach across it?

NORA: I'm no wife for you, as I am now.

HELMER: I'm strong enough to become a different man.

NORA: Maybe—if your doll is taken away.

HELMER: To separate—to be separated from you! No, Nora, no, I can't conceive of that.

NORA: All the more reason it has to happen.

HELMER: Nora, Nora, not now! Wait until morning.

NORA: I can't spend the night in a stranger's bedroom.

HELMER: But couldn't we live here together as brother and sister—?

NORA: (*Touches Helmer's hand.*) You know very well that wouldn't last long. (*Rises.*) Good-bye, Torvald. I don't want to see the children. I know they're in better hands than mine. There's nothing I could do for them now, the way I am.

(*Long pause.*)

HELMER: But later, Nora—later?

NORA: (*Bitterly.*) How do I know that? I don't even know what will become of me.

HELMER: But you're my wife, now and forever.

NORA: Listen to me, Torvald—when a wife deserts her husband's house, the way I'm doing now, I believe that the law absolves him of all obligations toward her. At any rate, I absolve you of all obligations. You mustn't feel bound by anything, any more than I will. There must be complete freedom on both sides. Here is your ring back. Give me mine.

HELMER: That, too?

NORA: That, too. (*They exchange rings.*) There. And now it's over. (*Lays her keys on the night table beside the bed.*) I'll leave the keys here.

Tomorrow, after I've gone away, Christine will come and pack the things I brought with me from home. I want those sent on to me.

(*Pause.*)

HELMER: Nora, won't you ever think of me?

NORA: I'm sure I'm going to think of you often, and of the children and of this house.

HELMER: May I write to you, Nora?

NORA: No, never. I forbid you to do that.

HELMER: But at least I can send you—

NORA: Nothing; nothing.

HELMER: —help you if you need it.

NORA: No, I say. I'll accept nothing from strangers. (*Prepares to go.*)

HELMER: Nora—can't I ever be more than a stranger to you?

NORA: Oh, Torvald, then the most wonderful thing of all would have to happen.

HELMER: What is this most wonderful thing—tell me!

NORA: Then we, you and I, would have to change so much that—Oh, Torvald, I don't believe in wonders any more.

HELMER: But I want to believe in them. Tell me! We'd have to change so much that—?

NORA: That our life together could become a marriage. Good-bye.

(*Exit* NORA. HELMER, *bathed in a searing white light, is left weeping on the bed.*)

FINIS MALORUM

August Strindberg

JULIE

Stage version of *Miss Julie* by Ingmar Bergman
Stage design and costumes by Gunilla Palmstierna-Weiss

Miss Julie...Anne-Marie Kuster

Jean, *valet* ....Michael Degen

Christine, *cook* ....Gundi Ellert

Servants .... Solveig Samzelius

Karin Romig

Irene Fischer

Peter Thom

Michael Tietz

Udo Weinberger

Directed by Ingmar Bergman
Premiere 30 April 1981

CHARACTERS

MISS JULIE, *twenty-five years old, ash blond, well-developed*

JEAN, *valet, thirty years old, dark*

CHRISTINE, *cook, thirty-five years old, still young-looking*

  Servants:

CLARA, *housemaid*

SOFIE, *scullery-maid*

ANNA, *stable-girl*

LARS, *coachman*

JOHAN, *stable foreman*

NILS, *a boy*

The action takes place in the Count's kitchen on Midsummer Eve.

A large kitchen. Running the width of the rear wall are four high windows, opaque rather than transparent, through which figures and movements outside the kitchen can be discerned. Roughly in the middle of the rear wall are two swinging glass doors, reached by a short flight of four stairs, that lead to the park outside. A cast-iron stove, equipped with an exhaust hood, occupies the left wall of the kitchen. A chair is placed beside the stove. To the right stands a simple kitchen table, of white pine, with three chairs and three backless stools. In the right wall behind the table, a door leads to Jean's bedroom. The kitchen is decorated with birch branches, and white lilac blooms are heaped in a bowl on the table. A water barrel with a ladle, an icebox, and a washstand concealed by a folding screen occupy the background. A large cupboard with porcelain and glassware stands around the corner to the left. A large old-fashioned bell hangs above the glass doors, to the left of which is a speaking tube. A coffee pot is on the stove.

Empty stage. Fiddle music in the distance. CHRISTINE *enters, stands at the stove, and begins frying in a pan.* JEAN *enters quickly, running down the flight of stairs. He is in livery and carries a pair of high riding boots, which he sets down on the floor. He removes his cap and wipes the sweat from his forehead, then goes to the water barrel and drinks from the ladle. He picks up a newspaper on the table.*

JEAN: Miss Julie's crazy again tonight—absolutely crazy!

CHRISTINE: Well, so here you are at last.

JEAN: I took the Count to the station. And as I was passing the barn on my way back, I went in and was dancing when I see Miss Julie leading the dance with the gamekeeper. But the minute she catches sight of me, she rushes straight into my arms and invites me for the ladies' waltz. And she's been waltzing like that since—I've never seen the like of it before. She *is* crazy!

CHRISTINE: Always has been. But never so bad as during these past couple of weeks, after the engagement was broken off.

JEAN: Yes, what was all that business about, anyway? He was a fine man, even if he wasn't rich. Oh well, they're always full of their little whims. (*Finishes reading.*) Funny, though, a young lady like her. Hmm. Rather stay home with the servants, wouldn't she? Instead of going with her father to visit her relatives.

CHRISTINE: She's probably a little embarrassed after the breakup with her fiancé.

JEAN: Most likely. He certainly was a man to stand his ground, though.

Know how it happened, Christine? I saw it, you know, though I didn't want to let on I did.

CHRISTINE: So you saw it, did you?

JEAN: I certainly did. One evening they were down in the stable yard, and Miss Julie was putting him through his training, as she called it. And do you know what that meant? She made him jump over her riding whip, like a dog you'd teach to jump. He hopped twice, and each time he was given a rap. But the third time he grabbed the whip out of her hand and struck her across the left cheek with it. Then off he went.

CHRISTINE: You don't say. And you actually saw it happen? You don't say. So that's the reason she paints her face so white now?

JEAN: That's what happened all right. And now, Christine, what nice things have you got for me tonight?

CHRISTINE: (*Serves from the frying pan and places a plate before him.*) Oh, just a bit a kidney I cut from the veal roast.

JEAN: (*Sniffs the food.*) Superb? *Délicieux!* (*Feels the plate.*) You might have warmed the plate, though.

CHRISTINE: You can be more finicky than the Count himself when you've got a mind to be. (*Pulls his hair affectionately.*)

JEAN: (*Angry.*) Leave my hair alone! You know I can't stand that.

CHRISTINE: Now, now, it's only meant to be affectionate. You know that. (Jean *eats.* CHRISTINE *opens a bottle of beer.*)

JEAN: Beer—on Midsummer Eve? No, thank you! I can do better than that for myself. (*Opens a drawer in the table and extracts a bottle of red wine. The cork is sealed with yellow wax.*) Yellow seal—not bad eh? Now bring me a glass! A wine glass, naturally—this is the *real* thing I'm drinking.

CHRISTINE: (*Returns to the stove and puts a small saucepan on.*) God help whoever gets you for a husband! What a fusspot you are.

JEAN: Don't talk nonsense. You'd be glad enough to get a fine man like me. And I don't think you've been damaged by having people say that I'm your fiancé, either. (*Tastes the wine.*) Good. Very good indeed. Not quite the proper room temperature, though. (*Warms the glass in his hand.*) We bought this in Dijon. Four francs a liter it cost us—in bulk. Not counting the duty. What are you cooking now? Smells like devil's brew.

CHRISTINE: Oh, just some damned slop Miss Julie wants for Diana.

JEAN: You should express yourself less vulgarly, Christine. And why should you have to be cooking for that little beast on a holiday evening, anyway? Is it sick or something?

"Good! Very good indeed!" Michael Degen as Jean.

CHRISTINE: You might say that. It sneaked our with the porter's mutt, and now it's in trouble—not that our young lady would admit any such thing.

JEAN: Miss Julie's too haughty in some ways and not proud enough in others—just the way the Countess was in her time. She was more at home in the kitchen or the stables, but ride in a carriage behind one horse, that she'd never do. Her cuffs were filthy, but she had to have the family crest stamped on every button. Miss Julie, now, to come back to her—she never takes proper care of herself or her person. I must say she has no finesse. (*Drinks.*) Just now when she was dancing in the barn, she grabbed the gamekeeper away from Anna and made him dance with her. We'd never do a thing like that, but that's how it is when the gentry try to mingle with the common people—they just become common. She's a fine-looking woman, though! Magnificent! Ah, those shoulders and those—etcetera.

CHRISTINE: Don't overdo it! I've heard what Clara says, and she dresses her.

JEAN: Clara! You women are always jealous of one another! I know her, I've been out riding with her—and when she dances—umm! (*Pause.*)

CHRISTINE: Listen here, Jean, aren't you going to dance with me when I'm through?

JEAN: Of course I am.

CHRISTINE: Promise?

JEAN: Promise? (*Corks the bottle.*) When I say I'll do a thing, I do it. And thanks for dinner. It was superb.

JULIE: (*In the doorway, talking to someone outside.*) I'll be right back, don't wait.

(JEAN *hides the bottle in the drawer, stands respectfully.*)

JULIE: (*Crossing to Christine at the stove.*) Well, is it ready?

(CHRISTINE *indicates that* JEAN *is present.*)

JEAN: (*Gallantly.*) Have the ladies their secrets?

JULIE: (*Strikes his face with her handkerchief.*) Curious?

JEAN: Ah, what a delicious smell of violets that had.

JULIE: Naughty! Are you an expert in perfumes, too? You certainly know how to dance! Now no more looking. Off with you!

JEAN: (*Pertly but politely.*) Is this some magical potion you ladies are brewing for Midsummer Eve? Something to help you read your lucky star and see a future husband?

JULIE: (*Sharply.*) You'd need good eyes to see him. (*On her way out, to* CHRISTINE.) Put this in a bottle and cork it well. Now, come along and dance a schottische with me. Jean.

JEAN: (*Hesitates.*) No offense intended, but I promised this dance to Christine.

JULIE: Well, then she can have another one—can't you, Christine? You will let me borrow Jean, won't you?

CHRISTINE: I've no say in the matter. If you're kind enough to ask him, Miss, it's hardly his place to refuse. (*To* JEAN.) Go along now! And be grateful for the honor.

JEAN: Frankly speaking, and having no wish to hurt your feelings, Miss Julie, I wonder if it's wise for you to dance twice in a row with the same partner. Especially since people here are so ready to jump to conclusions.

JULIE: (*Flares up.*) What's this? What sort of conclusions? What are you trying to say?

JEAN: (*Submissively.*) If you choose not to understand, Miss, then I'll have to speak more plainly. It doesn't look well to show preference for one of your servants, when others are expecting the same unlooked-for favor . . .

JULIE: Preference! What is it you imagine? I'm astonished! I, as mistress of this house, am honoring the servants' party by my presence. And when I decide to dance, I wish to do so with someone who can lead properly, so I don't become a laughingstock.

JEAN: As you wish, Miss Julie. At your service.

JULIE: Don't take it as an order. Tonight we're all part of the same happy celebration. No social distinctions. Now, your arm, please! And don't worry, Christine, I won't carry off your fiancé.

[The "Pantomime" described in Strindberg's stage directions was replaced in Ingmar Bergman's production by the following sequence of actions:*

JEAN offers JULIE his arm, and they leave quickly through the swinging doors at the rear. CHRISTINE is alone. A fiddle is heard in the distance, playing a schottische.

CHRISTINE clears Jean's plate away, drinks the wine remaining in his glass, and carries the plate and glass to the sink. She fetches a washbasin and pitcher, and removes her apron and cook's top. After pouring water into the basin, she washes her face, neck, arms, and between her breasts. Then she dries herself with a towel, and unpins her hair before a small mirror. As she does so, two servant girls, Clara and Sofie, appear outside the windows, peering in. CLARA enters and whispers something to CHRISTINE, giggling and sniggering as she does so. Angrily, CHRISTINE pushes her away and then chases her out the door with the towel. The girls run off and disappear. CHRISTINE pushes open the door and looks outside. Then she returns to the table and tries on a wreath of white flowers. JEAN returns, alone. He sits on the steps by the doorway, laughing and combing his hair, as CHRISTINE empties out the washbasin.]

JEAN: Yes, she's crazy, all right. And what a way to dance! Why, people were standing at the doors laughing at her behind her back. What do you make of it, Christine?

CHRISTINE: Oh, she's probably getting her period—she always turns so queer then. Are you going to dance with me now?

JEAN: Not angry because I went off and left you, I hope?

CHRISTINE: Not a bit. Not on account of a small thing like that. Besides, I know my proper place.

JEAN: (*Embraces her.*) You're a sensible girl, Christine. You'd make a fine wife.

* Bracketed material throughout indicates similar changes.

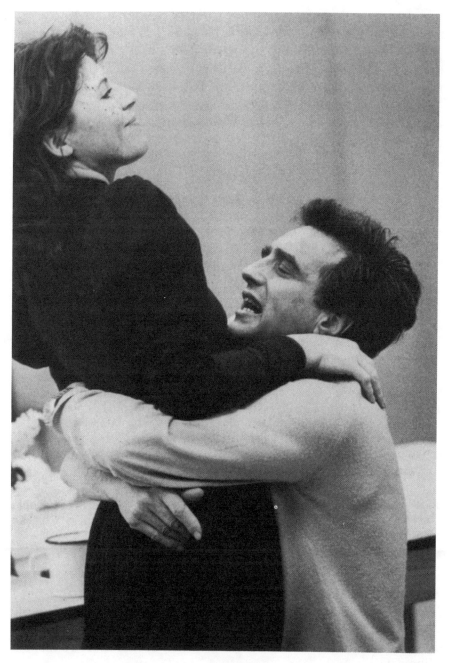

"You're a sensible girl, Christine. You'd make a fine wife." Gundi Ellert (Christine) and Michael Degen (Jean) in rehearsal.

JULIE: (*Enters. Disagreeably surprised, with forced levity.*) What a charming partner you turn out to be—deserting your lady like that!

JEAN: On the contrary, Miss Julie. As you can see, I hurried back to find the partner I had deserted.

JULIE: (*Changing her tone.*) You know, no one can dance like you! But why are you wearing that livery when it's a holiday? Take it off at once.

JEAN: Then I'll have to ask you to step out for a moment, Miss. I have my black coat hanging right over here.

JULIE: Embarrassed by me, are you? Just to change a coat? You can go into your room and come back, then. Otherwise stay here, and I'll turn my back.

JEAN: By your leave, Miss. (*He goes out to change his coat.*)

JULIE: Tell me, Christine, is Jean your fiancé? You two séem to be on very familiar terms.

CHRISTINE: Fiancé? Yes, if you like. We call it that.

JULIE: Call it that?

CHRISTINE: Well, Miss Julie, you had a fiancé yourself, but . . .

JULIE: We were formally engaged.

CHRISTINE: But it came to nothing all the same.

> (JULIE *is about to walk out, changes her mind, comes back, and sits at the table as* JEAN *reenters wearing a black frock coat.*)

JULIE: *Très gentil, monsieur Jean! Très gentil!*

JEAN: *Vous voulez plaisanter, Madame!*

JULIE: *Et vous voulez parler français!* Where did you learn that?

JEAN: In Switzerland. I was the wine waiter in one of the biggest hotels in Lucerne.

JULIE: You look the perfect gentleman in that redingote. *Charmant!*

JEAN: Now you're flattering me.

JULIE: (*Annoyed.*) Flattering you?

JEAN: My natural modesty prevents me from believing you'd pay sincere compliments to anyone like me. So I allowed myself to presume that you were exaggerating—or flattering me, as it's also called.

JULIE: Where did you learn talk like that? You must have gone to the theatre a lot.

JEAN: Oh, yes. And to a great many other places as well.

JULIE: But you were born right here in the neighborhood, weren't you?

JEAN: My father worked the land on the crown attorney's estate right across the way. And I used to see you as a child, Miss, though you never noticed me.

JULIE: Is that so.

JEAN: Yes. And I recall one time in particular—no, I don't ever want to talk about that.

JULIE: Oh, yes! Please do. Make an exception!

JEAN: No, I can't. Not now. Some other time, perhaps.

JULIE: Some other time is no time. Why, is it so dangerous now?

JEAN: Not dangerous, just very difficult for me, that's all.—Will you look at that! (*Indicates* CHRISTINE, *who has fallen asleep in a chair by the stove.*)

JULIE: She'll make a nice wife, that one! Do you suppose she snores, too?

JEAN: She doesn't, but she talks in her sleep.

JULIE: (*Cynically.*) How do *you* know she talks in her sleep?

JEAN: (*Impudently.*) I've heard her.

(*Pause. They watch one another.*)

JULIE: Why don't you sit down?

JEAN: I couldn't do that in your presence.

JULIE: But if I order you to?

JEAN: Then I'll obey.

JULIE: Sit down, then.—Wait a moment! Can't you give me something to drink first?

JEAN: I don't know what we've got in the icebox. Only beer. I think.

JULIE: Why the *only*? My tastes are simple. I prefer it to wine.

JEAN: (*Takes a bottle of beer from the icebox, opens it, finds a glass and plate from the cupboard, and serves her.*) Here you are!

JULIE: Thank you. Won't you have some yourself?

JEAN: Beer's no great friend of mine—but your wish is my command.

JULIE: Command? As a proper gentleman you ought to keep a lady company, it seems to me.

JEAN: Very aptly put. (*Opens another bottle, takes a glass.*)

[As Julie drinks her beer, the shadowy figures of two men, Lars and Johan, were seen in Bergman's production crouching outside the windows, peering into the kitchen.]

JULIE: Now, drink my health. (JEAN *hesitates.*) I do believe the boy is bashful.

JEAN: (*Goes down on his knees, raises his glass.*) My lady's health!

JULIE: Bravo! Now kiss my shoe and the ritual will be complete.

(Jean *is reluctant, then grasps her foot firmly and kisses it lightly.*)

JULIE: Excellent. You ought to have become an actor.

JEAN: (*Stands up.*) This has to stop, Miss Julie! Someone might come by and see us.

[The watching figures disappear.]

JULIE: Why would that matter?

JEAN: Because people would gossip, that's why! If you knew how they were chattering away up there just now . . .

JULIE: What were they saying? Tell me!—And sit down!

JEAN: (*Sits.*) I have no wish to hurt you—but the expressions they used—hinting at things that . . . well, you can guess for yourself! You're no child. When a lady is seen drinking alone with a man—and a servant at that—at night, then . . .

JULIE: Then what? Besides, we're not alone. Christine's here, isn't she?

JEAN: Asleep, yes!

JULIE: Then I'll wake her up. (*Gets up.*) Christine! Are you asleep! Christine! The woman sleeps like a stone.

JEAN: (*Angrily.*) Don't disturb her!

JULIE: (*Sharply.*) I beg your pardon!

JEAN: People who stand over a stove all day long have a right to be tired at night. Their sleep deserves to be respected.

JULIE: A very noble thought—it does you credit. I'm grateful for your advice! (*Reaches out her hand to* JEAN.) Now, come along outside and pick me some lilacs.

(*During the following,* CHRISTINE *awakens and wanders wearily off to the right to lie down.*)

JEAN: With you, Miss Julie?

JULIE: With me.

JEAN: Impossible. Out of the question.

JULIE: I don't understand what's in your mind. Surely you couldn't possibly imagine . . .

JEAN: I don't, no, but other people might.

JULIE: What—that I've fallen for one of my own servants?

JEAN: I'm not a vain man. But such things have been known to happen before—and to these people nothing is sacred.

JULIE: He's an aristocrat, no less.

JEAN: Yes, I am.

JULIE: If I step down . . .

JEAN: Don't step down, Miss Julie, take may advice! No one would believe that you did it freely. People would always say you fell!

JULIE: I have a higher opinion of people than you have. Come and find out! Come! (*Very close to Jean, looks at him searchingly.*)

JEAN: You are strange, you know.

JULIE: Perhaps. But then so are you. (*Sits.*) Everything in the world is so strange. Life, people, everything—all of it scum drifting on the water, drifting along, until it sinks, sinks down! I have a dream that comes back from time to time, and I'm reminded of it now. I'm perched high up atop a pillar and can see no means of getting down. I grow dizzy when I look down, and I must get down, but I lack the courage to let myself fall. I can no longer hold on, and I long to fall, but I don't fall. Yet I shall have no peace until I descend, no rest till I come down, back down to the ground! And were I to reach the ground, I'd want to go deep into the earth. . . . Have you ever felt anything like that?

JEAN: No. I dream that I'm lying under a high tree in a dark forest. I want to climb, climb to the top, into the sunshine, where I can look out across the bright landscape, and plunder the bird's nest way up there where the golden eggs are found. And I climb and I climb, but the trunk is so thick and so slippery, and the first branch is so difficult to reach. But I know that if I could just reach that first branch, I could mount the tree like a ladder, straight to the top. I haven't reached it yet, but I will reach it, if only in my dream.

JULIE: And here I am prattling on with you about dreams. Come now and dance. In the park. (*She offers him her arm, and they move to leave.*)

JEAN: Tonight we must sleep on nine Midsummer flowers, Miss Julie, then our dreams will come true!

(*They stop in the doorway, and* JEAN *puts a hand to one eye.*)

JULIE: Let me see what you have in your eye.

JEAN: Oh, it's nothing. Only a speck of dust. I'll be fine in a moment.

JULIE: I must have brushed against you with my sleeve. Come and sit down and I'll help you. (*She takes his arm and guides him to a chair, holds his head and bends it backwards. She tries to remove the speck with a corner of her handkerchief.*) Sit still, absolutely still! (*Slaps his hand.*) Behave yourself, now. I do believe the big strong boy is trembling! (*Feels his upper arm.*) And with such strong arms!

JEAN: (*Warningly.*) Miss Julie!

JULIE: *Oui, Monsieur Jean.*

JEAN: *Attention! Je ne suis qu'un homme!*

JULIE: Just sit still! There! It's out. Now kiss my hand and thank me.

JEAN: (*Stands.*) Now listen to me, Miss Julie! Christine's gone to bed! Will you listen to me!

JULIE: Kiss my hand first!

JEAN: Listen to me!

JULIE: Kiss my hand first!

JEAN: Very well, then, it's your responsibility!

JULIE: For what?

JEAN: For what? Are you still a child at twenty-five? Don't you realize that playing with fire is dangerous?

JULIE: Not for me. I'm insured.

JEAN: No, you're not! And even if you are, there's combustible material nearby.

JULIE: Meaning you?

JEAN: Yes! Not because I am who I am, but just because I'm a young man . . .

JULIE: . . . with an attractive appearance. What incredible conceit! A Don Juan, perhaps? Or a Joseph? I'm prepared to believe you're a Joseph!

JEAN: You think so?

JULIE: I almost fear so.

(Jean *makes a bold move to embrace and kiss her.*)

JULIE: (*Slaps him*) Insolence!

JEAN: Serious or joking?

JULIE: Serious.

JEAN: (*Takes up the boots and starts to polish them.*) Then what happened a moment ago was serious, too! You play your games far too seriously, and that's dangerous. And now I'm tired of this game—so if you'll excuse me, I'll get back to my work. The Count's boots have to be ready on time, and it's already long past midnight.

JULIE: Put those boots down!

JEAN: No, that's a duty I'm expected to carry out. But I'm not expected to serve as your playmate. And I never will. I consider myself above that.

JULIE: You're a proud one!

JEAN: Yes, sometimes. Sometimes not.

JULIE: Have you ever been in love?

JEAN: That's not a word we'd use. But I've run after plenty of girls. And once, when I couldn't have the one girl I wanted, I became sick. Really sick, I tell you, like those princes in the Arabian Nights who could neither eat nor drink for love.

JULIE: Who was she? (Jean *is silent*.) Who was she?

JEAN: You can't make me answer that.

JULIE: If I ask you as an equal? As a—friend? Who was she?

JEAN: You.

JULIE: (*Sits.*) Priceless!

JEAN: Yes, if you like. It was ridiculous! This, you see, was the story I didn't want to tell you before. But now I will tell you! Do you know what the world looks like from down below? You haven't any idea! Like the hawks and the falcons whose backs are rarely seen because they glide along way up there. I grew up in a farmer's cottage with seven brothers and sisters and a pig, in the middle of gray fields where not a single tree grew. But from our window I could see the wall around the Count's park, with apple trees growing above it. It was the Garden of Paradise, and an army of bad angels with flaming swords stood guard over it. But despite them, the other boys and I found our way to the Tree of Life. Now you despise me?

JULIE: Oh—all boys steal apples, I suppose.

JEAN: You say that now, but you despise me all the same. No matter! One day I entered this Paradise with my mother, for the sole purpose of weeding the onion beds. Behind the vegetable garden stood a Turkish pavilion, shaded by jasmine trees and overgrown with honeysuckle. I had no idea what it might be used for, but I'd never seen such a lovely place before. People went inside and came out again, and one time the door was left standing open. I crept nearer and saw that the walls were covered with pictures of kings and emperors. Red curtains with tassels hung before the windows—ah, now you understand what I'm getting at. I—you're holding your nose!—(*He breaks off a lilac blossom and holds it under her nose.*)—I had never been inside the castle, had never seen anything except the church—but this place was far more lovely, and my racing thoughts returned to it incessantly, until I couldn't stand

it any longer. I wanted to experience, just once, the full pleasure of it—
enfin, I stole inside, sat down in there, and looked and marveled. But
then someone came. There was only one way out, at least for the gentry,
but for me there was another way, and I had no other choice but to
make use of it.

(*What is being described here is one of those splendidly appointed lav-
atory facilities that were usual among the stately houses of Sweden.* JULIE
lets the lilac blossom she has taken fall to the table.)

Running as fast as I could, I plunged through a raspberry hedge, dashed
across a strawberry patch, and found myself up on the rose terrace.
Then I caught sight of a pink dress and a pair of white stockings—it
was you. I crawled under a pile of weeds—under it, mind you—beneath
thistles that stung me and wet earth that stank. And I watched you
walking among the roses, and I thought to myself: If it's true that a
thief can enter Paradise and dwell among the angels, then isn't it
strange that a poor farmer's child cannot enter the castle park and play
with the Count's daughter!

JULIE: (*Elegiacally.*) Do you suppose that all poor children have the same
thoughts that you did?

JEAN: (*Hesitates at first, then with conviction.*) If all poor . . . why, yes—
naturally! Naturally!

JULIE: It must be a boundless misfortune to be poor!

JEAN: (*Deep sorrow, strongly exaggerated.*) Oh, Miss Julie! Oh!—A dog
can lie on the Countess's sofa, a horse may have its muzzle stroked by
a young lady's hand, but a servant boy—(*Changes his tone.*) Ah, well.
Now and then you see someone who has what it takes to pull himself
up in the world—but how often does that happen! Anyway, want to
know what I did then? I jumped into the millrace, clothes and all, and
was dragged out and given a beating. But the very next Sunday, when
my father and the rest of the family went off to visit Grandma, I fixed
things so I could stay at home. Then I scrubbed myself with soap and
hot water, put on my best clothes, and went to church, where I knew
I'd be able to see you! I saw you and went back home, with my mind
made up to die. But I wanted to have a beautiful and pleasant death,
with no pain. Then I remembered it was dangerous to sleep underneath
an elderberry bush. We had a big one in full bloom. So I stripped it of
every single blossom, and then I lay down in the oat-bin. Have you
ever noticed how smooth oats are? As soft to touch as—human skin!
Meanwhile, I shut the lid and closed my eyes and woke up really very
sick. But I didn't die, as you can see. What I actually wanted—I don't
know. I had no hope of winning you. To me you were a symbol of the
hopelessness of ever reaching above the class I was born into.

JULIE: You tell a charming story, you know. Did you attend school?

JEAN: Very little. But I've read a lot of novels, and have been to the theatre. And besides, I've listened to how the better classes speak. Most of what I've learned I got from them.

JULIE: You mean you stand around listening to what we say?

JEAN: Certainly! And I've heard plenty too, I can tell you that. While sitting on the coachman's box or rowing the boat. One time I overheard you and another young lady—

JULIE: Oh? And just what did you overhear?

JEAN: Well, it's best not to repeat it. But I *was* a little surprised—I couldn't imagine where you'd learned all those words. Perhaps, I said to myself, there isn't so great a difference between one human being and another after all.

JULIE: Shame on you! We don't behave the way *you* do when we're engaged.

JEAN: (*Looks fixedly at her.*) Quite sure? No need to act so innocent with me, Miss Julie. I saw it all and heard it all.

JULIE: The man I gave my love to was contemptible.

JEAN: They always say that—afterward.

JULIE: Always?

JEAN: Seems to be always—at least I've heard the word used several times before on similar occasions.

JULIE: What occasions?

JEAN: Like the one in question. Last time I . . .

JULIE: (*Rises.*) Silence! I will not listen to any more of this!

JEAN: Funny—*she* didn't want to listen to it, either. Well, if you'll forgive me, I must be getting to bed.

JULIE: (*Softly.*) To bed? On Midsummer Eve?

JEAN: Yes. Dancing with those people up there doesn't amuse me greatly.

JULIE: Go take the key to the boat, and row me out on the lake. I want to watch the sun come up.

JEAN: Is that wise?

JULIE: You sound worried about your reputation?

JEAN: Why shouldn't I be? I wouldn't like to make myself ridiculous, I wouldn't want to be sent away without references, just when I'm getting started. And I think I owe a certain responsibility to Christine.

JULIE: I see, so now it's Christine . . .

JEAN: Yes, and you as well. If you'll take my advice, you'll go straight upstairs to bed.

JULIE: Am I to take orders from you?

JEAN: Just this once, for your own good! Please! It's late, and our tiredness makes us drunk and sets our brains on fire. Go up to bed. Besides, unless I'm wrong I hear the others coming this way to look for me. If they catch us here together, you're finished.

VOICES: (*Singing as they approach.*)

> She came from the woods in distress
> Tridiridi traralala
> With mud on her face and her dress
> Tridiridi lala.
>
> Her dreams were of gold and roast veal
> Tridiridi traralala
> Of a castle and coach with a seal
> Tridiridi lala.
>
> Her cupboard's now bare, it's too bad
> Tridiridi traralala
> There's no more roast veal to be had
> Tridiridi lala.

JULIE: I know these people, and they love me just as I love them. Let them come. Then you'll see!

(*They stand close together inside the glass doors.*)

JEAN: No, Miss Julie, they don't love you. They take your food—but they spit at you afterward. Take my word for it! Listen! Just listen to what they're singing! No, it's better you didn't hear.

JULIE: (*Listening.*) What are they singing?

JEAN: A dirty song. About you and me.

JULIE: Outrageous! God! How rotten of them!

JEAN: A crowd like that is always cowardly. But in a fight with them, the only thing to do is to run.

JULIE: Run? Run where? We can't get out? And we can't go into Christine's room!

JEAN: Into mine, then. Necessity knows no law! You can count on me— as a truly loyal and respectful friend.

JULIE: But wait, think a moment—what if they look for us in there?

JEAN: I'll bolt the door. And if they try to break in, I'll shoot. Come! Come!

JULIE: (*Meaningfully*) You promise me—?

JEAN: I swear.

(JULIE *hurries out to the right.* JEAN *follows quickly.*)

[The "Ballet" described in Strindberg's stage directions was replaced in Bergman's production by the following sequence of actions:

The stage has grown dark during the lewd song. It now becomes completely silent. Shadowy figures can be seen crouching outside the windows, peering in. CLARA, one of the two servant girls who had spied on Christine earlier, leads the way into the kitchen, followed by SOFIE and JOHAN, the stable foreman and Sofie's boyfriend. Stealthily these three seat themselves around the kitchen table and begin to drink whatever they can find. LARS, the coachman, appears, impudently buttoning his fly and pulling up his suspenders; with him is ANNA, a sluttish girl in a loud red dress. As the three around the table softly begin to sing again, LARS raps out the tempo of the song on Jean's bedroom door. The woman in red does a drunken, contorted dance. NILS, a youngster drunker than the rest, has been staggering in and out of the room; he now vomits violently and collapses at the foot of the water barrel.

The singing and tapping of the song stop as CHRISTINE enters. The man who has been rapping on Jean's door spits a mouthful of beer at it in disgust. One by one, each throwing a knowing glance at CHRISTINE, the dark figures leave, dragging their drunken companion with them. CLARA, who considers JEAN her personal property, is the last to depart. She rises slowly from the table, walks with deliberation to the door, and makes an obscene gesture in Christine's direction before disappearing outside.

Dawn begins to break, and the sky outside the windows grows red. CHRISTINE, left alone, sits wrapped in a black shawl, facing away from Jean's door. Then, as she turns to glance at the door, she hears a noise from inside and quickly disappears. At the same instant, JULIE rushes from Jean's room in complete disarray. The scar on her cheek has begun to bleed, and streams of blood can be seen down her right leg. Bent over double, she dashes across the kitchen, up the stairs to the swinging doors at the rear, and reaches the outside just in time to vomit. JEAN appears from his room, but darts back inside and then reappears with a train schedule in his hand.]

JEAN (*Excited.*) Can you possibly think of staying here now?

JULIE: No, I can't. But what should we do?

JEAN: Escape, travel, far away!

JULIE: Travel? But where?

JEAN: To Switzerland, to the Italian lakes! Have you ever been there?

JULIE: No—is it nice there?

JEAN: Eternal summer, oranges, laurel trees, beautiful!

JULIE: But what would we do there?

JEAN: I'll start a hotel. With first-class accommodations for first-class customers.

JULIE: Hotel?

JEAN: That's the life, let me tell you! Always new faces, new languages, never a moment to spare for worry or nerves. No need to wonder what to do with yourself next—there's work to be done all the time. Bells ringing night and day, trains whistling, the omnibus coming and going. And all the time the jingle of gold coins in the till. That's the life!

JULIE: Yes, that's one way to live. But what about me?

JEAN: Mistress of the inn, the pride of the establishment. With your looks—and your style—why, it's a sure thing! It'll be a big success! You'll sit in the office like a queen, setting your slaves in motion with one push of an electric bell. The guests will file past your throne, humbly placing their tribute on a table. You'd never believe how jumpy people get when they're handed a bill. And I'll salt the bills, and you'll sweeten them with your most charming smile. Oh, yes, let's get away from here. (*Consults the train schedule.*) Right now, on the next train! We'll be in Malmö by six-thirty, Hamburg eight-forty tomorrow morning, Frankfurt-Basel takes a day, then on to Como through the Gotthard Pass in, let's see, three days. Three days!

JULIE: It all sounds lovely. But Jean—you have to give me courage. Tell me you love me! Hold me in your arms!

JEAN: (*Hesitates.*) I'd like to—but I don't dare! Never again in this house. I do love you—no question about that—can you doubt it?

JULIE: (*Shy, very feminine.*) Call me by my first name, Jean. Call me Julie. There are no barriers between us now.

JEAN: (*Tormented.*) I can't do it! There *are* barriers between us, as long as we stay in this house. There's the past, there's the Count—I've never met anyone I have more respect for—just seeing his gloves on a chair makes me feel like a small boy again—just hearing that bell up there makes me jump like a scared horse. And when I look at his boots standing there now, all high and mighty, I get shivers down my back. (*Kicks the boots angrily.*) Superstitions, prejudices they drum into us from childhood—it's no easy matter to escape them. Just come to another country, to a republic, and people will grovel in the dust before a servant's livery like mine! Grovel in the dust, I tell you! But *I* won't! I wasn't born to grovel, because I have what it takes, I have character, and if only I can just reach that first branch, then watch me climb! Today I'm a servant, but in a year I'll own a hotel, in ten years I'll be an independent gentleman, and then I'll travel to Rumania, let them decorate me, and maybe—notice I said *maybe*—I'll end up as a Count after all!

JULIE: How wonderful.

JEAN: Oh, in Rumania you can buy a Count's title—but that makes you a Count all the same! My Countess!

JULIE: What do I care about all that? That's what I'm leaving behind now! Tell me you love me, otherwise—yes, otherwise, what am I?

JEAN: I'll tell you a thousand times—later on. But not here! And above all, no emotions, otherwise we lose everything. We have to look at things coolly, like sensible people. (*He takes a cigar, clips it, lights it.*) Now you sit down there, and I'll sit over here, and we'll talk things over as though nothing had happened.

JULIE: (*Desperate.*) Oh, dear God! Have you no feelings?

JEAN: Me? Nobody has more feelings than I do. But I can control myself.

JULIE: A little while ago you could kiss my shoe—and now—

JEAN: (*Harshly.*) That was a little while ago. Now we have something else to think about.

JULIE: Don't speak harshly to me.

JEAN: No, just sensibly. *One* foolish mistake is enough! The Count may come back at any time, and before he does we have to decide what lies ahead for us. What do you think of my plans for the future? Do you approve?

JULIE: They seem acceptable. But one question. A project of that scope requires a greal deal of capital. Do you have it?

JEAN: (*Chews his cigar.*) Me? Of course. I have my professional skills, my broad experience, my knowledge of languages! That's the kind of capital that's worth something, I should say.

JULIE: But it still won't buy you a railway ticket.

JEAN: Perfectly true. Which is why I'm looking for a backer to strengthen the finances.

JULIE: Where would you find one so quickly?

JEAN: You'll have to find him, if you want to be my partner.

JULIE: I can't, and I have no money of my own.

   (*Pause.*)

JEAN: Then the whole thing's off. (*Leaning back, the cigar in his mouth.*)

JULIE: And—?

JEAN: Everything stays the way it is.

JULIE: Do you imagine I'd stay under this roof, as your lover? Do you imagine I'm going to let people point their finger at me? Do you think I could ever look my father in the face again after this? No! Take me with you, away from here, away from the humiliation and the shame! Oh, dear Jesus, what have I done? Oh, my God! (*Weeps.*)

JEAN: Aha, now we strike up the wailing aria! What *have* you done, anyway? Only what plenty of others have done before you.

JULIE: (*Screaming, in a convulsive fit.*) And now you despise me! I'm falling! I'm falling!

JEAN: Just fall on me, I'll pick you up again.

JULIE: What terrible power drew me to you? The attraction of the weak to the strong? Or of the loser to the winner? Or was it love? Is this what love is? Do you know what love is?

JEAN: Me? Yes, you bet I do. You don't suppose this is my first time around, do you?

JULIE: What a language you talk, and what thoughts you think!

JEAN: That's what I've learned, and that's what I am. Now don't be hysterical, and stop putting on airs. We're two of a kind now. There, there, my dear, come let me give you a glass of something extra nice.

   (*He opens the drawer of the table, takes out the wine bottle, and fills two used glasses.*)

JULIE: Where did you get that wine?

JEAN: From the cellar.

JULIE: My father's burgundy!

JEAN: Not good enough for his son-in-law?

JULIE: And I—*I* drink beer!

JEAN: Just goes to show your taste is inferior to mine.

JULIE: Thief!

"What terrible power drew me to you?" Anne-Marie Kuster as Julie, with Degen as Jean.

JEAN: Going to tell on me?

JULIE: Oh! Oh God! (*Pause. She sits, drinks.*) Have I been out of my mind tonight, was I walking in my sleep? Midsummer Eve! A time for innocent games . . .

JEAN: Innocent—well! (*Laughs.*)

JULIE: Is there anybody on earth at this moment who's more miserable!

JEAN: But why? After a conquest like this! Think of Christine in there. Don't you think she has feelings, too?

JULIE: I thought so before, but I don't any longer. No, a servant is still a servant . . .

JEAN: And a whore's still a whore!

JULIE: (*On her knees on the floor.*) Dear God in heaven, put an end to my wretched life! Take me away from the filth I'm sinking into! Save me! Save me! (*Another convulsion.*)

JEAN: (*Patting her on the back, cigar in hand.*) I can't deny I pity you. When I was lying in the onion bed and saw you in the rose garden, well—I have to admit it—I had the same dirty thoughts all boys have.

JULIE: And you wanted to die for my sake!

JEAN: In the oat-bin? That was only a story.

JULIE: A lie, in other words!

JEAN: Something like that. I think I read the story in a magazine— about a chimney sweep who got down into a woodbox with some lilacs, because he'd been charged in a paternity suit . . .

JULIE: I see. That's the sort you are . . .

JEAN: What else could I think of? You always need a fancy story to catch the women with, you know.

JULIE: Swine!

JEAN: *Merde*!

JULIE: So now you've seen the hawk's back—

JEAN: Not exactly its back.

JULIE: And I was to be the first branch—

JEAN: The branch was rotten.

JULIE: I was to have been the signboard on the hotel—

JEAN: On my hotel.

JULIE: —sitting behind your counter, enticing your customers, falsifying your bills—

JEAN: I'd take care of that myself.

JULIE: That a human soul could be so deeply soiled.

JEAN: Launder it, then.

JULIE: Servant, flunkey, stand up when I speak!

JEAN: Servant's slut, flunkey's whore, shut up and get out of here. Are you trying to pretend that *I'm* coarse? Nobody of my class would ever behave as coarsely as you did tonight. What scullery maid do you think would play up to a man the way you did? Have you ever seen any girl of my class cheapen herself like that? I've only seen it happen among animals and loose women. But I know it's done among your class. That's what they call being liberated or emancipated or something educated like that.

JULIE: (*Crushed.*) That's right! Hit me. Trample on me. I don't deserve anything better. I'm the contemptible one—but help me! Help me out of this—if there is a way out.

JEAN: I'm not trying to diminish my share of the blame—or the credit— for having seduced you. But do you suppose somebody in my position would have so much as dared to look at you if you hadn't issued the invitation? I'm still amazed, though . . .

JULIE: And proud.

JEAN: Why not? Though I have to admit I found the conquest too easy to be really exhilarating.

JULIE: Hurt me more.

JEAN: No. Please forgive me for everything I said. I don't strike defenseless people, least of all women. I can't deny that it gives me a certain satisfaction to have discovered it was only cat's-gold that dazzled us down here, that the hawk's back was as gray as the rest of it, that the whiteness of the cheeks was nothing but powder, that polished fingernails could have black edges, and that the handkerchief was dirty, even if it did smell of perfume.—But on the other hand, it saddens me to have seen that what I was striving for was no loftier, no more solid, just as it hurts me to see autumn flowers torn to shreds by the rain and turned into muck.

JULIE: You speak as if you were already above me.

JEAN: But I am. You see, although I'm able to turn you into a Countess, you could never make me a Count.

JULIE: But I'm the child of a Count, and you'll never be that!

JEAN: True enough. But I can be the father of a Count if . . .

JULIE: You're a thief. I'm not.

JEAN: A thief isn't the worst thing you can be! There are lower categories than that. Besides, when I'm in service in a house, I consider myself a member of the family, in a way, a child of that house. And nobody calls it stealing when a child plucks a berry from a loaded bush. (*His passion becomes aroused again.*) You're a fine figure of a woman, Miss Julie! Far too good for somebody like me. You let yourself be seduced, and now you want to cover up that mistake by telling yourself you love me. You don't, unless perhaps I attract you physically—and then your love's no better than mine. But that's not enough for me. I couldn't be content just being your stud—and I can never make you love me.

JULIE: Are you so sure?

[At this point in Bergman's production, the following sequence of actions replaced the business described in Strindberg's stage directions:

JEAN has begun again to make love to JULIE. He fondles her breasts, then reaches underneath her dress and roughly thrusts his hand between her legs. As she struggles, he pulls her savagely from her chair, forces her down backward against the table, and straddles her. With great effort she finally fights him off and pushes him to the floor.]

JEAN: You mean to say it could happen? That I could love you, there's no question about that. You're beautiful, you're refined—educated, lovable when you want to be, and once you've aroused a flame in a man, it will never ever be quenched.—You're like hot wine, strongly spiced, and one kiss from you . . .

JULIE: Leave me alone! You won't win me that way!

JEAN: How, then? Down on my knees, kissing your shoe? I won't do it! It won't happen that way. No caresses and tender words, no plans for the future, no saving you from humiliation! So how?

[JEAN has by this time retreated to the chair beside the stove, where he sits.]

JULIE: How? How? I don't know. I don't know anything! I hate you the way I hate rats—but I can't run away from you.

JEAN: (*Nonchalantly.*) So run away with me!

JULIE: Run away? Why not stay here? Does it really matter what I do? Yes, we have to run away. But I'm so tired. Give me a glass of wine. (JEAN *pours for her. She looks at her watch.*) But first we must talk. We still have a little time. (*Empties her glass and holds it out to be refilled.*)

"You're like hot wine, strongly spiced . . ." Degen (Jean) and Kuster (Julie).

JEAN: Don't drink like that. It'll make you drunk.

JULIE: What does it matter?

JEAN: What does it matter? It's stupid to get drunk. Now, what do you want to say to me?

JULIE: We have to run away. But first we have to talk—or rather I have to talk, because you've been doing all the talking so far. You've told the story of your life, now I'm going to tell mine, and then we'll know all there is to know about one another before we set out on our journey together.

JEAN: One moment! Excuse me! Consider carefully whether you won't be sorry later for putting your life's secrets in my hands.

JULIE: Aren't you my friend?

JEAN: Sometimes, yes. But don't rely on me.

JULIE: You're just saying that. Besides, my secrets are common knowledge anyway. You see, my mother wasn't noble by birth, she came from simple origins. She was brought up under the influence of the ideas of her time about equality, women's freedom, and all the rest of it, and that gave her a decided aversion to marriage. So when my father proposed to her, she told him she would never become his wife, but he could be her lover. He explained to her that he had no desire to see the woman he loved enjoy less respect than he did. She told him she cared nothing for the respect of the world, and so, under the influence of his passion, he gave in to her conditions. But then he found himself expelled from society and left with only his life at home, which didn't satisfy him. I came into the world—much against my mother's wishes, so far as I could gather. I was to be brought up by her as a child of nature— what's more I was to be taught all the things a boy is taught, so I could be an example of the fact that women are just as good as men. I had to wear boy's clothes, learn to take care of the horses, but was never allowed in the cowshed. I had to groom and harness the horses and go hunting and even learn to slaughter. That was horrible! Meanwhile, the men on the estate were put to performing women's tasks and women the men's—with the result that the property was on the verge of bankruptcy and we became the laughingstock of the district. At last my father must have awakened from my mother's spell—he revolted, and everything was changed back to suit his wishes. After that my parents were married quietly. My mother became ill—what kind of illness it was, I don't know—but she suffered convulsions, hid herself in the attic or the garden, and sometimes stayed out all night. Then came the great fire you've heard stories about. The house, the stables, and the cowshed all burned to the ground, under such peculiar circumstances that arson was suspected. The catastrophe came one day after the term of our insurance policy had expired, and the premium sent by my father had been delayed by a careless servant and hadn't arrived on time.

(*She fills her glass and drinks.*)

JEAN: Don't drink any more!

JULIE: Oh, what difference does it make? So we were left penniless and had to sleep in the carriages. My father was at a loss where to raise the money to rebuild the house. His old friends had all forgotten him. So then my mother advises him to borrow the money from a friend of her youth, a brick manufacturer living nearby. Father gets the loan but pays no interest on it, which surprises him greatly. And so the house is rebuilt. (*Drinks again.*) Do you know who set fire to the house?

JEAN: The Countess, your mother!

JULIE: Do you know who the brick manufacturer was?

JEAN: Your mother's lover.

JULIE: Do you know whose money it was?

JEAN: (*Silent.*)—no, that I don't know.

JULIE: It belonged to my mother.

JEAN: And to the Count, too, if no separate property agreement had been signed.

JULIE: There was no agreement. My mother had a modest capital of her own and she didn't want it to fall into my father's hands, so she placed it in the safekeeping of—her friend.

JEAN: Who pinched it.

JULIE: Quite right. He held on to it. My father learns of all this. He can't press charges, he can't repay his wife's lover, he can't prove that the money belonged to his wife. That was my mother's revenge on him for having seized control of the house. He was ready to shoot himself at the time—there were rumors that he had actually tried to and failed. He lived on, though, and my mother was made to pay for what she'd done. Those were five hellish years for me, let me tell you! I loved my father, but being ignorant of the facts I took my mother's side. She was the one who taught me to hate men—she detested all men, as you've heard—and I swore to her I'd never become any man's slave.

JEAN: And so you got engaged to the county commissioner!

JULIE: Exactly—so that he should become my slave.

JEAN: And he wasn't willing?

JULIE: He was willing enough, but he didn't get the chance. I grew tired of him.

JEAN: I saw it all—down by the stable.

JULIE: What did you see?

JEAN: What I saw. The way he broke off the engagement. You can still see it there on your cheek.

JULIE: That's a lie! I was the one who broke the engagement. Has he been saying he did, that contemptible liar?

JEAN: He wasn't contemptible at all, I suspect. You hate men, don't you.

JULIE: Yes—most of the time. But sometimes—when the weakness comes over me, when nature takes over—(*With an expression of disgust.*) Will the fire never die!

JEAN: You hate me, too?

JULIE: Boundlessly! I'd like to see you put to death like an animal.

JEAN: Two years at hard labor for the sodomite and the animal to be killed. Correct?

JULIE: Yes!

JEAN: But we have no judge here—and no animal either. So what do we do, then?

JULIE: Go away together!

JEAN: To torment each other to death?

JULIE: No—to enjoy ourselves for two days, or a week, or for as long as it's possible to enjoy oneself. And then—die.

JEAN: Die? That's crazy! I'd rather start a hotel.

JULIE: (*Not listening to him.*) On the shores of Lake Como, where the sun always shines, and the laurel trees are green at Christmastime, and the orange groves gleam.

JEAN: Lake Como is a rainy hole, and the only oranges I ever saw there were in grocery stores. But it's a good spot for the tourist trade, because it has plenty of villas that are rented out to loving couples. That's a very lucrative business. Know why? Because they sign a rental agreement for six months—and then they leave after three weeks.

JULIE: (*Naively.*) Why after three weeks?

JEAN: They quarrel, of course! But they have to pay the full price all the same. And then you rent the villa out again. It goes on and on like that—because there's lots of love in the world, even if it doesn't last so long. (*Pause.*)

JULIE: You don't want to die with me?

JEAN: I don't want to die at all. For one thing, I like living—and for another, I believe that suicide is a sin against the Providence that gave us life.

JULIE: *You* believe in God?

JEAN: Of course I do. And I go to church every other Sunday. Now, to be frank, I'm tired of all this and I'm going to bed.

JULIE: I see. And you suppose I'll let myself be satisfied with that? Do you know what a man owes a woman he has seduced?

JEAN: (*Returns from his room and slams a silver coin down on the table.*) Here. I always pay my debts.

JULIE: Do you know what the law provides?

JEAN: Unfortunately the law doesn't include a penalty for a woman who seduces a man.

JULIE: Do you see any other way out of this for us except to go away, get married, and then be divorced?

JEAN: And if I refuse to agree to such a misalliance?

JULIE: Misalliance?

JEAN: From my point of view, absolutely! I come from a better background than you do. At least I have no arsonists in my family!

JULIE: Can you prove you don't?

JEAN: You can't prove I do, because we have no family tree—except what's in the police files. But I looked up your family tree in the peerage. Do you know who the founder of your line was? He was a miller who let the king sleep with his wife one night during the war with Denmark. I have no ancestors like that! I have no ancestors at all, but I can make myself an ancestor!

JULIE: This is what I get for opening my heart to someone unworthy, compromising my family's honor . . .

JEAN: Lack of it, you mean! Don't say I didn't warn you. Drinking's bad because it loosens people's tongues. And loose tongues are bad!

JULIE: Oh, how I regret it! How I regret it! If you at least loved me—

JEAN: For the last time—what is it you want? Am I supposed to weep for you, am I supposed to jump over your riding whip, am I supposed to kiss you and entice you down to Lake Como for three weeks? And what am I supposed to do after that? What do you want? This is becoming unbearable. It's what comes of getting mixed up with women. Miss Julie, I can see you're unhappy, I know you're suffering, but I can not understand you. We don't have these little whims. We don't have this hatred. We take love as a game, whenever our work gives us time for it. But we don't have time all day and all night long, as you do. I think you're sick, and your mother was certainly crazy, too—why, we've had whole parishes that went crazy from pietism, and this thing that's raging now is a pietism of a kind! Yes, you're definitely sick.

JULIE: Please be kind to me. Speak to me like a human being.

JEAN: Fine, then act like a human being. You spit on me, and then you won't allow me to wipe it off on you.

JULIE: Help me! Just help me! Tell me what I should do! Which way should I turn?

JEAN: Christ, if only I knew!

JULIE: I've been out of my mind, I've been crazy, but is there nothing that can save me?

JEAN: Stay here and keep quiet. No one knows a thing.

JULIE: Impossible! The others know, and Christine knows.

JEAN: They don't know. It's something they'd never dream was possible.

JULIE: (*Hesitates.*) But—it could happen again.

JEAN: That's true!

JULIE: And the consequences?

JEAN: (*Pause. He gets an idea.*) The consequences! What an idiot I've been not to have thought of that! Yes, there's only one thing left to do—get away from here! At once! At once! I can't come with you, that would ruin everything. You must go away alone—far away—any-where.

JULIE: Alone? Where? I can't!

JEAN: You must! And before the Count gets back, too. If you stay here, we both know what'll happen. Once you make a mistake, you go on repeating it because the damage is already done. And you get more and more reckless—until in the end you get caught! So you must leave! Then you can write to the Count and confess everything—except that it was me! He'll never guess that. Not that I think he'll be too eager to find out!

JULIE: I'll go if you come with me.

JEAN: Are you insane, woman? Miss Julie Flees with Servant! In two days time the newspapers would be full of it. The Count would never survive that.

JULIE: I can't go. I can't stay here. Help me! I'm so weary, so terribly weary. Order me! Set me in motion! I can't think any longer, I can't move any longer . . .

JEAN: And now you see what poor, spineless creatures you really are! So why is it you strut around with your noses in the air, as if you were the lords of creation? Very well, then, I'll give you your orders. (*Pause. Planning.*) Go upstairs, get dressed, take some money for the trip, and come back here!

JULIE: (*Softly.*) Come up with me!

JEAN: To your room? Now you've lost your mind again! (*Hesitates a moment.*) No! Go, at once!

(JEAN *takes hold of her and virtually propels her up the stairs and through the swinging doors at the rear.*)

JULIE: (*As she is leaving.*) Speak kindly to me, Jean.

JEAN: No order ever sounds kind. Now see how it feels! See how it feels!

[In Bergman's production, the following sequence of actions replaced the business described in Strindberg's stage directions:
JULIE disappears and JEAN is alone. He sits at the table, hunched over it in utter exhaustion, with his back to the audience. CHRISTINE enters briskly from her room. She carries a basin of water across the kitchen and empties it. Then she disappears into Jean's room and returns with a stiff shirt front and a white tie in her hand.]

CHRISTINE: Blessed Jesus, what a mess in here! What have you been up to?

JEAN: Oh, Miss Julie dragged all the others down here. Did you sleep so soundly you didn't hear anything?

CHRISTINE: I slept like a log.

JEAN: Getting ready for church?

CHRISTINE: That's right. You promised you'd come to communion with me this morning.

JEAN: Yes, I did, didn't I. And here you are with my best bib and tucker. Well, come on, then. (*He sits up wearily as* CHRISTINE *dresses him in the shirt front and tie.*) What's the lesson for today?

CHRISTINE: The beheading of John the Baptist, I expect.

JEAN: Oh, then we're in for a long one. Hey! You're strangling me! Oh God, I'm so tired. So tired.

> [During the following exchange in Bergman's production:
> CHRISTINE fills a kettle with water, puts it on the stove to boil, opens the stove and blows up the fire, grinds fresh coffee in a mill, clears the kitchen table, and washes the table top. Her angry impatience is evident in the noise and vigor with which these various actions are accomplished. JEAN, meanwhile, remains seated in his chair, motionless.]

CHRISTINE: Well, what have you been doing, up all night? You look positively green in the face.

JEAN: I've been sitting here, talking with Miss Julie.

CHRISTINE: She's got no sense of what's proper, that one!

JEAN: (*After a pause.*) Know something, Christine?

CHRISTINE: Well?

JEAN: It's strange, you know, when you stop to think about it. With her.

CHRISTINE: What's strange?

JEAN: Everything.

  (*Pause.* CHRISTINE *notices the half-empty glasses on the table.*)

CHRISTINE: Have you been drinking together, too?

JEAN: Yes.

CHRISTINE: Disgusting—Look at me straight in the eye!

JEAN: Yes.

CHRISTINE: Is it possible? *Is it possible?*

Christine (Ellert): "I'd never have believed it! Never!" Michael Degen is Jean.

JEAN: (*After a moment's reflection.*) Yes, it's possible.

CHRISTINE: Ugh! I'd never have believed it! Never! Ugh!

JEAN: You aren't jealous of her, are you?

CHRISTINE: No, not of her. Had it been Clara or Sofie—then I'd have scratched your eyes out! Why I don't know, but that's the way it is.—No, it's simply disgusting!

JEAN: Are you angry with her, then?

CHRISTINE: No, I'm angry with you! That was a rotten thing to do, really rotten. Poor young woman. No, I don't care who hears me, I won't stay in this house any longer—not in a house where you can't have respect for your employers.

JEAN: Who says you have to have respect for them?

CHRISTINE: Oh yes, that's what you say, you're so smart! But I wouldn't want to work for people who can't behave decently. Would you? You just drag yourself down in the dirt by doing it, that's my opinion.

JEAN: Well, at least it's some consolation to know they're no better than we are.

CHRISTINE: Not in my opinion. If they aren't any better, then there's nothing to inspire us to become better ourselves. And think of the Count! Just think of all the sorrows he's had in his time. Blessed Jesus! No, I'm not staying in this house any longer!—And with somebody like yourself, at that! Had it been the young commissioner now, had it been someone finer . . .

JEAN: What's that supposed to mean?

CHRISTINE: Oh well, you're not so bad in your way, but there's still a difference between people and people.—No, I'll never get over it with her. Miss Julie, who's always been so proud, so standoffish with men—who'd ever believe she'd go and give herself just like that? And to somebody like you? Why, she all but had poor Diana shot for chasing after the porter's mutt! I mean, honestly! But I'm not staying here any longer. When the new term comes round in October, I'm leaving!

JEAN: And then?

CHRISTINE: Well, since we happen to be on the subject, it's high time you looked for something yourself, since we're getting married.

JEAN: What would I look for? I can't get another position like this once I'm married.

CHRISTINE: No, of course not. I suppose you could find a job as a concierge, or else try to get in as superintendent of a public building someplace.

Government pay is low but it's secure, and the wife and children get a pension—

JEAN: (*With a grimace.*) Wonderful! But it's not quite my style to plan an early death just to oblige my wife and children. I have bigger prospects than that in mind, I assure you.

CHRISTINE: You and your prospects. You've got responsibilities, too! Just keep that in mind!

JEAN: Now don't start in pestering me by talking about responsibilities. I know perfectly well what I have to do. Besides, we've got plenty of time to worry about that. Now, off you go and get yourself dressed. Then we'll go to church.

[In Bergman's production, JULIE could be seen approaching during the previous speech, dressed in traveling clothes. Pausing outside the windows, she watches JEAN and CHRISTINE in a laughing, eager embrace. She quickly retreats out of sight.]

CHRISTINE: Who was that walking around upstairs?

JEAN: I don't know. Clara, probably.

CHRISTINE: (*As she leaves.*) It couldn't be the Count, could it? We'd have heard him come home.

JEAN: (*Alarmed.*) The Count? No, it can't be. He would have rung.

CHRISTINE: (*Exits.*) Well, God help us! I've never experienced anything to equal this.

[In Bergman's production, the following sequence of actions replaced the business described in Strindberg's stage directions:

The sun has now risen. The strength of the sunlight flooding in through the windows increases steadily. JULIE enters, dressed for travel. She hurries down the steps inside the door, and kisses JEAN with an air of feverish excitement. Her head is covered by a light, off-white shawl which she removes and places on a chair. In her hand she carries a birdcage, covered with a cloth, which she also sets down.]

JULIE: I'm ready now.

JEAN: Shh, Christine's awake!

JULIE: Does she suspect anything?

JEAN: She knows nothing at all. But my God, you're a sight!

JULIE: Why, what's wrong?

JEAN: You're white as a sheet—and forgive me for saying so, but your face is filthy.

JULIE: Let me wash myself, then. (*She goes to the washbasin and washes her face and hands.*) There. Now give me a towel. Oh—the sun's coming up!

JEAN: And the spooks vanish.

JULIE: Yes, there really were spooks abroad this night!—Listen, Jean, listen to me! Come with me, I have money now.

JEAN: Enough?

JULIE: Enough for a start. Come with me! I can't go alone, not today. Just imagine—Midsummer Day, on a stifling train, crammed in with crowds of people who stare at you. Long waits at stations when all you want is to rush on. No, I can't do it, I can't! And then the memories begin—childhood memories of Midsummer Days—the church all hung with leaves—birch leaves and lilacs—dinner at a festive table, among relatives and friends—afternoon in the park, dancing, music, flowers, games! Oh, you can try to run! You can try to run away, but the memories follow behind in the baggage car—and the remorse and the guilt!

[JEAN has been counting her money furiously during the previous speech. When he has finished his counting, he replies with a satisfied smile.]

JEAN: I'll come with you—but right now, this very minute, before it's too late. Now, at once!

JULIE: Then hurry and get dressed! (*She picks up the birdcage.*)

JEAN: But no baggage! That would give us away.

JULIE: No, nothing—only what we can have with us in the compartment.

JEAN: (*Has taken his hat.*) What have you got there? What is it?

JULIE: It's only my greenfinch. I can't leave that behind.

JEAN: What? We're supposed to drag a birdcage along with us? You *are* out of your mind. Put down that cage!

JULIE: It's the one thing I'm taking with me from my home! The one living creature that loves me, after Diana was so faithless. Please! don't be cruel! Let me take it!

JEAN: Put down that cage, I tell you! And don't talk so loud—Christine will hear us!

JULIE: No, I can't leave it in the hands of strangers. I'd rather you killed it.

JEAN: Give it here to me, then. I'll chop off its head.

JULIE: Just don't make it suffer! Don't . . . no, I can't do it!

JEAN: Give it here. I can.

JULIE: Oh, my little Sarina, must you leave me now?

JEAN: Please stop making scenes! Our lives depend on this, our whole future. Now, hurry! (*He snatches the bird from her, takes it to the chopping block, and picks up a kitchen axe.* JULIE *turns away.*) You should have been taught how to butcher chickens instead of how to shoot. (*Brings down the axe.*) Then you wouldn't be so bothered by a drop or two of blood. (*Goes to wash his hands.*)

JULIE: (*Screams.*) Kill me, too! Kill me, since you can butcher an innocent creature and never even tremble! Oh, how I hate and despise you! There is blood between us now! I curse the moment I laid eyes on you, I curse the moment I was conceived in my mother's womb.

JEAN: And what good does all your cursing do? Just go!

JULIE: (*Approaches the chopping block, as though drawn to it against her will.*) No, I don't want to go yet. I can't—I must look—shh! There's a carriage outside. (*Listens, while her eyes remain fixed on the block and the axe.*) Do you think I can't bear the sight of blood! Do you think I'm so weak!—Oh, how I wish I could see your blood, your brains on a chopping block—how I wish I could see your whole sex swimming in a pool of blood like this—I think I could drink from your skull, I'd like to bathe my feet in your gaping chest, I'd gladly eat your heart, roasted whole! You think I'm weak—you think I love you just because my womb craved your seed, you think I'll carry your brat under my heart and nourish it with my blood—give birth to your child and take your name! Listen—what is your name anyway? I've never heard your last name— I'll bet you don't even have one. I'd have to be Mrs. Porterlodge or Mrs. Garbageheap! Dog with my collar around your neck, flunkey with my crest on your buttons—I share you with my own cook, I'm in competition with my own scullery maid! Oh—Oh! You think I'm a coward who'll run away? No, now I'm staying—and then let the storm break! My father will come home—find his desk broken into—his money gone. Then he'll ring the bell—that bell, right there—twice to summon his lackey. Then he'll send for the police—and I shall tell everything! Everything! Oh, it will be wonderful to put an end to it all—if only it could all end!—And then he'll have a stroke and die—and we'll be finished with everything at last, and there will be peace—stillness— eternal rest! And the coat of arms will be broken over the coffin—and the Count's line will become extinct. And the lackey's line will continue in an orphanage—win laurels in the gutter—and end in prison!

JEAN: (*Clapping his hands sarcastically.*) Bravo! There speaks the blue blood of royalty! Very fine, Miss Julie!

(CHRISTINE *enters, dressed for church, a psalmbook clasped in her hands.* JULIE *hurries toward her, seeking protection.*)

JULIE: Help me, Christine! Protect me from this man!

CHRISTINE: (*Cold and unmoved.*) What kind of rumpus is this on a holy-day morning? (*Looks at the chopping block.*) Shouting and screaming the way you've been doing!

JULIE: Christine, you're a woman and you're my friend. Don't trust this swine!

JEAN: (*Stealing off to his room.*) While you ladies talk things over, I'll just go in and shave.

JULIE: You must understand me! You have to listen!

CHRISTINE: No, I understand nothing at all about such loose ways. Where are you off to dressed like that? And him with his hat on—well? What's that supposed to mean?

JULIE: Listen to me, Christine. Listen and I'll explain everything . . .

CHRISTINE: I have no wish to know anything.

JULIE: You must listen to me . . .

CHRISTINE: About what? Your foolishness with Jean? See, I'm not worried about that one bit, and I don't intend to mix myself up in it either. But if you've got some idea of tricking him into running away, we'll soon put a stop to that!

JULIE: (*Very nervous.*) Now try to be calm, Christine, and listen to me. I can't stay here and Jean can't stay here either. And so we have to go away . . .

CHRISTINE: Hmm, hmm!

JULIE: (*Pulling herself together.*) But, you see, I just had an idea—we could go away, all three of us—abroad—to Switzerland and start a hotel together. I have money, you see—and Jean and I could run the whole thing—and you, I thought you could take charge of the kitchen.— Wouldn't that be fine! Say yes, now! (*Clasps Christine's arms in a gesture of entreaty.*)

CHRISTINE: (*Cold and thoughtful.*) Hmm, hmm!

JULIE: (*Tempo presto.*) You've never been away on a trip, Christine— you should travel and have a look at the world. You've no idea how much fun it is to travel on a train—new people all the time—new countries—and then we'll come to Hamburg and stop to see the zoological gardens along the way—you'll love that—and then we'll go to

"Wouldn't that be fine! Say yes, now!" Kuster as Julie and Ellert as the unyielding Christine.

the theatre and hear an opera—and when we get to Munich we'll have the museums, Christine, with Rubens and Raphael, those great painters, you know.—You've heard of Munich, where King Ludvig lived— you know, the King who lost his mind.—And then we'll see his castles—he had castles that are built just like the ones in fairytales—and from there it isn't far to Switzerland—with the Alps—just imagine, Christine—the Alps with snow in the middle of summer—and oranges grow there, and laurel trees that are green all year round—(JEAN *stands in the doorway to his room, his face covered in shaving lather. He whets his razor on a strap that he holds with his teeth and his left hand. He listens with satisfaction to what is being said, occasionally nodding approval.*)

JULIE: (*Tempo prestissimo.*) And then we'll get ourselves a hotel—and I'll sit in the office while Jean stands and receives the guests—I'll do the shopping—and write letters.—That's the life, let me tell you!— And then the train will whistle, and the omnibus will arrive, and electric bells will ring on all the floors, and then they'll ring in the res taurant—and I'll make up the bills—and I can salt them, too, I can tell you—because you'd never believe how nervous people get when they have to pay a bill!—And you, Christine—you'll be mistress of the kitchen.—Naturally you won't have to stand at the stove yourself anymore—and you'll be able to wear nice, new clothes for the guests to see you in—and with your looks, you know—I'm not flattering you now—you're sure to catch yourself a man one bright day, one of those rich Englishmen, you know—people like that are so easy—

(*Slower.*)

—to catch—and then we'll get rich—and we'll build ourselves a villa on Lake Como—it's true it rains there now and then—but—

(*Spent.*)

—the sun must shine once in a while—even though it looks dark—and—so—otherwise we can come back—come back home again—

(*Pause.*)

Back here—or someplace else.

CHRISTINE: Look here, do you really believe all this?

JULIE: If I really believe it?

CHRISTINE: Yes.

JULIE: I don't know. I don't believe anything any longer. (*She collapses at the table, and her head sinks down between her arms.*) Nothing. Nothing whatsoever.

CHRISTINE: (*In Jean's direction.*) So, you were thinking of running off, were you?

(JEAN *comes in with the razor in his hand, dries his face in a towel, and places the razor on the table.*)

JEAN: Running off? Well, that's overstating it, I'd say! You heard Miss Julie's plan, and even if she is tired now from being up all night, it still sounds like a good enough idea to me.

CHRISTINE: Will you listen to him! Do you suppose I'd work as a cook for the likes of her . . .

JEAN: (*An angry fight breaks out between them.*) You keep a civil tongue in your head when you talk about your mistress! Understand?

CHRISTINE: Mistress?

JEAN: That's right.

CHRISTINE: Just listen to that, will you!

JEAN: Yes, and you'd better listen to it for your own good! And talk less!

Miss Julie's your mistress, and what you despise her for now you ought to despise yourself for, too!

CHRISTINE: I've always had enough respect for myself . . .

JEAN: To be able to look down your nose at others!

CHRISTINE: . . . that I've never stepped beneath my station. You tell me if you've ever caught the Count's cook getting mixed up with the stableboy or the swineherd! Just tell me that!

JEAN: Just because you're lucky enough to have gotten hold of a fine man for yourself!

CHRISTINE: A fine man indeed, who sells the Count's oats out of his own stable—

JEAN: You should talk—extorting percentages on the groceries and taking kickbacks from the butcher!

CHRISTINE: What did you just say!

JEAN: And you're the one who can't have respect for your mistress anymore! (*As they scuffle violently.*) You—you—you!

CHRISTINE: Are you coming with me to church now? You could use a good sermon, after all you've done!

JEAN: No, I am not going to church today. You can go by yourself, and get all your misdeeds off your conscience.

"It still sounds like a good enough idea to me," Jean (Degen) tells Christine (Ellert), as Julie (Kuster) sits exhausted at the table.

CHRISTINE: Yes, I'll do just that, and I'll come home with forgiveness for myself, and enough for you besides! Our Saviour suffered and died on the cross for all our sins, and if we turn to Him with faith and humility in our hearts, He will take all our sins upon Himself.

JEAN: Including the groceries?

JULIE: Do you believe that, Christine?

CHRISTINE: That is my living faith, as truly as I stand here, and it's the faith I have kept from my childhood, Miss Julie. And where the sin is exceedingly great, there shall His mercy overflow.

JULIE: Oh, if only I had your faith. Oh, if . . .

CHRISTINE: Ah, but that, you see, is something you can never have, except by God's special grace, and that isn't given to everyone!

JULIE: To whom is it given, then?

CHRISTINE: That is the great secret of the Almighty, for the Lord takes no notice of persons, except that the last shall be first . . .

JULIE: So He does take notice of the last, then?

CHRISTINE: (*Continues.*) . . . and it is easier for a camel to pass through the eye of a needle, than for a rich man to enter into the kingdom of God. So you see, Miss Julie, that's the way it is. And now I'm going—by myself—and on my way I'll warn the stableboy not to allow any

"And it is easier for a camel to pass through the eye of a needle," Christine (Ellert) warns Julie (Kuster).

horses to be taken out, just in case someone might be thinking of leaving before the Count gets back. Good-bye! (*She goes out.*)

JEAN: That little bitch! And all on account of that greenfinch!

JULIE: (*Dully.*) Forget about the greenfinch.—Do you see any way out of this, any end to it?

JEAN: (*Ponders.*) No.

JULIE: What would you do in my place? (*Strong sunlight.*)

JEAN: In your place? Let me think. As a Count's daughter, as a woman, after this kind of mistake. I don't know. Yes, now I do know!

JULIE: (*Makes a gesture.*) Like this?

JEAN: Yes. But *I* wouldn't do it—be clear about that! There's a difference between us.

JULIE: Because you're a man and I'm a woman? What difference does that make?

JEAN: Same difference as between—a man and a woman!

(*Strong light on* JULIE *as she reaches out for the razor.*)

JULIE: (*With the razor in her hand.*) I want to do it! But I can't! My father couldn't do it, either, that time he should have.

JEAN: No, he shouldn't have done it. He had to get his revenge first.

JULIE: And now my mother revenges herself in turn, through me.

JEAN: Didn't you ever love your father, Miss Julie?

JULIE: Yes, beyond all limits, but I think I hated him, too! I must have hated him without ever realizing it. But he was the one who taught me to despise my own sex, the one who turned me into half a woman and half a man! Who's to blame for everything that happened? My father, my mother—or is it all my own fault? But what is my own? I have nothing of my own! I don't have one single thought that I haven't gotten from my father, not one single emotion I haven't gotten from my mother, and this latest idea—about everyone being equal—I got that from him, my fiancé, and because of it I called him contemptible. How can it be my fault, then? Shift the guilt over to Jesus, as Christine did—no, I'm too proud for that, and too intelligent—thanks to my father's wisdom.—And all that about a rich man not being able to get into heaven, that's a lie, and Christine, with her money in a savings account, won't get there in any case! So whose fault is it, then? And what does it matter whose fault it is? I'm still the one who has to shoulder the guilt, bear the consequences . . .

"Order me and I'll obey you like a dog." Kuster and Degen in dress rehearsal.

JEAN: Yes, but . . .

> (*Two sharp rings of the bell are heard.* JEAN *jumps up, and quickly changes into his livery coat.*)

JEAN: The Count's home! You don't suppose that Christine—

> (*Hurries to the speaking tube, knocks on it and listens.*)

JULIE: Now he's been to his desk!

JEAN: Jean here, sir. (*Listens. The audience cannot hear what the Count says.*) Very good, sir. (*Listens.*) Very good, sir. At once. (*Listens.*) Right away, sir. (*Listens.*) Yes, sir. In half an hour.

JULIE: What did he say? For God's sake, tell me what he said!

JEAN: He wants his boots and his coffee in half an hour.

> [JEAN hastens to fetch a covered silver tray, places it on the table, and begins afterwards to polish the Count's boots.]

144

JULIE: In half an hour, then. Oh, I'm so tired! I'm unable to do anything any longer! Unable to feel remorse, unable to run, unable to stay, unable to live—unable to die! Help me! (*She stands and walks, with the razor in her hand, toward the middle of the room.*) Order me, and I'll obey you like a dog. Do me this last service, save my honor, save my name! You know what I should do, but can't—will me to do it! Order me to do it!

JEAN: I don't know why—but now I can't, either—I don't understand it. It's as though this jacket here actually kept me—from being able to order you—and now, since the Count spoke to me—now—how can I explain it—ah—it's this damned servant boy sitting on my back! I think if the Count were to come down here right now—and he ordered me to cut my throat—I'd do it on the spot.

JULIE: Then make believe you're my father, and I'm you. You were such a good actor before, when you got down on your knees—you were the gentleman then—or—haven't you ever been to the theatre and watched a hypnotist? (JEAN *nods affirmatively.*) He says to the subject, take the broom! And the subject takes it. He says, sweep! And the subject sweeps—

JEAN: But the other one has to be asleep.

JULIE: (*Ecstatic.*) I'm already asleep.

JEAN: (*Seated beside the stove.*) Go now—go out to the barn and—

JULIE: (*Standing still.*) Thank you. Now I am going to rest! But just tell me one more thing—that the first can also obtain the gift of grace. Tell me that, even if you don't believe it.

JEAN: The first? No, I can't do that. But wait—Miss Julie—now I have it! You aren't among the first any· longer—you are among the last!

JULIE: That's true. I am among the very last—I am the last. Oh! But now I can't go! Tell me once more that I must go.

JEAN: No, now I can't either. I can't.

JULIE: And the first shall be the last.

JEAN: Don't think, don't think! You're taking all my strength from me, too, and making me a coward. Wait! I thought the bell moved. No! Should we stuff paper into it?—Imagine being so frightened of a bell! But it's not just a bell—someone is sitting behind it—a hand sets it in motion—and something else sets the hand in motion. Then cover your ears, that's all you have to do, just hold your hands over your ears! Yes, but then he'll ring louder! And keep on ringing until somebody answers—and then it'll be too late! Then the police will come—and then—

(*Two loud rings of the bell.*)

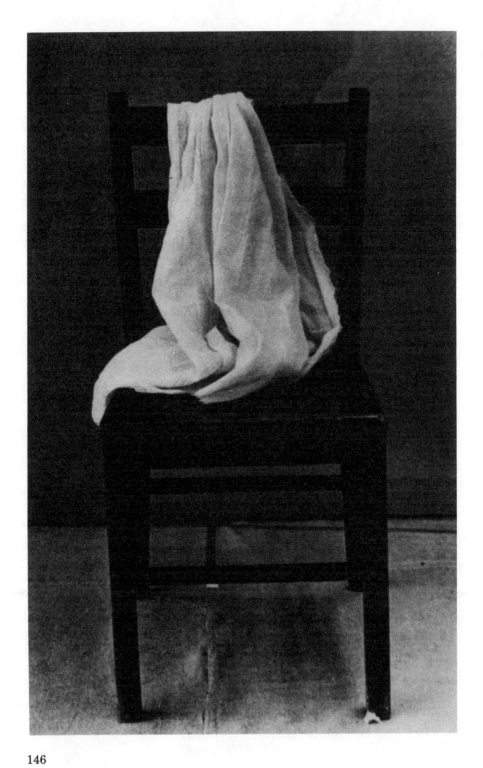

JEAN: (*Dashes to where he has left Julie's money, snatches up the bills, and stuffs them haphazardly into the side pockets of her dress.*) This is terrible! But it can't end any other way! Go!

[JULIE smiles calmly, walks firmly up the steps, and exits through the glass doors. As her figure disappears outside, JEAN pulls the cover off the tray, pours coffee into the silver coffee pot, takes up the tray in one hand and the Count's boots in the other, and hurries away to answer his master's summons.]

Ingmar Bergman

SCENES FROM A MARRIAGE

Dialogue and a prologue arranged for the stage
by the director and the actors

Set arranged by Elizabeth Urbancic

Marianne ....Gaby Dohm

Johan.. Erich Hallhuber

Mrs. Palm... Monika John

Photographer... Gündüz Bizde

Karin⎱   *The children of*   Monika Schlüter/Elke Schüssler

Eva ⎰   *Marianne and Johan*   Patricia Schwöbel/Melanie Weigl

Directed by Ingmar Bergman
Premiere 30 April 1981

The Interview

The house lights remain on and the audience continues to talk as the play gets underway. MARIANNE *and* JOHAN *are being interviewed in their home. The Interviewer,* MRS. PALM, *leads the way into the room. It is furnished with an ornate mahogany sofa—a monstrosity of bourgeois taste, upholstered in green velvet—and a small side table. In the interviewer's wake come* MARIANNE *and* JOHAN *and their two young daughters, accompanied by a caricature of a photographer, called Ingmar, who hops about the room continually snapping pictures. The family is posed in suitable groupings around the sofa. The girls,* EVA, 12, *and* KARIN, 11, *are delighted to perform "cute" little tricks for the benefit of the camera. Another absurd family composition is arranged in the doorway, after which the children are allowed to disappear and "Ingmar" is sent off on his next two assignments.* MARIANNE *and* JOHAN *sit, rather stiffly and on their best behavior, beside each other on the sofa.* MRS. PALM *takes a seat in the front row of the audience, from which she conducts the first part of the interview.*

MRS. PALM: (*Gaily.*) For our series, "Marriages that Cope with Job and Love," we always begin with a standard question. The question is: How would you describe yourselves in a few words?

JOHAN: That's not an easy one.

   (*The house lights dim.*)

MRS. PALM: Not so difficult either, surely?

JOHAN: I mean, there's risk of a misunderstanding.

MRS. PALM: Do you think so?

JOHAN: Yes. It might sound conceited if I described myself as extremely intelligent, successful, youthful, well-balanced, and sexy. A man with a world conscience, cultivated, well-read, popular, and a good mixer. Let me see, what else can I think of . . . friendly. Friendly in a nice way even to people who are worse off. I like sports. I'm a good family man. A good son. I have no debts and I pay my taxes. I respect our government whatever it does. I've left the state church. Is this enough or do you want more details? I'm a splendid lover. Aren't I, Marianne?

MRS. PALM: Perhaps we can return to the question. How about you, Marianne? How would you describe yourself?

MARIANNE: I doubt if I have the same natural appreciation of my own excellence as Johan. But to tell the truth, I'm glad I can live the life I do. It's a good life, if you know what I mean. Well, what else can I say . . . Oh dear, this is difficult!

JOHAN: She has a nice figure.

MARIANNE: You're joking. I'm trying to take this thing seriously.

MRS. PALM: Perhaps we can take up the question again later. Well, let's start with a few facts. I'd like to know your ages.

JOHAN: I'm thirty-six. But you wouldn't think so to look at me, would you?

MARIANNE: I'm thirty-five.

JOHAN: Both of us come from almost indecently middle-class homes.

MARIANNE: Johan's father is a doctor.

JOHAN: And my mother's the motherly type. Very much so.

MARIANNE: My father's a lawyer. It was decided from the outset that I was to be a lawyer too. I'm the youngest of seven children. Mother ran a big household. Nowadays she takes it easier.

JOHAN: She does?

   (*Polite smiles.*)

MARIANNE: The funny thing about us both is that we actually get along very well with our parents. We see quite a lot of each other. There has never been any friction to speak of.

MRS. PALM: Perhaps we'd better say something about your professions.

JOHAN: I teach at the Psychotechnical Institute.

MARIANNE: I specialize in family law and am employed by a law firm. Most of my work has to do with divorces and so on.

JOHAN: And our work has to do with translating the scientific-experiential theories of applied psychology into potentially practical applications. My own research concerns the consequences of the psychopathological blocking mechanism that prevents a person in a dark room from being able to touch concentrated beams of light with a sharp instrument—I experiment with the optimum size of the light beams, you see.

MRS. PALM: Ah yes, I understand completely. How did you meet?

MARIANNE: Let Johan tell you.

JOHAN: Good Lord, *that's* interesting!

MARIANNE: At any rate, it wasn't love at first sight.

JOHAN: Both of us had a large circle of friends and we used to meet at all sorts of parties. Also, we were politically active for several years and we went in for amateur dramatics quite a lot as students. But I can't say we made any very deep impression on each other. Marianne thought I was stuck-up.

MARIANNE: He was having a much-discussed affair with a pop singer and that gave him a certain image and made him insufferable.

JOHAN: And Marianne was nineteen and married to a fool, whose only saving grace was that he was the apple of his rich father's eye.

MARIANNE: But he was awfully kind. And I was madly in love. Besides, I got pregnant almost at once.

MRS. PALM: But how was it that . . .

JOHAN: That we two came together? That was Marianne's idea, actually.

MARIANNE: My child died soon after it was born.

MRS. PALM: Oh, dear.

MARIANNE: And then my husband and I got a divorce, rather to our relief. Johan had been dropped by that pop singer and was a little less stuck-up. We were feeling a bit lonely and tousled. So I suggested trying to make a go of it.

JOHAN: We were not in the least in love with one another.

MARIANNE: We were just miserable.

JOHAN: We got along very well together and really got down to our studies.

MARIANNE: So we started living together. Suddenly we were accepted as Johan and Marianne. After six months we got married.

JOHAN: Besides, by then we were in love.

MARIANNE: Terribly.

JOHAN: We were considered an ideal married couple.

MARIANNE: And so it has gone on.

MRS. PALM: No complications?

MARIANNE: We've had no material worries. We're on good terms with friends and relations on both sides. We have good jobs that we like. We're healthy.

JOHAN: And so on and so on, to an almost vulgar degree. Security, order, comfort, and loyalty. It all has a suspiciously successful look, doesn't it?

MARIANNE: Naturally, like other people, we have our differences. That goes without saying. But we agree on all the important things.

MRS. PALM: Don't you ever quarrel?

JOHAN: Oh yes, Marianne does.

MARIANNE: Johan is very slow to anger, so it calms me down.

MRS. PALM: It sounds fantastic. The whole thing.

MARIANNE: Someone was saying to us just last night that the very lack of problems is in itself a serious problem. I suspect it's true. A life like ours always has its dangers. We're well aware of that.

JOHAN: The world is going to the devil and I claim the right to mind my own business.

MARIANNE: I don't agree with Johan.

MRS. PALM: Oh, what do you think then?

MARIANNE: I believe in fellow-feeling.

MRS. PALM: What do you mean by that?

MARIANNE: If everyone learned to care about each other right from childhood, the world would be a different place. I'm certain of that.

(MARIANNE *hurries out, saying she must look after her daughters.* JOHAN *fills his pipe and exchanges a rather uncertain but polite smile with the interviewer.*)

JOHAN: To tell you the truth, it's not such a simple matter.

MRS. PALM: No?

JOHAN: We used to think that nothing could happen to us. Now we know that everything can happen. That's the real difference.

MRS. PALM: Are you afraid of the future?

JOHAN: If I stopped to think I'd be paralyzed with fear. Or so I imagine. So I don't think. I'm fond of this cozy old sofa, because it gives me an illusion of security. I like Bach's "St. Matthew Passion" though I'm not religious, because it gives me a sense of piety and belonging. I depend very much on close contact with our families, because that reminds me of my childhood when I felt protected. I think you must have a kind of technique to be able to live and be content with your life. The people I admire most are those who can take life as a joke. I can't. I have too little sense of humor for a feat like that. You won't print this, will you?

MRS. PALM: No, I'm afraid it's a little too complicated for our women readers. If you forgive my saying so.

(MARIANNE *has returned and sits down on the sofa. The telephone rings.* JOHAN *excuses himself and vanishes.* MRS. PALM *seizes the opportunity. After all, it's a woman's magazine looking for a story here. She comes up and joins* MARIANNE *on the sofa.*)

MRS. PALM: I don't think you and I have met since our school days.

MARIANNE: Do you often see our old schoolmates?

MRS. PALM: Actually I don't. (*Going right to the point.*) I gather that you and Johan have a good life together. Haven't you? I mean, you're really happy. Everything you tell me sounds simply marvelous. But then why shouldn't some people be granted perfection.

MARIANNE: I don't know that we've got perfection. But we do have a good life. I mean, we're happy. Oh yes.

MRS. PALM: (*Seizing on this.*) How would you define the word happiness?

MARIANNE: Must I really?

MRS. PALM: (*Gravely.*) This is a woman's magazine, Marianne.

MARIANNE: If I thought up something to say about happiness, Johan would only laugh at me. No, I can't. You must hit on something yourself.

MRS. PALM: (*Roguishly.*) Don't try to wriggle out of it now.

MARIANNE: I suppose happiness is being content. I don't long for anything. Except for the summer, of course. (*Pause.*) I wish it could always be like this. That nothing ever changed.

MRS. PALM: What do you have to say about fidelity?

MARIANNE: Well, really!

MRS. PALM: You must help me put some body into this. Johan's awfully sweet, but I didn't get much out of him.

MARIANNE: Fidelity?

MRS. PALM: Yes, fidelity. Between man and woman. Of course.

MARIANNE: Fidelity. Hmm, what can one say about that . . .

MRS. PALM: In your profession you must surely have come across—

MARIANNE: I wonder if fidelity can exist other than as a matter of course. I don't think fidelity can ever be a compulsion or a resolution. You can never promise anyone fidelity. Either it's there or it isn't. I like to be faithful to Johan, therefore I am faithful. But naturally I don't know how it will be tomorrow or next week.

MRS. PALM: Have you always been faithful to Johan?

MARIANNE: (*Coldly.*) Now I think we're getting *too* personal.

MRS. PALM: Forgive me. Now I have only one last question, while Johan is busy out there. What do you have to say about love?

MARIANNE: Why, Elfriede!

MRS. PALM: You *must* say something about love. It's part of this series to give your views on love.

MARIANNE: And if I don't want to?

MRS. PALM: Then I'll have to make up something myself and it won't be half as good.

MARIANNE: No one has told me what love is. And I'm not even sure it's necessary to know. I think it's enough if you're kind to the person you're living with. Affection is also a good thing. Comradeship and tolerance and a sense of humor. Moderate ambitions for one another. If you can supply those ingredients, then . . . then love's not so important. I wish that . . .

MRS. PALM: Why are you so upset?

MARIANNE: I don't know. I can't see through this problem, so I'd rather not talk about it. But I wish that people . . . that we were not forced to play a lot of roles we don't want to play. That we could be simpler and gentler with each other. Don't you think so too?

MRS. PALM: (*Alert.*) That life could be a little more romantic!

MARIANNE: No, I didn't mean that actually. In fact, I meant just the opposite. You see how badly I express myself. Can't we talk a bit about children and upbringing instead? It's something more concrete, anyway.

MRS. PALM: Perhaps we did digress.

MARIANNE: Yes, I think we did. Perhaps you'd like me to show you the other rooms?

(*They disappear.*)

Interlude

(JOHAN *wanders in, reading a woman's magazine.*)

JOHAN: The outcome of this interview was inevitable. It appeared six weeks later in a magazine called *Woman's World of Fashion.* (*Reads aloud.*) "Marianne has folksong-blue eyes that seem to light up from within. When I ask her how she manages both job and home she gives a little introspective smile as though she were keeping a sweet secret and answers rather evasively that she copes all right, that she and Johan help each other. 'It's a question of *mutual understanding,*' she says suddenly, brightening as Johan comes in and sits down beside her on the handsome heirloom sofa. He puts a protective arm around her shoulders and she snuggles up to him with a smile of security and trust. So I leave them, and I can't help noticing that they are secretly pleased when I go, so that they can once more be alone together. Two young people, strong, happy, with a constructive attitude toward life in general, but who have never forgotten all the same to give love first place."

(*As he speaks, the sofa is replaced by a large double bed, two chairs and a table covered with breakfast things, and a low table with a telephone.*)

JOHAN: We would now like to present some scenes from the daily life of Johan and Marianne. Scenes from a perfectly ordinary day—or, as it might also be called. "The Art of Sweeping Things under the Rug."

At Breakfast

(MARIANNE *is awake, watching* JOHAN *sleeping beside her. She gets out of bed, goes out, and returns in a moment with the newspaper. She tosses the paper onto the bed beside* JOHAN, *and begins her morning exercises.*)

MARIANNE: Good morning.

JOHAN: Good morning.

MARIANNE: Did you sleep well?

JOHAN: Like a log. And you?

MARIANNE: Stupidly I woke up at five o'clock and couldn't get back to sleep.

JOHAN: Why not?

MARIANNE: I lay there getting all worked up.

JOHAN: Should I have a bad conscience?

MARIANNE: For once you're not to blame, my darling. I lay fuming about that wretched Sunday dinner with my parents.

JOHAN: But we always have Sunday dinner with our parents. Either yours or mine.

MARIANNE: It's utterly absurd.

JOHAN: We do it for their sake. (*Gets out of bed.*)

MARIANNE: I'm going to call anyway and say we can't come.

JOHAN: Can't come!

MARIANNE: Yes.

JOHAN: Whatever will your mother say?

MARIANNE: She can say what she darn well pleases. You and I are going to have a nice Sunday to ourselves together with the children. (*Whistles.*)

JOHAN: Well, if you can accomplish *that*!

MARIANNE: I'm beginning to lose my temper.

JOHAN: Is it the curse?

MARIANNE: You always think it's that.

JOHAN: . Well, isn't it?

MARIANNE: Even if my period *is* due on Monday, that's not necessarily why I feel like blowing my top.

JOHAN: But Marianne dear, what is it?

MARIANNE: Just think about it. Our life's mapped out into little squares—every day, every hour, every minute. And on every square it's written down what we're supposed to do. If there's suddenly an empty square we're dismayed and scrawl something onto it at once.

JOHAN: But we have our vacation.

MARIANNE: (*With a laugh*) Johan! You haven't a clue to what I mean. On our vacation we have more of a schedule than ever. It's all Mummy's fault, actually. And your mother's not much better.

JOHAN: (*Laughing.*) What have the dear old ladies done wrong?

MARIANNE: You don't understand anyway, so there's no point talking about it.

JOHAN: Aren't you going to wake up the girls?

MARIANNE: No, they're having a late morning. Karin has the day off from school and Eva had rather a sore throat last night, so I thought I'd let her stay home. (*Angry.*) So that she can come with us to dinner on Sunday. Otherwise there'll be a hell of a fuss with comments and questions. You must admit.

JOHAN: You were going to phone and say we can't come.

MARIANNE: I'd rather you did.

JOHAN: Oh no, thank you! I'm not getting tangled up in making excuses to your mother. You can do that yourself.

MARIANNE: Then I'm going to call up your sister and tell her I don't want to go with her to the fashion show on Friday. Then I'm going to cancel our date with the Bergmans for dinner on Friday. They'll be madly hurt but I don't give a damn. Then you can refuse the invitation to the Peruvian ambassador's cocktail party. And I have no intention of going to your mother's French course, nor am I going to the theatre this evening. And you can take next week off and we'll go away somewhere together with the children. And not come back for two whole years. My God, this is stupid. Johan!

JOHAN: Hmm.

MARIANNE: We work hard, both of us. That's not it. We're always meeting people. That's not it either. We spend time with our children as often as we can. We hardly ever quarrel, and if we do we're sensible and listen to each other and make a valid compromise. Things couldn't be better.

JOHAN: It sounds ideal.

MARIANNE: It's troubling all the same.

JOHAN: (*Smiling.*) And our mothers are to blame.

MARIANNE: Yes, I think so, though I can't prove it.

JOHAN: Then we can only express a pious wish that the dear ladies die as soon as possible.

MARIANNE: (*Earnestly.*) Someone should have killed them long ago!

JOHAN: Doesn't the Bible say someplace that thou shalt leave thy father and thy mother, for thus shalt thou prosper and enjoy a long life? Anyway, why don't you call up your mother now? She's an early riser.

MARIANNE: Didn't we agree that *you* were going to make our excuses?

JOHAN: Oh no, my darling. Go on, call her. I'll hold your hand and be your moral support.

MARIANNE: All right, I will. Feel how my heart's pounding. But sooner or later we must take the first step.

JOHAN: The first faint cries of the great revolution. No answer? What a relief?

MARIANNE: Hello. Good morning, Miss Alm. Is Mother there? Oh, good. May I have a word with her? By the way, Miss Alm, how is your knee? Oh, not any better. Is it worse? Oh, I *am* sorry. What does the doctor say? Not much sympathy, eh? No, that's how it is these days. (*With a change of tone.*) Good morning, Mummy. How are you? That's good to hear. Has Daddy gone yet? Oh yes, of course, he was going to the country. Can you let him go off on his own like that? Oh, Erik's with him. That's good. Er, Mummy, I have something to tell you. (*Long pause, while her mother speaks.*) Yes, how did you guess? What are our reasons? I just want to be alone with Johan and the children for a whole Sunday. No, we're not going anywhere. No, we just don't want to come to dinner. (*Her mother talks.*) I don't think for a moment that Daddy was looking forward to Sunday dinner. (*Her mother talks.*) Yes, but Mummy, it should be a pleasure, not a duty. (*Her mother talks.*) Yes, I see. I see. I didn't know that. You didn't tell me. (*Her mother talks.*) Bored stiff, to be quite honest. No, no, forget all about it, Mummy. No, no, please! (*Her mother talks.*) We'll come as arranged. Yes, we'll manage. Yes, that's all right. Johan sends his love. Bye for now, Mummy dear. Yes—fine, then. Bye, bye. We'll look forward to it. (*She puts down the phone.*)

JOHAN: The revolution was smothered at birth.

MARIANNE: Aunt Elsa was coming to dinner. She hasn't been up to town for over six months. And she was *particularly* looking forward to seeing us. And she was bringing a present for you. (*Angry.*) Shit!

JOHAN: And your mother had asked Mrs. Danielson to come and cook the dinner. And your father was *so* looking forward to seeing us.

MARIANNE: Hell and damnation!

JOHAN: I admire your pluck all the same. (*Kisses her.*) We'll say no some other time. Don't upset yourself.

MARIANNE: Will you be home for dinner?

JOHAN: No, we'd better meet at the theatre. I'll be there in plenty of time to pick up the tickets.

MARIANNE: Do you like coming home?

JOHAN: (*Kindly.*) Is everything so awfully complicated today?

MARIANNE: I'd like us to hide in bed and just hold each other tight and not get up for a whole week. And we'd both have a good cry.

JOHAN: We haven't chosen that sort of life.

MARIANNE: If only I were sure that it's we who have chosen, and not our mothers. Imagine if you and I started being unfaithful to each other.

JOHAN: (*Embarrassed.*) Why, Marianne!

MARIANNE: I don't mean temporarily. But all the time. I mean if we seriously fell in love with someone else. What would you say?

JOHAN: I'd kill you of course.

MARIANNE: (*With a sigh.*) Sometimes I wish . . .

JOHAN: What?

MARIANNE: Nothing. (*Kiss.*) So long, darling!

JOHAN: So long!

   (*After* MARIANNE *has left,* JOHAN *picks up the phone, dials, hesitates, and quickly puts it down again as* MARIANNE *suddenly returns.*)

MARIANNE: Oh, Johan, I nearly forgot. I went around to a few travel agents and got all these brochures—look. I think you and I ought to go away together next summer.

JOHAN: And what do we do with the summer house?

MARIANNE: We can be there all the spring and fall.

JOHAN: Where did you think of going?

MARIANNE: Anywhere. We've never been to Florence, for instance. Or what about the Black Sea? That's an idea. Or Africa? There are some fantastically cheap trips to Morocco. Or Japan. Suppose we went to Japan!

JOHAN: Why this sudden urge to travel?

MARIANNE: Don't *you* think it would be fun? Just to go off like that?

JOHAN: I don't know.

MARIANNE: Then let's forget it.

JOHAN: Are you disappointed?

MARIANNE: When you're in a bad mood you always come out with a very funny accusation: You say I couldn't care less about our marriage. Isn't that what you say? Well, now I *am* caring about it.

JOHAN: How thoughtful of you.

MARIANNE: Why the sarcasm?

JOHAN: It's not sarcasm at all. I do think it's thoughtful. It's just that I don't think I want to go gallivanting about the world in the middle of summer. When I could be sitting in a boat fishing.

MARIANNE: It'll all be the same as usual then.

JOHAN: Why not send the children to your sister? That would be a big relief.

MARIANNE: Not if we stay at home.

JOHAN: Why not?

MARIANNE: It would look awfully funny.

JOHAN: So what?

MARIANNE: It won't do. And what do you think Mother would say? She'd grumble and fuss and we'd never hear the end of it. Besides, the children would also think it was funny. Of course, we could ask Kattrin to look after them for a week, or ten days at most, but certainly no more.

JOHAN: Must we be so dependent on what everyone thinks?

MARIANNE: I don't understand what you're getting at.

JOHAN: Marianne . . .

MARIANNE: (*Serious suddenly.*) Yes, Johan.

JOHAN: Do you find life tedious?

MARIANNE: No. What a question! Do you?

JOHAN: I don't know.

MARIANNE: I still think life's exciting.

JOHAN: (*Looking at her.*) You *are* sweet, you know.

MARIANNE: Oh, come on . . .

JOHAN: Marianne!

MARIANNE: Is there something you want to tell me?

JOHAN: Can the scheme of things be so treacherous that life suddenly goes wrong? Without your knowing how it happens. Almost imperceptibly.

MARIANNE: (*Softly.*) Do you mean us?

JOHAN: Is it a matter of choosing, and making the wrong choice? Or of jogging along in the same old rut without thinking. Until you lie there on the garbage dump.

MARIANNE: (*Searchingly.*) Has something happened, Johan?

JOHAN: Absolutely nothing. I swear.

MARIANNE: We're pretty honest with each other, you and I. Aren't we?

JOHAN: I think so.

MARIANNE: You have to speak out, however painful it is. It's awful to go around bottling things up. Don't you think?

JOHAN: (*Irritably.*) Hell, yes. What time is it?

MARIANNE: Seven fifteen.

JOHAN: My watch is always stopping. What were you saying? Oh yes, honesty. I suppose you mean over sex, to put it bluntly.

MARIANNE: Sometimes I think we . . .

JOHAN: (*Briefcase in hand*) You can't live side by side with someone and always be totally frank. It would be too tiring.

MARIANNE: Yes, that is the big question.

JOHAN: Anyway, I must go now.

MARIANNE: I'll take a little walk. I have to buy some new jeans for Karin, too.

JOHAN: Good Lord, you bought a pair of new jeans just last week.

MARIANNE: Those were for Eva.

JOHAN: Can't their clothes be handed down? It certainly had to be done in my childhood.

MARIANNE: Well, it's not done nowadays, you see, my poor darling. (*Waits for* JOHAN *to sit down.*) I'm terribly fond of you, do you know that? Do you know that I'm terribly scared of losing you? I ought to tell you these things much more often, I know they mean a lot to you. I'm not very good at it, I'm afraid. I'll try to improve. You're so sweet. And I'm terribly, terribly fond of you.

JOHAN: I'll try to remember that.

MARIANNE: So long, and drive carefully.

Interlude

JOHAN: At the theatre, Johan and Marianne have seen Ibsen's *A Doll's House*, and at home afterward, Marianne has once again taken the book from the shelf to read the third act. There she has come upon the following statement.

MARIANNE: (*Reading aloud.*) So Helmer says: "Above all else you are a wife and a mother." And then Nora replies: "I no longer believe that. I believe that, above all else, I'm a human being, just as you are—or at least I have to try to become one. Oh, I know most people would agree with you, Torvald, and I know it's the kind of argument that's found in books. But I can't let myself be satisfied anymore with what most people say or what's found in books. I have to think these things through for myself and try to make sense of them."

> (*As they speak, the furniture for the previous scene is replaced by a comfortable modern armchair and a matching two-seater sofa. Between the two stands a coffee table. Small side tables are placed in front of the sofa and armchair, to serve as footstools.*)

Nora

(JOHAN *is seated in the armchair*, MARIANNE *occupies the sofa. Between them, a late-night snack of wine and cheese is arranged on the table.*)

JOHAN: Yes, but the play damn well creaks. Even Strindberg thought so.

MARIANNE: He was just envious.

JOHAN: A few things have happened during the last hundred years, after all. Though not in the way Ibsen hoped.

MARIANNE: Have they?

JOHAN: (*Yawns.*) Feminism is a dead issue, Marianne. Women nowadays can do whatever they like. The trouble is they can't be bothered.

MARIANNE: (*Smiles.*) Oh, that's very interesting!

JOHAN: I always thought there was something absurd and pathetic about the women's rights movement. Especially when they try to bring their sisters into line. A stupid, ineffectual, moronic mob who brainwash themselves from birth. It's too damn heartbreaking for words.

MARIANNE: We're only starting. Just you wait and see.

JOHAN: I'll never see anything. Have you ever heard of a female sym-

"Yes, but the play damn well creaks. Even Strindberg thought so." Erich Hall-huber (Johan) and Gaby Dohm (Marianne) in rehearsal.

phony orchestra? Imagine a hundred and ten women with menstrual cramps trying to play Rossini's overture to *The Thieving Magpie*.

MARIANNE: Lucky no one can hear you.

JOHAN: Women pinched the best role at the outset. No wonder they're not giving it up now that they've learned to play it to perfection. Besides, they've achieved what they've always been after: man's collective bad conscience, which gives them unbelievable advantages without their having to lift a finger. (*Eats.*) I don't mean a word of what I say, and anyway I couldn't care less about it.

MARIANNE: When we were younger we were so hopeful.

JOHAN: Do you remember when our parents practically turned us out because we joined the May Day procession? You were more fanatical than I was.

MARIANNE: And you accused me of neglecting both you and the children.

JOHAN: That was the winter when we all had the Asian flu. And you tried to crawl off to your political meetings, and on top of that insisted you could manage the kids without help *and* hold down your job. That was a quarrel.

164

MARIANNE: We believed in humanity's future, anyway.

JOHAN: It's always nice to have a belief, I grant you. Besides, we had the pleasure of annoying our parents, and that meant a lot. You weren't even-tempered in those days. Cute and hot-tempered. In fact, you were damned attractive as a socialist.

MARIANNE: Aren't I now?

JOHAN: What?

MARIANNE: Damned attractive.

JOHAN: Yes, of course you're attractive. Why?

MARIANNE: I've also been thinking about it.

JOHAN: Must it always be that two people who live together for a long time begin to tire of each other?

MARIANNE: We haven't tired.

JOHAN: Almost.

MARIANNE: (*Indulgently.*) We work too hard—that's what's so banal. And in the evenings we're too tired.

JOHAN: Marianne, that wasn't a reproach.

MARIANNE: I'm not so sure.

JOHAN: Word of honor.

MARIANNE: But we like each other in every way.

JOHAN: Not in that way. Not very much anyhow.

MARIANNE: Oh yes, we do.

JOHAN: It's just that our life together has become full of evasions and restrictions and refusals.

MARIANNE: (*Hurt.*) I can't help it if I don't enjoy it as much as I used to. I can't help it. There's a perfectly natural explanation. You're not to accuse me and give me a bad conscience about this.

JOHAN: You needn't get so upset!

MARIANNE: I think it's all right as it is. God knows it isn't passionate, but you can't expect everything. There are those who are much worse off than we are.

JOHAN: Without a doubt.

MARIANNE: Sex isn't everything. As a matter of fact.

JOHAN: (*Laughing.*) Why, Marianne!

MARIANNE: (*On the verge of tears.*) If you're not satisfied with my performance you'd better get yourself a mistress who is more imaginative and sexually exciting. I do my best, I'm sure.

JOHAN: (*Sourly.*) There we have it.

MARIANNE: You've got that look again.

JOHAN: I haven't got any look.

MARIANNE: That look and that tone of voice. Whatever it is you're brooding about, come out with it.

JOHAN: It's no use. You lose your temper at whatever I say on this subject.

MARIANNE: No, I promise. I'm listening. Quite objectively.

JOHAN: Sometimes I wonder why we complicate this problem so frightfully. This business of lovemaking is pretty elementary, after all. It was surely never meant to be a huge problem overshadowing everything else. It's all your mother's fault, if you ask me. Though you don't like my saying so.

MARIANNE: I just think it's so damn superficial of you to talk like that.

JOHAN: Don't be so sour, Marianne. I'm being kind.

MARIANNE: I'm not sour, I'm not sour at all. All the same, you think it's my fault that we don't enjoy it any more.

JOHAN: You said just now that you do your best.

MARIANNE: Yes, indeed I do. I do, Johan.

JOHAN: Can't you hear yourself how awful that sounds?

MARIANNE: So you think I'm lying?

JOHAN: No, for Christ's sake! No! No!

MARIANNE: Then I don't understand.

JOHAN: Let's drop this subject now and go to bed. It's late anyway.

MARIANNE: Isn't that just like you. First you start a huge discussion and then, having got me all worked up, you yawn and say you're sleepy and want to go to bed.

JOHAN: Marianne! You suffer from devastatingly high standards. But can't our poor sex life be spared your ambitions.

MARIANNE: Why must you always wrangle with me on this particular point? First you abuse me for not trying, and then you abuse me because I exert myself.

JOHAN: (*Gently.*) Oh, God. Now look what I've gone and done.

MARIANNE: Yes, haven't you. Can't you be nice and kind instead. It would help a lot more.

JOHAN: Yes. (*Giving up.*) There, there, Marianne, don't be upset. It was silly of me to bring all this up.

MARIANNE: You can talk too much about these things.

JOHAN: (*Giving up.*) I suspect you're right.

MARIANNE: I know you're supposed to tell everything and not keep anything secret, but in this particular matter I think it's wrong.

JOHAN: (*Who has heard this before.*) Yes, you're probably right.

MARIANNE: (*Following up her advantage.*) There are things which must be allowed to live their life in a half-light.

JOHAN: (*Total retreat.*) You think so?

MARIANNE: I'm quite convinced of it. We upset and hurt each other all to no purpose when we carry on like this. And all the barbs are still there when we get into bed. My God, it's like lying on a bed of nails.

JOHAN: (*Laughing.*) Ha . . .

MARIANNE: What are you laughing at?

JOHAN: The bed of nails.

MARIANNE: (*More graciously.*) It's all very well for you to laugh.

JOHAN: Can't we go to bed now?

MARIANNE: You must admit you've been unusually stupid and cocky and tactless.

JOHAN: I apologize.

MARIANNE: Do you think I don't give you enough affection?

JOHAN: Affection takes time.

MARIANNE: Then you *don't* get enough.

JOHAN: *We* don't get enough. And don't give enough.

MARIANNE: That's why I wanted us to go away together this summer.

JOHAN: I don't think affection should be kept only for vacations.

MARIANNE: (*Kissing him.*) You're kind anyway, even if you *are* an idiot.

JOHAN: Then it's lucky I'm married to you.

MARIANNE: You have your great moments, but in-between you're horribly mediocre.

JOHAN: At our age tens of thousands of brain cells snuff out every day. And they're never replaced.

MARIANNE: With you it must be ten times as many, you're so silly.

JOHAN: You're sweet even if you do scold and make a fuss. (*He kisses her and touches her breasts. She moves his hand gently away. He gives a short laugh, stands up, and yawns. MARIANNE smiles a little guiltily.*) I'm nearly asleep.

MARIANNE: I'll just look in on the children.

"You're sweet even if you do scold." Hallhuber and Dohm in performance as Johan and Marianne.

Interlude

JOHAN: A few months later, or maybe only a few days later, on a completely ordinary evening, Johan and Marianne are lying in bed as usual, reading their books as usual, eating sweets—possibly even macaroons—when Marianne, as usual, closes her book and puts her glasses aside. Usually, Marianne then says goodnight, rolls over on her side, and falls asleep immediately. This time, however, something extraordinary happens in the life of Johan and Marianne . . .

(As he speaks, the furniture for the previous scene is removed and the large double bed is placed in the middle of the stage.)

The Child

(JOHAN and MARIANNE are lying in the double bed, reading. A box of sweets lies on the bed between them.)

MARIANNE: I'm pregnant.

JOHAN: That's what I said three weeks ago. And you denied it.

MARIANNE: I didn't want to worry you.

JOHAN: I'm not a bit worried.

MARIANNE: What are we going to do about it?

JOHAN: Do you want to keep it?

MARIANNE: I want us to talk it over. Then we'll do what we've both decided.

JOHAN: I think it's for you to say.

MARIANNE: Why is it up to me?

JOHAN: Well, naturally. You'll have all the discomfort and the onus. Alternatively, the joy and the satisfaction.

MARIANNE: You mean it's all the same to you if we have another child?

JOHAN: I wouldn't put it like that.

MARIANNE: I want to know what you think. Give me a straight answer.

JOHAN: It's not so easy.

MARIANNE: Is it so hard to be honest?

JOHAN: You're being unreasonable now, Marianne.

MARIANNE: What was your first impulse?

JOHAN: It's not in my nature to have first impulses. In that respect I'm an invalid.

MARIANNE: Do you *want* another child?

JOHAN: I have no objections anyway. It might even be rather nice.

MARIANNE: But you can't pretend you're enthusiastic. Can you? Be honest now.

JOHAN: You keep harping on *my* being honest. Can't you tell me what *you* want instead? It would be much simpler.

MARIANNE: I happened to ask you.

JOHAN: I'm trying to think when we slipped up. You've been on the pill the whole time. Or haven't you?

MARIANNE: I forgot to take it that time we were away.

JOHAN: Did you now. Why didn't you say so?

MARIANNE: I didn't think it mattered.

JOHAN: Did you do it on purpose?

MARIANNE: I don't know.

JOHAN: That's no answer.

MARIANNE: I suppose I thought, if I get pregnant now, then we're meant to have another child.

JOHAN: Oh my God! My God! My God!

MARIANNE: What's wrong?

JOHAN: And you're supposed to be a modern, efficient professional woman who is always going on about how important family planning is. My God!

MARIANNE: I agree it's rather irrational.

JOHAN: Then you've made up your mind. And in that case there's nothing to be done. Is there?

MARIANNE: I thought you might be pleased.

JOHAN: Oh yes, I'm quite pleased.

MARIANNE: It's the third month.

JOHAN: You haven't been sick at all.

MARIANNE: On the contrary. I've never felt so well.

JOHAN: Our mothers will be overjoyed, at any rate. What do you think our daughters will say?

MARIANNE: Their tolerance is unlimited at the moment. They will forgive us.

JOHAN: Well, well, Marianne. You know, I'm quite beginning to look forward to it. Besides, you're so pretty when you're big-bellied. (*A long silence ensues. Then* MARIANNE *begins to weep.* JOHAN *looks at her astonished.*) What's wrong now?

MARIANNE: Nothing.

JOHAN: There must be something.

MARIANNE: Absolutely nothing.

JOHAN: But I can see there's something.

MARIANNE: No, nothing, really.

JOHAN: Just what do you want yourself?

MARIANNE: I don't know.

JOHAN: What it really amounts to is that neither you nor I want any more children.

MARIANNE: Do you think so?

JOHAN: I think we're both appalled at the thought of a squalling brat and feedings and diapers and nursing and getting up at night and the whole damn circus. We like to think that's all behind us.

MARIANNE: I have such a bad conscience.

JOHAN: Why?

MARIANNE: I have a bad conscience because first I go and long for a child and toy with the idea and look forward to it, and then, when it's a fact, I regret it no end. It doesn't make sense.

JOHAN: Why must you always take a moral view of everything?

MARIANNE: It's my fourth child, Johan. One died, and I take the life of another.

JOHAN: Good God, you can't reason like that.

MARIANNE: I do, anyway.

JOHAN: It's a question of being practical.

MARIANNE: No, it isn't.

JOHAN: What, then?

MARIANNE: It's a question of love, Johan!

JOHAN: Aren't you too worked up now?

MARIANNE: No.

JOHAN: Then can't you explain what you mean?

MARIANNE: No, I can't, because it's a feeling. It's as if I no longer felt I was real. You're not real either. Nor are the children. Then along comes this baby. *That's* real.

JOHAN: You might say just the opposite.

MARIANNE: And then we're left with all our damned wretched comfort and cowardice and unreality and are ashamed. And we have no affection. And no love. And no joy. We could easily welcome this baby. And I think I was right in looking forward to it when I went around daydreaming about it. I had the right feeling. I'd be *ready* now to have a baby.

JOHAN: I don't know what you're talking about.

MARIANNE: No.

JOHAN: You speak as if you'd already had an abortion.

MARIANNE: In one way I have.

JOHAN: One can't blame oneself for thoughts.

MARIANNE: (*Shouting.*) This is serious, Johan. The whole of our future's at stake. Suppose we now do something irrevocable. Suppose it's crucial and we don't know it is.

JOHAN: What are these ridiculous, ghostly, intangible demands you're making? They're pure superstition.

MARIANNE: You don't understand.

JOHAN: No, I'm damned if I do understand a single word of what you've been saying.

MARIANNE: We're only trying to get out of it.

JOHAN: We're trying to avoid dramatic decisions and anything rash, if that's what you mean. And I think that's sensible. (*Gives* MARIANNE *a glum look.*)

MARIANNE: You don't look so happy either.

JOHAN: This conversation makes me feel sick.

MARIANNE: Johan!

JOHAN: Yes?

MARIANNE: Couldn't we have this baby and look forward to it? Couldn't we spoil it a little and be fond of it?

JOHAN: I've already said it would be nice, so there's no need to harp on it. You're the one who has made it all so complicated. Not I.

MARIANNE: Let's make up our minds then.

JOHAN: Excuse me, but what are we making up our minds about?

MARIANNE: Let's make up our minds to have another baby.

JOHAN: Fine, let's do that.

MARIANNE: I feel quite relieved.

JOHAN: (*Kindly.*) There's nothing so strange about both wanting to and not wanting to.

MARIANNE: No, I suppose not.

JOHAN: If anything, it's the rule.

MARIANNE: Actually, it had nothing to do with the baby.

JOHAN: No?

MARIANNE: It had to do with you and me.

JOHAN: You're not still crying?

MARIANNE: I don't know what's the matter with me.

JOHAN: I think you need a brandy.

MARIANNE: Yes, I think I do. (*To the audience, after a pause.*) Two weeks later, Marianne underwent a small operation.

Interlude

MARIANNE: Johan and Marianne's summer house, an old family property located on the seacoast outside of Stockholm. It is a late evening at the end of August. Johan has been staying in town for the past two days.

Marianne and the girls have gone to bed early—there was nothing on TV on this particular evening.

(*As she speaks, the double bed is moved to a new position. A straight chair is placed at its foot.*)

Paula

(MARIANNE *jumps out of bed excitedly as* JOHAN *enters and she senses his presence.*)

MARIANNE: Here already! What a lovely surprise. You weren't coming until tomorrow. Are you hungry? How good of you to come this evening. The children are asleep. There was nothing on TV and we thought it would be nice to have an early night. The girls and I have been dieting today. Would you like an omelet or a sandwich and some beer?

JOHAN: That sounds good.

MARIANNE: Or would you like a real meal? Shall I fry some eggs and bacon? Or heat some soup?

JOHAN: Sandwiches and beer are fine. While I think of it, I have a message from Peter and Katarina. They're going to call you up on Monday at the office.

MARIANNE: That's a long and nerve-racking business, poor things.

JOHAN: *Are* they getting divorced? It seems to me as if they don't know what they want to do.

MARIANNE: You can believe I've been worrying that you were angry with me.

JOHAN: Why should I be angry with you?

MARIANNE: You know quite well! I was beastly on the phone last night.

JOHAN: That was nothing.

MARIANNE: I called you right back, but you must have pulled the plug out.

JOHAN: I was pretty tired last night.

MARIANNE: I still think I was nasty to you last night. I really do.

JOHAN: Can't we just forget it?

MARIANNE: You *are* funny, you never finish talking about anything. I won't be long-winded, darling. All I want to say is that I think you're right. And I'm right too. In a different way. If you don't want to go out to dinner in a tuxedo, then that's your business. You're right there. On the other hand, I do think you could get yourself a new tuxedo.

JOHAN: I don't like tuxedos. I feel like a dressed-up chimpanzee in a tuxedo.

MARIANNE: Yes, I remember you said that. (*Laughs.*) Well, let's not start quarreling again. I love you, even if you won't dress up in a tuxedo. It's not absolutely essential to our marriage.

JOHAN: It seemed like it last night.

MARIANNE: I told you I was wrong. God, I am getting hungry watching you eat. I'll simply have to have a sandwich. It can't be helped. I'm dizzy with hunger. I've lost over four pounds this last week. Does it show?

JOHAN: No.

MARIANNE: I feel it anyway, let me tell you. Why can't we be big and fat and good-tempered? Do you remember Aunt Miriam and Uncle David? They were perfect dears and got along so well together, and they were so *fat*! And every night they lay there in the big creaky double bed, holding hands and content with each other just as they were, fat and cheerful. What is it, Johan? Are you worried about something? Has something happened? What's wrong? Tell me what it is.

JOHAN: I came here this evening to tell you something. I've gone and fallen in love, you see. It's quite absurd and maybe it's all a goddamn mistake. It probably is a goddamn mistake. I met her during the convention in June. She was the interpreter and secretary. Actually, she's studying for her degree. She's going to teach Slavic languages. She's nothing much to look at. In fact, you'd undoubtedly think she was ugly. I have no idea what this will lead to. I have no idea about anything. I'm completely bewildered. Of course I'm pleased in one way. Though I have a hell of a bad conscience about you and the children. We've always got along well, haven't we? I mean, things haven't been any better or worse for us than for most people. Say something.

MARIANNE: I don't know what to say.

JOHAN: I suppose you think it was wrong of me not to tell you about this before. But I didn't know how it would turn out. I thought: I'll soon get over it. It's just a passing phase. So I didn't want to worry you.

MARIANNE: It's so strange.

JOHAN: What's strange?

MARIANNE: That I haven't realized anything. That I haven't been suspicious or noticed anything. Everything has been as usual, better in fact. You've been so kind. And I've just gone around like a silly fool, blind and unsuspecting. It's sickening. What are we to do now then?

JOHAN: I don't know.

MARIANNE: Do you want a divorce? Are you going to marry her? Anyway, why do you have to tell me about this tonight of all times? Why the sudden hurry?

JOHAN: We're going to Paris tomorrow afternoon.

MARIANNE: I see. Are you finished eating?

JOHAN: I want to get away from all this. At any rate for a time. I was going down anyway in the fall to see Grandin and his assistant. And Paula has a study grant and was going to use it up this fall. I want to be with her. I can't be without her. So we're leaving together tomorrow afternoon. (MARIANNE *looks at him in silence.*) Now that I'm talking to you, now that I'm at home, I'd prefer to scrap the whole damn thing. I feel tired and scared. (MARIANNE *looks at him in silence.*) Nothing could be sillier or more commonplace and absurd than this. I know just what you're thinking and I have no excuses to offer.

MARIANNE: How can you know what I'm thinking?

JOHAN: I'm trying not to have a bad conscience, but it's only affectation. This is the way it *is,* Marianne. There's nothing to be done about it. (MARIANNE *looks at him in silence.*) You know the truth now and that's the main thing.

MARIANNE: I know nothing. Shouldn't we get some sleep? It's late. And I suppose you're off early.

JOHAN: I have a meeting at nine.

MARIANNE: Then I suggest we go to bed. (MARIANNE *watches* JOHAN *undress. He is embarrassed by her gaze, and to make matters worse he has some incriminating marks on his chest.*) You have marks on your chest.

JOHAN: I know.

MARIANNE: How indiscreet of you both.

JOHAN: Do you know if my gray suit is here or in town? I've been hunting for it.

MARIANNE: It's at the dry cleaners.

JOHAN: Shit.

MARIANNE: Are you planning to wear it?

JOHAN: Naturally.

MARIANNE: I have the ticket if you'd like to call for it tomorrow.

JOHAN: I won't have time. I'll be busy all day until three o'clock, and then we're off.

MARIANNE: If you like, I'll drive in and pick it up for you. And I'll gladly do your packing. You're not very good at it.

JOHAN: No thank you.

MARIANNE: You're being silly.

JOHAN: Yes, I am in fact rather conventional.

MARIANNE: Otherwise I think you have all you need. There are clean shirts and underclothes here, so you can take those with you. Can't you travel in your jacket and flannel pants? They look nice on you.

JOHAN: Whatever you say.

MARIANNE: How long will you be away?

JOHAN: I don't know. It all depends.

MARIANNE: What do you mean?

JOHAN: I have requested and been given six months' leave of absence. Before then I have about a month's work which I'm taking with me. So it will be seven or eight months at least.

MARIANNE: (*Thunderstruck.*) Oh.

JOHAN: It's just as well to make a clean break.

MARIANNE: Do you suppose I'll still be here when you come back?

JOHAN: I don't give a damn.

MARIANNE: I see.

JOHAN: Do you know how long I've had this in mind? Can you guess?

MARIANNE: Don't tell me.

JOHAN: I don't mean Paula, I mean the idea of leaving you and the children. Can you guess at all?

MARIANNE: Don't tell me.

JOHAN: For four years I've wanted to get rid of you.

MARIANNE: No more now, please.

JOHAN: No, you're right.

MARIANNE: What are you going to live on? I mean now, during your leave of absence. You'll have to pay an allowance to the children in any case.

JOHAN: Don't worry. I have enough to get by on.

MARIANNE: Then you must have income that I don't know of.

JOHAN: How right you are.

MARIANNE: How is that possible?

JOHAN: (*Beside himself.*) Listen now, for Christ's sake, though it's no
goddamn business of yours. For one thing I've sold the boat, and for
another I've taken a loan, which Frid has been kind enough to put his
name to. From the first of September the bank will pay one thousand
six hundred kronor a month to you and the girls. For the time being.
Then we'll make some other arrangement when I come home. You'd
better talk to one of your lawyer colleagues at the office. I don't give
a damn. Name your price. I'm not taking anything with me, except
perhaps my books, if you have no objection. I'll just vanish, do you hear?
Into thin air. I will pay all I reasonably can to support you and the
children. My needs are nil. All that interests me is to take the step out
of all this. Do you know what I'm most fed up with? All this fucking
harping on what we're supposed to do, what we must do, what we must
take into consideration. What your mother will think. What the children will say. How we had best arrange that dinner party and shouldn't
we invite my father after all. We must go to the coast. We must go to
the mountains. We must go to St. Moritz. We must celebrate Christmas,
Easter, Whitsun, birthdays, namedays, the whole fucking lot. I know
I'm being unfair. I know that what I'm saying now is all goddamn
nonsense. I know that we've had a good life. And actually I think I still
love you. In fact, in one way I love you *more* now since I met Paula.
But can you understand this bitterness? I don't know what to call it.
This bitterness, I can't hit on any better word. No one can explain it
to me for the simple reason that I have no one to talk to. No, I don't
understand. I don't understand this thing I call bitterness, which has
kept getting worse and worse.

MARIANNE: Why haven't you said anything?

JOHAN: How can one talk about something which hasn't any words? How
can one say that it's boring to make love although technically everything is perfect? How can I say that it's all I can do not to strike you
when you sit there at the breakfast table all neat and tidy eating your
boiled eggs? And the girls giving themselves airs in that silly spoiled
way. Why have we indulged them so hysterically? Can you tell me that?
I'm not blaming you, Marianne. Everything has just gone to pot. And
no one knows why.

MARIANNE: I must have been doing wrong the whole time.

JOHAN: Stop that. It's an easy way out always to take the blame. It
makes you feel strong and noble and generous and humble. You haven't
done wrong and I haven't done wrong. It's no use trotting out guilty
feelings and a bad conscience, though God knows my conscience is so

bad it's nearly choking me. It's all sheer chance, a cruel coincidence. Why should you and I of all people be able to dodge the humiliations and the disasters? It's all perfectly logical. So why start talking about guilt and doing wrong.

MARIANNE: Won't you change your mind and not go?

JOHAN: That's impossible.

MARIANNE: But if I plead with you.

JOHAN: It's no use, and it's only distressing.

MARIANNE: Can't you at least postpone the trip for a month or two? You're not giving me a chance. I think we could repair our marriage. I think we could find a new form for our life together. Perhaps Paula would understand me better than you do. I ought to meet her and talk to her.

JOHAN: Marianne . . .

MARIANNE: It's a mistake to cut everything off just when we're starting to be honest with each other. Can't we let the disaster sweep over us together? I mean, we're destroying so much by tearing down all we've built up. You must give me a chance, Johan. It's unkind of you just to present me with a *fait accompli.* You're putting me in a ridiculous and intolerable position. Surely you can see that.

JOHAN: I know just what you mean: What are our parents going to say? What will my sister think, what will our friends think? Jesus Christ, how tongues are going to wag! How will it affect the girls, and what will their school friends' mothers think? And what about the dinner parties we're invited to in September and October. And what are you going to say to Katarina and Peter? To hell with all that! I intend to behave like a pig, and what a relief!

MARIANNE: That wasn't what I meant.

JOHAN: Oh, what did you mean?

MARIANNE: (*Softly.*) Nothing. (*They've gotten into the big double bed and put out the light. Neither can get to sleep. They lie for a long time silent and unmoving, deeply distressed. There is complete silence around them.*) I forgot to set the alarm. What time do you have to get up?

JOHAN: Set it for five thirty, will you. I must do some packing too. I have to be at the institute at nine for a conference.

MARIANNE: I've been meaning to get another alarm clock. This one is loud enough to wake the dead. It's not terribly reliable either. There, it's set for five thirty. Anyway, I usually wake up without an alarm. Don't worry. (*Suddenly.*) I want you to tell me about Paula.

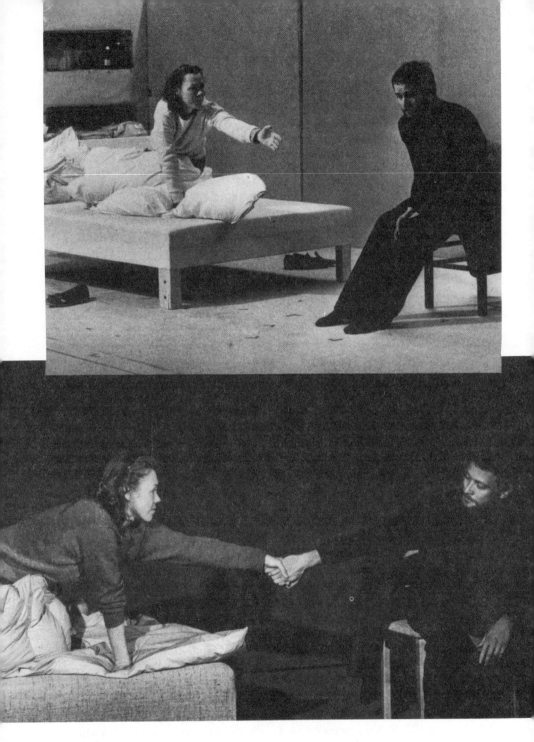

"Won't you change your mind and not go?" asks Gaby Dohm in this rehearsal shot. The same scene in performance: "But if I plead with you."

JOHAN: What's the point of that?

MARIANNE: Please.

JOHAN: Why do you want to torment yourself?

MARIANNE: It's not self-torment. I want to know what she's like. Do you have a photo of her? You must.

JOHAN: Please, Marianne, can't we be spared?

MARIANNE: I beg you. Can't you help me with this?

JOHAN: Very well, as you wish. Where's my wallet? Here are two photos. One was taken two years ago, when she was on vacation down by the Black Sea. The other's a passport photo taken a couple of weeks ago. It's a good likeness, I think.

MARIANNE: She has a nice figure. Lovely breasts, it seems. Are they?

JOHAN: Yes, she has lovely breasts.

MARIANNE: Does she dye her hair? It looks like it, I mean.

JOHAN: It hadn't occurred to me, but it's possible.

MARIANNE: She has a nice smile. How old is she?

JOHAN: Twenty-three. She hasn't been very lucky in love. She's been engaged twice and I think in that particular respect she's made a muddle of her life with all kinds of men.

MARIANNE: Does that upset you?

JOHAN: I'll say it does. Her outspokenness can sometimes be rather unpleasant. I would prefer not to know anything, but she insists on giving me the details of her erotic past. It's rather trying, since I suffer from retrospective jealousy. She has no illusions. She says she knows that I'll go back to you, that she doesn't have a chance against you.

MARIANNE: Are you good together in bed?

JOHAN: At first it was dreadful. I suppose it was my fault too. I'm not really used to it. I mean with other women. I couldn't do a thing. But she said that no one had ever been so kind and tender toward her. I wanted to break the whole thing off, although I was in love with her. You see, I realized that if I couldn't have sex with her, the whole affair was doomed. But she got in an awful state when I wanted to end it all. I was afraid she would hurt herself. Then we were out of town for a week.

MARIANNE: You went away together?

JOHAN: Yes. You remember I gave some lectures in Copenhagen in April.

MARIANNE: Oh, it was then. In April.

JOHAN: We lived it up in the evenings and behaved like pigs. We got mixed up in drunken brawls and were kicked out of the hotel. We ended up in a squalid little place on a back street, and suddenly we clicked and made love day and night. She said that it had never been so good for her before. I felt terrifically high, of course. I know what you're thinking, Marianne, and it's true. You and I also had much better times together after that trip. And more fun.

MARIANNE: Did you tell Paula that?

JOHAN: No, I didn't dare.

MARIANNE: All I ask is that you postpone the trip.

JOHAN: Paula would never agree to put if off and I feel the same way. I've made up my mind.

MARIANNE: Can't I meet her?

JOHAN: What's the use? Besides, she won't hear you spoken of. I hardly dare to mention your name.

MARIANNE: You *are* in a spot.

JOHAN: It depends how you look at it. Paula and I get along well together. She's cheerful and kind and tender. We always have lots to talk about. In-between we have the most awful fights. But I'm beginning to wonder if it isn't pretty salutary. All my life I've been so goddamn well-behaved and sensible and balanced and cautious. I don't know. I don't know anything.

MARIANNE: Come and lie beside me. I want you to make love to me. You can do that anyway. I mean for old times' sake.

JOHAN: I don't think I can. The best thing would be to have some coffee and pack and leave at once.

MARIANNE: No, lie down and close your eyes. You'll go to sleep, you'll see. We need some sleep both of us. It will be a strenuous day tomorrow.

JOHAN: I'm so ashamed.

MARIANNE: Let's wait with all that. It's only you and me now. We have these few hours to ourselves. Just you and me.

(*It is five thirty.* MARIANNE *wakes up, cautiously awakens* JOHAN. *He tries to draw her to him; she remains stiff and unwilling.* JOHAN *gets out of bed quickly and goes into the bathroom.* MARIANNE *gets out a suitcase and places it on the bed. She begins to pack.* JOHAN *comes back into the room with a nail scissors.*)

JOHAN: Can you help me, please? I've split a nail and can't manage it.

MARIANNE: You're biting your cuticles again.

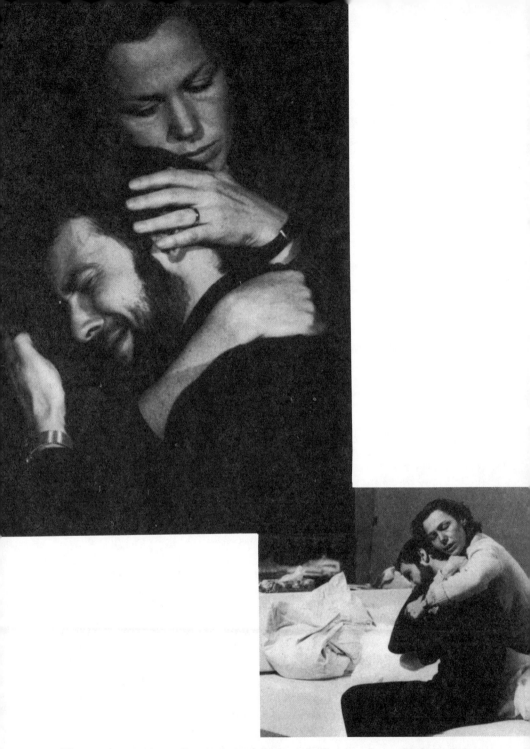

The same scene in performance and rehearsal: "I'm so ashamed." Gaby Dohm as Marianne and Erich Hallhuber as Johan.

JOHAN: Do you know what has become of Speer's memoirs? I'm sure I left the book on the bedside table.

MARIANNE: I thought you'd finished it, so I lent it to Mother.

JOHAN: Oh. Decent of you. Ow! Christ!

MARIANNE: I must cut down here. You've broken the nail. It's bleeding slightly, I'll have to put on a bandaid. What *do* you do to your nails?

JOHAN: Thank you, that's fine.

MARIANNE: Shall I pack the shaver, or will you take the one you have in town?

JOHAN: I have to go up to the apartment anyway to fetch some things, so you can leave it.

MARIANNE: Do you want the ticket for the dry cleaners?

JOHAN: I might as well take it, in case I have time. Where is it?

MARIANNE: Almost opposite the church.

JOHAN: Oh, I know. I'm not lugging those heavy shoes with me, if that's what you think.

MARIANNE: They might come in handy in the winter. Which pajamas are you taking?

JOHAN: Look, get out of here and make breakfast, while I finish packing.

MARIANNE: Does it bother you my helping you pack?

JOHAN: I can't deny that I think it's indecent, though I don't know why.
   (MARIANNE *leaves the room for a few moments to prepare a breakfast tray.*)

MARIANNE: What shall I do with your mail?

JOHAN: I'll write and tell you my address. Then you can send important letters on, if you don't mind. And if you'd be good enough to pay bills and so on in the usual way.

MARIANNE: Another thing. The plumber was supposed to come and repair the bathroom before we move back to town. Have you spoken to him, or shall I call him up? You said you'd get in touch with him. I mean, if you've forgotten it in all the muddle, I could see to it that he comes and gets those jobs done at least.

JOHAN: I've phoned him dozens of times, but he's never there. So I have *not* forgotten, as you seem to think.

MARIANNE: What are you going to do with your car while you're away? Will you keep it in the garage?

JOHAN: I've asked Paula's sister to look after it. There's no point in its standing idle, and she has just moved out of town.

MARIANNE: I see.

JOHAN: But if you wouldn't mind canceling my appointment with the dentist. I'm sure to forget.

(JOHAN *wants to make a final break. He gets his coat from the hallway, and comes back into the room with his briefcase in his hand.*)

MARIANNE: What do you want me to tell the children?

JOHAN: Tell them anything you like.

MARIANNE: Shall I tell them you've fallen in love with another woman and have cleared out and left us?

JOHAN: I don't think you could put it better. It also has the advantage of being true. I don't look for understanding from that quarter.

MARIANNE: Karin is going to take it badly. She's so attached to you right now. She never stops talking about you.

JOHAN: Don't paw at me. It hurts enough as it is. I must go now. So long, Marianne, take care of yourself.

MARIANNE: So long.

JOHAN: I may be home in a week.

MARIANNE: If only you were. We'd make a fresh start in every way. We'd get rid of all the routine and the slack habits. We'd talk over the past. We'd try to find where we've gone wrong. You'd never hear any accusations. I promise you. It's all so unreal. I don't know what to do about it. You're shutting me out. Can't you promise to come back? Then I'd know *something*. I mean, you can't just leave me without any hope. It's not fair. Even if you have no intention of returning, you could at least *say* you're coming home again.

JOHAN: I must go now, Marianne.

(MARIANNE *tries to hold on to* JOHAN, *but he tears himself free and leaves. She stands for a long time without moving, then goes to the telephone and dials a number.*)

MARIANNE: Hello, Fredrik, it's Marianne. Sorry to wake you. Is Birgit there? No, it doesn't matter. Let her sleep. How are things? Oh, you like puttering around alone at this hour. No, I won't keep you long. No, it's cloudy here. Oh, how nice for you. Well, I wanted to talk to you about something. No, I just wanted someone to talk to. You and Birgit *are* our friends. I must have . . . I must . . . it's all so unreal, Fredrik. You see—(*Pause.*)—I'm about to burst into tears any moment and I don't *want* to cry. You see, Johan has fallen in love with another woman. Her name's Paula, and they're going off to Paris today. Can't you talk to Johan and ask him to wait a bit? He needn't rush off headlong like

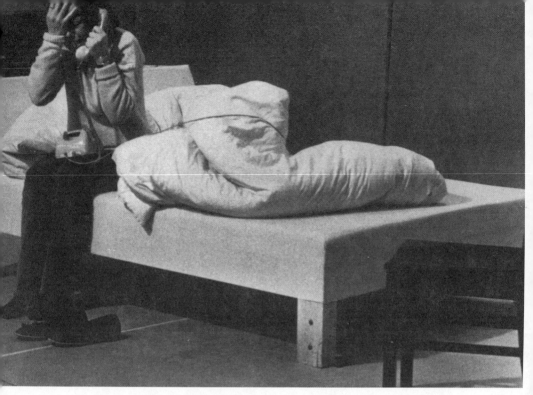

"I just wanted someone to talk to." Gaby Dohm as Marianne.

that. What? You've already talked to him? Oh, I see. I see. So you and Birgit have known all along. You've known the whole time and not said a word to me? What the hell kind of friends are you anyway? How could you be so goddamn rotten and unfair to me? I don't care what you say. And all the times we've met and talked and you have known and never said anything. (*In a fury.*) Nice friends you are! You can go to hell with your explanations. Just how many people have known of this? Oh, quite a number. I'm glad to know. (*She flings the phone down. She bites her hand to stop herself from screaming.*)

INTERMISSION

The Reunion

(*Sofa, armchair, and side tables, in a new constellation.* Marianne *enters and speaks to the audience.*)

MARIANNE: Two years have elapsed. Johan and Marianne haven't seen each other. Then, one afternoon Johan telephoned and arranged a meeting.

(*The doorbell rings. She goes to open the door after a quick check-up in front of the mirror.*)

JOHAN: Hello.

MARIANNE: Hello. Come in!

JOHAN: Sorry if I'm late. I had trouble with the car. It wouldn't start. How pretty you are. And what a nice dress.

MARIANNE: I'm glad you like it. I bought it a couple of days ago but regretted it afterward. I didn't think it suited me. And it suddenly seemed much too red.

JOHAN: It suits you admirably.

MARIANNE: Do come in, Johan. I feel nervous standing here in the hall, making polite conversation.

JOHAN: I'm nervous too. I haven't been able to settle down to anything all day. It's ridiculous, really. But I haven't seen you for quite a long time. Over six months.

MARIANNE: How was it that you suddenly . . . ?

JOHAN: Paula's in London for a week.

MARIANNE: Oh, I see. Oh. Would you like a drink?

JOHAN: Yes, please, I'd love a whiskey. Straight. It settles the stomach. I mean, it calms you down.

MARIANNE: Have you taken to drinking whiskey?

JOHAN: Yes, just imagine.

MARIANNE: I asked Aunt Johanna to take charge of the girls for tonight. So they're staying with her until the day after tomorrow. They're going to the theatre this evening, and tomorrow they have a holiday from school and are going to the country.

JOHAN: How practical.

MARIANNE: Practical?

JOHAN: I mean, it would have been pretty rough going to meet the children too. How are they?

MARIANNE: You needn't ask after them out of politeness. But we'll write down their birthdays in your appointment book, so that you don't forget them again as you did this year.

JOHAN: Fine.

MARIANNE: I bought them each a present from you, but they saw through me. And that wasn't very nice.

JOHAN: Yes, I can see that.

MARIANNE: It's pretty awful the way you never get in touch with them. They hardly ever mention you nowadays.

JOHAN: That's understandable.

MARIANNE: Why can't Paula let you see us without raising Cain for days on end . . . ?

JOHAN: If we're meeting just to give you the chance of moralizing, I'd better go at once.

MARIANNE: You've said yourself that Paula is so jealous that you can't see either me or the children without there being a godawful fight.

JOHAN: What do you expect me to do about it?

MARIANNE: Are you such a damned coward that you can't tell her what *you* want to do?

JOHAN: Yes.

MARIANNE: I'm sorry.

JOHAN: It doesn't matter. I realize you think the situation is absurd. But don't scold me. It's no use.

MARIANNE: Would you like some more whiskey?

JOHAN: Yes, please.

MARIANNE: How are things otherwise?

JOHAN: Hmmm.

MARIANNE: You look a fright with that haircut. And you've put on weight, I think.

JOHAN: I must admit you really turn me on when we're close together like this. What are we going to do about it?

MARIANNE: Let's have dinner first. Then we'll see.

JOHAN: I don't mind telling you that things are going pretty well for me just now. I've been offered a guest professorship at a university in Cleveland for three years.

MARIANNE: How nice.

JOHAN: It's a splendid chance, both career-wise and financially. After all, it's over there that things happen in our field. There's nothing to keep me here. I'm fed up with the academic duck pond. So I leave in the spring, if all goes well.

MARIANNE: Congratulations.

JOHAN: And now for the unspoken question: Are you taking Paula with you to America? And the answer is no. Call it running away, if you like. Okay, I'm decamping. I've had just about enough. Maybe the time is right. Paula has been good for me. She has taught me a few things about myself which I'm glad to know. But there's a limit. To be quite frank, I'm pretty tired of her. I suppose you think it's disloyal of me to sit here running Paula down. But she forfeited my loyalty long ago. I'm fed up with her. With her emotional storms and scenes and tears and hysterics, then making it all up and saying how much she loves me. (*Checking himself.*) I'll tell you this, Marianne. The best thing about Paula was that she taught me to shout and brawl. It was even permissible to strike her. I wasn't aware that I had any feelings at all. If I were to tell you . . . you'd think I was lying. I'm talking your ear off. But I'm in such a terribly good mood. I've felt on top of the world ever since I was offered that professorship.

MARIANNE: (*Quietly.*) In that case perhaps we could discuss the divorce. I mean, if you're going to be away for several years it would be better to clinch the matter before you do. Don't you think?

JOHAN: I agree with whatever you think.

MARIANNE: Then I suggest that we do get a divorce. One never knows what may happen. I might want to remarry. And it would be awfully complicated if you're in America.

JOHAN: Is something up?

MARIANNE: That made you curious, didn't it?

JOHAN: Look here, Marianne! Suppose you tell me something about yourself. How are things, Marianne? Judging by your appearance, your hairdo, your dress, your figure, and your general amiability, they must be pretty good. What I'm most anxious to know, of course, is whether you have a lover.—You've changed things around, I see.

MARIANNE: Any objections?

JOHAN: Oh, none at all.

MARIANNE: I've moved into your study.

JOHAN: And what have you done with my things?

MARIANNE: (*Gaily.*) They're in storage.

JOHAN: But . . .

MARIANNE: I'm paying for it. I decided finally that I had a right to a workroom of my own. So I bought some furniture and put up new curtains and my own pictures which there wasn't room for here in the old days and which you didn't like. Was that tactless, perhaps? Do you think I should have waited until the divorce was over? Should I have observed a year of mourning? Oh, and I've also changed the telephone, so it's in my name now.

JOHAN: Oh, that's good.

MARIANNE: You're a tiny bit bitter about something all the same.

JOHAN: By no means. I think you did right.

MARIANNE: Thank you. Oh, and I've taken away the double bed.

JOHAN: What was the point of that?

MARIANNE: I nearly went crazy sleeping in one corner of a huge bed.

JOHAN: And what about your lover? Where do you house him?

MARIANNE: For the time being I think it's better for us to meet at his place.

JOHAN: You mean because of the girls?

MARIANNE: (*With a smile.*) No, silly. They're always after me to get married again.

JOHAN: Well, I'll be damned. —Anyway, this place is fit to live in.

MARIANNE: You live out of town, don't you?

JOHAN: We live in three rooms of a concrete silo. On the tenth floor. With a view of another concrete silo. At the downstairs entrance drunken thirteen-year-olds stagger about. They amuse themselves by knocking down the old people. The building has cracks everywhere. The windows fit so badly that the curtains flutter in the draft. For two whole weeks not long ago I had to get every drop of water from a hydrant. None of the toilets worked. If possible, people avoid the subway after eight in the evening. In the middle of it all is something which a demented architect has called the piazza. Not that I'm complaining. In fact I think it's interesting. But Paula likes it out there. She says it all fits in with her picture of the world. And that it feels safe. I don't really care where I live. To me every domicile is only temporary. You must have your security inside yourself.

MARIANNE: And have you?

JOHAN: I didn't, as long as I was living here at home.

MARIANNE: Aha.

JOHAN: Everything around us then was so confoundedly important. We were forced to make a ritual of security.

MARIANNE: I don't know what you mean.

JOHAN: All security was anchored in the things outside ourselves. Our possessions, our country house, the apartment, our friends, our income, food, holidays, parents. Do you know what my security looks like? I'll tell you. I think this way: Loneliness is absolute. It's an illusion to imagine anything else. Be aware of it. And try to act accordingly. Don't expect anything but the worst. If something nice happens, all the better. Don't think you can ever do away with loneliness. It is absolute. You can invent fellowship on different levels, but it will still only be a fiction about religion, politics, love, art, and so on. The loneliness is nonetheless complete. What's so treacherous is that sometime you may be struck by an idea of fellowship. Bear in mind that it's an illusion. Then you won't be so disappointed afterward, when everything goes back to normal. You must live with the realization of absolute loneliness. Then you will stop complaining, then you will stop moaning. In fact, then you're pretty safe and are learning to accept with a certain satisfaction how pointless it all is.

MARIANNE: I wish I were as certain as you.

JOHAN: It's nothing but words. You put it into words so as to placate the great emptiness. I'm astonished sometimes at Paula's tremendous political faith. She's incessantly active within her group. Her conviction answers her questions and fills the emptiness. I wish I could live as she does. I really mean that, without any sarcasm. Why are you laughing? Do you think I'm talking rubbish? I think so too as a matter of fact. But I don't care.

MARIANNE: I don't know what you're talking about. It seems so theoretical. I don't know why. Perhaps because I never talk about such big matters. I think I move on another plane.

JOHAN: A more select plane, oh. A special plane reserved for women with a privileged emotional life and a happier, more mundane adjustment to the mysteries of life. Paula too likes to change herself into a priestess of life. It's always when she has read a new book by some fancy preacher of the new women's gospel.

MARIANNE: It sounds as if somewhere you were disappointed.

JOHAN: That's what you think.

MARIANNE: (*Quietly.*) I want you to know that I'm nearly always thinking of you and wondering if you're all right or whether you're lonely and afraid. Every day, several times a day, I wonder where I went wrong. What I did to cause the breach between us. I know it's a childish way of thinking, but there you are. Sometimes I seem to have got hold of the solution, then it slips through my fingers.

JOHAN: Why don't you go to a psychiatrist?

MARIANNE: I do go to a doctor who has also had psychiatric training, and we have a couple of talks a week. Sometimes we meet privately.

JOHAN: Is *he* your lover?

MARIANNE: We've gone to bed together a couple of times but it was a dead loss. So we gave up the attempt and devoted ourselves to my interesting mental life instead.

JOHAN: And where has that got you?

MARIANNE: Nowhere. I'm trying hard to learn to talk. Oh yes, and I moved into your study.

JOHAN: That was one result anyway. (*Yawns.*)

MARIANNE: What a huge yawn. Are you tired?

JOHAN: It's just the whiskey. I'm sorry. And I don't sleep terribly well. That added to the tension, I suppose.

MARIANNE: If you'd like to go home, don't mind me.

JOHAN: Oh, come now.

MARIANNE: You can lie down and have a nap if you like. I'll wake you in an hour.

JOHAN: What a fuss about that one wretched yawn. I don't *want* to lie down. Please tell me about your explorations inside yourself instead. That's much more interesting. I promise you.

MARIANNE: There's not really very much to tell. Though something funny did strike me. It only occurred to me last night.

JOHAN: (*Not very interested.*) Oh, that sounds exciting.

MARIANNE: The doctor said I should write down whatever came into my head. It didn't matter how irrelevant. Anything at all. Dreams, memories, thoughts. There's nothing much so far. It's hard to write when you're not used to it. It sounds so stilted and you can't find the right words and you think how silly it all is.

JOHAN: (*Politely.*) Won't you read me what you wrote last night? I'd like very much to hear it.

MARIANNE: Would you really? Are you sure? I'll go and get the book. I wrote for several hours and didn't get to sleep till about three o'clock. I looked a fright this morning and thought it *would* be today, just when I was going to see you after so long.

(MARIANNE *runs out to get the notebook. She comes back, cheerfully excited and smiling. She sits down and is about to begin reading.*)

JOHAN: You really are pretty.

MARIANNE: Now don't start paying compliments. You must take an interest in my soul instead. Sit down, please.
(*But* JOHAN *takes the notebook out of her hand, embraces and kisses her.*) No, don't. Sit down and be good and I'll read to you instead.

JOHAN: One good thing needn't exclude another.

MARIANNE: Johan! I've been thinking about that the whole time. What would it matter if we made love this evening? I've been longing for it and have worked myself up. But then I thought—what about afterward? I mean after you've gone. I'd be left longing for you again. And I don't want that. I'm in love with you, Johan. Don't you see? Sometimes I hate you for what you've done to me. And sometimes I don't think of you for several hours at a stretch. It's lovely. Oh no. I have everything I could want. I have friends and even lovers. I have my children and I hold down a good job and like my work. No one need feel sorry for me. But I'm bound to you. I can't think why. Maybe I'm a perverted masochist or else I'm just the faithful type who forms only one attachment in life. I don't know. It's so difficult, Johan. I don't want to live with anyone else. Other men bore me. I'm not saying this to give you a bad conscience or to blackmail you emotionally. I'm only telling you how it is. That's why I just can't bear it if you start kissing me and making love to me. Because then all my defenses break down. I can't explain it in any other way. And then it's so lonely again after you've gone. When I keep you at a distance like this it's all right. In fact, it's awfully nice. But don't let's fondle each other. Because then it's hopeless after you've gone.

JOHAN: I'm still in love with you. You know that.

MARIANNE: Why do you say that when it's not true?

JOHAN: Why should my feelings for you have changed? If we feel like making love now, why shouldn't we? Why think about how it's going to feel tomorrow? Isn't that being very silly?

(*His attempts at lovemaking become more and more passionate. Then* MARIANNE *breaks free of him.*)

MARIANNE: No, I don't want to. No! No, I won't under any circumstances. I don't want to moon about here, pining and weeping and longing. Please understand. There's nothing sillier than this. If you persist, you might just as well go. I mean it, Johan. I don't want us to make love. I really don't. Please try to understand.

JOHAN: I'll try to understand although I don't. So I'll sit down here. Then we'll devote ourselves to reading aloud instead and then I'll go home at a respectable hour and call Paula in London and tell her I've been to the theatre.

MARIANNE: I feel like an awful fool now. I want to go and hide and have a good cry.

JOHAN: I'll go now if you like. We can meet tomorrow instead and go out and have dinner or something.

MARIANNE: Perhaps it would be better. No, stay after all. Besides, I don't have time tomorrow.

JOHAN: (*Gently.*) Hey!

MARIANNE: Hey!

JOHAN: I'm awfully fond of you.

MARIANNE: I'm behaving like a child.

JOHAN: (*Gently.*) It's all right again now. The situation is under control. We've pulled through the crisis.

MARIANNE: It's such a scrawl that I can hardly ready my own writing. All this first part is nothing important. Yes, here. (*Reads aloud.*) "Suddenly I turned and looked at the old picture of my school class, when I was ten. I seemed to be aware of something that had been lying in readiness for a long time but beyond my grasp. To my surprise I have to admit that I don't know who I am. I haven't the vaguest idea. I have always done what people told me. As far back as I can remember I've been obedient, adaptable, almost meek. Now that I think about it, I had one or two violent outbursts of self-assertion as a little girl. But I remember also that Mother punished all such lapses from convention with exemplary severity. For my sisters and me our entire upbringing was aimed at our being *agreeable*. I was rather ugly and clumsy and was constantly informed of the fact. By degrees I found that if I kept my thoughts to myself and was ingratiating and farsighted, such behavior brought its rewards. The really big deception, however, occurred during puberty. All my thoughts, feelings, and actions revolved round sex. I didn't let on about this to my parents, or to anyone at all for that matter. Then it became second nature to be deceitful, surreptitious, and secretive. So it has gone on and on. In my relations with men. The same perpetual dissimulation. The same desperate attempts to please everybody. I have never thought: What do *I* want? But always: What does *he* want? What does he expect of me? What does he want me to want? It's not unselfishness as I used to think, but sheer cowardice, and what's worse—utter ignorance of who I am. I have never lived a dramatic life, I have no gift for that sort of thing. But for the first time I feel intensely excited at the thought of finding out what exactly I want to do with myself."

(JOHAN *is sitting with his head sunk on his chest and breathing deeply. He is asleep.* MARIANNE *wakes him gently.*)

JOHAN: What you were reading was so interesting. Please forgive me Marianne. Won't you read some more? I know you must be terribly hurt, but won't you read some more anyway?

MARIANNE: I think you ought to go home to bed now. (*With a smile.*) I'm not a bit hurt. Really.

JOHAN: Yes, I'd better push off now.

MARIANNE: Perhaps you'll call up some time. If only for the children's sake.

JOHAN: Yes, sure. Yes, of course I will.

MARIANNE: It's always nice to see you, you know that.

JOHAN: If only Paula weren't so goddamn jealous. But still, she has reason. It's hard on her too.

MARIANNE: When will you know definitely about America?

JOHAN: In about a month.

MARIANNE: You can let me know what happens.

JOHAN: Yes, I'll write.

MARIANNE: And what are we going to do about the divorce? We must make up our minds.

JOHAN: Are you going to marry again?

MARIANNE: I don't know yet.

JOHAN: I'd rather wait before deciding. Don't you think so too?

MARIANNE: I don't know what I think.
(JOHAN *leaves the room. For a while* MARIANNE *remains motionless and very sad. Then she senses that he has not left but is standing just behind her in the doorway. She reaches out her hand to him in silence. Suddenly they embrace.*) You'll stay with me tonight. Won't you?

JOHAN: Yes, I'll stay with you tonight.

Interlude

JOHAN: Finally Johan and Marianne have decided to arrange for the divorce. The meeting between them takes place in the Psychotechnical Institute at the University—to be more precise, in Johan's office, furnished in accordance with official equipment standard number three.

(*As he speaks, Johan's worktable and three chairs are placed at one side of the room, the sofa and armchair at the opposite side.*)

In Johan's Office

(JOHAN *is seated at the worktable, when* MARIANNE *rushes in.*)

MARIANNE: Sorry I'm late. But Daddy called just as I was leaving, and he went on and on and on. Hi. How are you?

JOHAN: I have a cold.

MARIANNE: Yes, you look pretty wretched.

JOHAN: At first I just had a sore throat that might have been anything and I thought, oh, it will go away. Then it turned into a runny nose and then went down into my chest. So now I cough all night long. I have a slight temperature and feel lousy. I very nearly phoned and put you off, but since you're going abroad I suppose it's essential to file the papers with the court before you leave, isn't it?

MARIANNE: Poor Johan. My heart bleeds for you. I hope Paula is looking after you properly.

JOHAN: She's also down with a cold.

MARIANNE: Is that so!

JOHAN: But with her it's a sort of gastric flu. It's all terribly romantic.

MARIANNE: You'll pull through, don't worry.

JOHAN: You seem in very good spirits.

MARIANNE: Hmm, I am, at that.

JOHAN: Any special reason?

MARIANNE: Oh, I'm always excited before a trip. And then it's spring. And I have a new coat and skirt. How do you like it, by the way? Smart, isn't it? But tell me. *Do* you like it?

JOHAN: Yes, it's very nice.

MARIANNE: I'm glad we could meet here in your workroom. It saves time, I mean.

JOHAN: It's not exactly cozy.

MARIANNE: Just the place for going through divorce papers. Now, if you'll just look at this. Here's the actual agreement that Henning has drawn up. It's word for word as we dictated it together.

JOHAN: Then I needn't read through it.

MARIANNE: One should always read before signing. Don't look so grumpy, Johan.

JOHAN: I'm not grumpy.

MARIANNE: You're as sulky as can be. Here's the inventory of goods and chattels we acquired jointly and how we've divided them up between us. It's only a reminder list. You needn't sign it.

JOHAN: It says here that you're to have Granny's wall clock. That's a mistake, anyway.

MARIANNE: My dear Johan, your grandmother gave it to me. We've discussed it, for that matter.

JOHAN: I can't recollect having discussed Granny's wall clock.

MARIANNE: If you're so attached to it, then keep it by all means. But it is actually mine.

JOHAN: No, no. You're right as always. Take the damned clock, I'm not going to squabble over trifles. (*Coughs.*)

MARIANNE: Is there anything else you think I have wrongfully appropriated?

JOHAN: (*Sulkily.*) Your sarcasm is wasted. I have a cold and I'm depressed. So there. Would you like a glass of fine old brandy?

MARIANNE: That's just what the doctor ordered.

JOHAN: Egerman gave me a bottle. He had been in Paris lecturing and was presented with a whole case by grateful colleagues. There we are. Skoal!

MARIANNE: Skoal!

JOHAN: Well, what do you say?

MARIANNE: Mmm. I don't really care for brandy, but this is something special.

JOHAN: I feel better now.

MARIANNE: (*After a pause.*) It's hard all the same.

JOHAN: What's hard?

MARIANNE: Getting divorced.

JOHAN: It's only a few goddamn papers.

MARIANNE: I still think it's hard. We've been living apart for ages. We've seen practically nothing of each other. We're agreed. Yet I'm sitting here with a bad conscience. Isn't it strange. Johan! Don't you think it's—

JOHAN: Yes, it's strange.

MARIANNE: Can't we sit over there on the sofa and put the overhead light out? The glare is frightful. How can you work in such a bleak room.

JOHAN: The sofa's not very comfortable either.

MARIANNE: Yes, it is, if you put your feet up on a chair.

JOHAN: Is that comfy? Like some more brandy?

MARIANNE: Yes, please. Are you all alone here this evening? Is the whole place empty?

JOHAN: There's a night watchman.

MARIANNE: How nice.

JOHAN: What do you mean, nice?

MARIANNE: I don't know, just nice.

JOHAN: When you have a cold, nothing's nice.

MARIANNE: Oh, stop feeling sorry for yourself! You're not going to die of it. Skoal! This gets better and better.

JOHAN: You *are* in good spirits.

MARIANNE: Yes, I think I am, though I'm not sure. (*Smiles.*) To tell the truth, I'm rather in love.

JOHAN: Still that David?

MARIANNE: David? Oh, him! No, that's over and done with.

JOHAN: Oh.

MARIANNE: For another thing, I'm beginning to feel free of you. And that's a relief. A *great* relief.

JOHAN: What do you mean by that?

MARIANNE: Never mind. Give me a kiss.

JOHAN: I have a cold.

MARIANNE: Don't you remember that I never catch your germs? Give me a kiss. I want you to.

JOHAN: (*Kissing her.*) Well, was it what you expected?

MARIANNE: Better. Now put your hand on my breast. Like that. Nice?

JOHAN: Are you going to seduce me?

MARIANNE: That's exactly my plan. In this very place, at this very moment. On the floor, right here on the carpet. What do you say to that? Wouldn't that be nice? Why do you look so anxious? Scared of the night watchman? Imagine if the night watchman did come in! (*Smiles.*) We'd ask him to join the party. We're so broadminded these days. Let's just drink and make love. And tomorrow we'll file the divorce papers.

Interlude

JOHAN: For the first time in Johan and Marianne's small, furiously discussed sex life, they did it on the rug.

JOHAN: A penny for your thoughts.

MARIANNE: Mmm, I'm not telling.

JOHAN: Perhaps you're hungry?

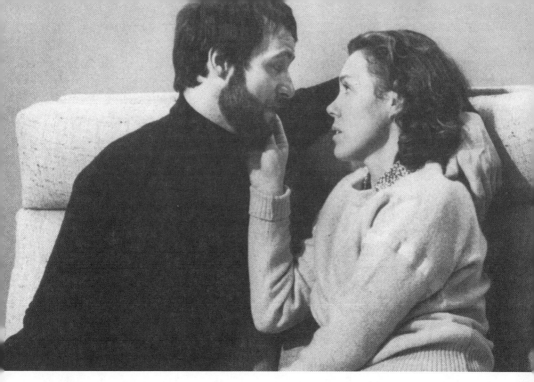

"I'm beginning to feel free of you." Dohm and Hallhuber rehearsing the scene in Johan's office.

MARIANNE: I always am.

JOHAN: What about a nice steak and a big glass of beer? Doesn't that sound good?

MARIANNE: But you're not allowed to take me out to a restaurant.

JOHAN: I'm in Uppsala this evening with my students.

MARIANNE: In that case you may take me to supper by all means. Let's sign the agreement and then go out and celebrate. Wouldn't that be a worthy end to a long and happy marriage.

JOHAN: I'd rather take the papers home and read through them quietly.

MARIANNE: What's this? Are we going to start chopping and changing after all our discussions?

JOHAN: You said yourself just now that one shouldn't sign anything without having read it through carefully. Didn't you?

MARIANNE: All right, we'll sit down opposite each other and read through the whole thing once more. So that you can see I haven't cheated you in some mysterious fashion.

JOHAN: Why are you so cross?

MARIANNE: I'm not in the least cross. Well, let's start.

198

JOHAN: You are. You're in a filthy temper.

MARIANNE: All right, I'm in a filthy temper, but I shall try to control it, since I'm used to controlling myself where you and your whims are concerned. (*Blandly.*) Can we leave this boring discussion now and get on with the reading. It's rather late, at that, and I have a busy day tomorrow.

JOHAN: So now we're not going to have supper?

MARIANNE: No, thank you. I'd rather not. I'm so grateful for the favors already bestowed upon me.

JOHAN: Whose whims now?

MARIANNE: Look here, Johan. (*Controlling herself.*) No, don't speak. There's no point. I'll try to keep my temper. (*Sweetly.*) Now, we'll put the papers in this envelope, like this, and you take them home with you and then you and Paula can go through the wording carefully together and see that I haven't cheated you.

JOHAN: Why, Marianne, what the hell's the matter?

MARIANNE: Nothing.

JOHAN: We were such good friends a moment ago.

MARIANNE: Exactly. By the way, don't forget it's Eva's birthday on Tuesday.

JOHAN: Am I in the habit of forgetting the children's birthdays?

MARIANNE: No, it has never happened, as I have always reminded you in good time. I'd be grateful if you'd kindly pay for her trip to France this summer. I can't afford it.

JOHAN: How much will it cost?

MARIANNE: I think about two thousand kronor.

JOHAN: What! Are you out of your mind? Where am I going to get two thousand kronor suddenly?

MARIANNE: Then you can ask your mother.

JOHAN: I've already borrowed far too much from her.

MARIANNE: Well, I have no money anyway.

JOHAN: Eva will just have to cancel her trip. *I* don't have any money. It won't hurt her to learn that you can't have everything you point to in this world. She's so goddamn spoiled for that matter that it's incredible. *And* ill-mannered.

MARIANNE: Now listen here! That's just . . .

JOHAN: She went to see Mother last week and Mother phoned me afterward and was quite shattered at the kid's behavior.

MARIANNE: (*Capitulating.*) Oh, did she say that?

JOHAN: Yes.

MARIANNE: Yes, it's hopeless. But she's at a difficult age.

JOHAN: I do think you might teach the girls a few manners. But you let them boss you around just as they like.

MARIANNE: It's not so easy, let me tell you. They say I'm never at home to look after them. They're always angry with me. It's as if everything were my fault.

JOHAN: Anyhow, I'm not going to pay for Eva's trip to France. You can tell her that.

MARIANNE: Tell her yourself.

JOHAN: Why? You have the custody of the children. I have to fork out a hell of a big maintenance, which incidentally I have to pay taxes on and which is completely ruining me. So I don't see why I should have a lot of idiotic expenses on top of that. There's nothing to that effect in the divorce agreement, at any rate. Or is there?

MARIANNE: It's not the children's fault if we're worse off because you went off with another woman.

JOHAN: I never expected that remark from you.

MARIANNE: No, I'm sorry. It was stupid of me.

JOHAN: Forget it. I will speak to our daughter. The difficulty is that we have no means of communication. Whenever she visits me she lolls on the sofa and reads *Donald Duck*. Or sprawls in an easy chair and watches TV. If I try to talk to her she mumbles something in a mono-syllable as if she were a half-wit. Paula can't get any answer out of her at all. The only thing that makes her condescend to answer in a sentence with subject, predicate, and direct object is if I bribe her with money or treat her to the movies. Otherwise she chatters away on the phone to her friends for hours. At any rate I have no paternal feelings. Though I must admit she has grown pretty. No, it's much easier with Karin. Though she's so damned childish. Do you think perhaps she's a bit retarded?

MARIANNE: How absurd you sound when you talk about the children like that. Absurd and childish.

JOHAN: I brought them into the world by mistake and since then I've paid a small fortune for their upkeep. That must suffice. I refuse to play the fond father and I permit myself to dislike the children as much as they dislike me. Who has said that *I* must always be the one to take the first step toward contact and affection and love and all that? No, I prefer to act my part of wallet on two legs. At least that doesn't give me a bad conscience, seeing that I'm practically bankrupt with all I have to cough up. And that's as it should be. If you make a blunder, you have to pay. And if, as in this case, you make two blunders, then it costs you double. I don't mind telling you that I loathe my stupid, spoiled, brainless, lazy, and selfish daughters. Anyway, the feeling is reciprocated. (*Pause.*) Why don't you say something? Are you angry now?

MARIANNE: I'm thinking back.

JOHAN: Thinking back?

MARIANNE: It used to be different. Do you remember? How pleased you were when I plodded around with my big belly. And how eager you were for Eva to have a baby sister or brother. You spent all your time with the children, you played with them, read them fairy tales, you were so gentle and kind and patient. Much more patient than I was. And they loved you. (*Sadly.*) Why did things turn out like this? What went wrong? When did the children get bored with you? When did you get bored with them? What became of all the love and solicitude? And all the joy?

JOHAN: There's no use crying over spilt milk. Children grow up, relations are broken off. Love gives out, the same as affection, friendship, and solidarity. It's nothing unusual. It just is so.

MARIANNE: Sometimes I feel that you and I were both born with silver spoons in our mouths, but we've squandered our resources and suddenly find ourselves poor and bitter and angry. We must have gone wrong somewhere, and there was no one to tell us what we did.

JOHAN: When it comes to emotions, we're illiterates.

MARIANNE: Illiterates?

JOHAN: We're taught everything about the body and about agriculture in Rhodesia and about the square root of pi, or whatever the hell it's called, but not a word about the soul. We're abysmally ignorant, about both ourselves and others. Our own fear and loneliness and anger. We're left without a chance, ignorant and remorseful among the ruins of our ambitions. To make a child aware of its soul is something almost indecent. You're regarded as a dirty old man. How can you ever understand other people if you don't know anything about yourself? Now you're yawning, so that's the end of the lecture. I had nothing more to say anyway. Some more brandy?

MARIANNE: Yes, please.

JOHAN: (*Coughing.*) Damn this cough. Oh, before I forget. I have something funny to tell you. That guest professorship has gone to hell.

MARIANNE: Why, Johan.

JOHAN: Not that it matters. But still.

MARIANNE: That's a terrible shame.

JOHAN: (*Drinking.*) Oh, I don't know. I was pretty disappointed, naturally. As usual there has been some goddamn hanky-panky. First the
trip was postponed. Then suddenly there was no money. Then next
thing I knew they'd sent Akerman! And fuck me. (*Laughs.*) Just goes
to show. Skoal!

MARIANNE: When did that happen?

JOHAN: In May. I don't understand how their minds work. A couple of
weeks ago we were supposed to go to a convention in Oslo. Suddenly
the department butts in and tells us we can't go. A, we're not getting
any money, and B, we're to stay at home and get on with our job. That's
no way to talk to us, for Christ's sake! We're not a lot of lousy little
school kids playing hooky. I went up to the Ministry to have the matter
out. I've never known anything like it. I asked to see the minister of
education but he didn't have time, so I had to content myself with some
confounded underlings. You should have seen them! You should have

Johan (Hallhuber): "When it comes to emotions, we're illiterates."

seen the way they behaved. At least I was taught manners. You should have heard the language they used! In the end I didn't know what I was saying, so I walked out. That's how they treat you nowadays. You're just a cipher. (*Drinks.*) People like me have become inconvenient. And of course we're not of the right political shade. Not progressive. Not to the left of left. Out of the race. I could die laughing. (*Drinks.*) I'm regarded as an expensive, unproductive unit which by rights should be got rid of by rationalization. I'm thirty-eight years old now, Marianne. And this is supposed to be the prime of life, when you could really make yourself useful, when you've gained a little experience. Shit, no. Throw the bugger out. Or let him creep around until he rots. I'm so goddamn tired, Marianne. If I had the guts I'd make a clean break and move to the country or ask for a job as teacher in a small town. Sometimes I wish I could . . . (*Drinks.*) Well, that's my sad story. Paula has a very ambivalent attitude toward the situation. And sometimes she says I'm a shit and starts packing her things. I don't know which of the alternatives would give me most relief. (*Laughs.*) Anyway, I think she has a lover. Not that I care. I'm not jealous any more. I'm not really anything any more. I hardly know who I am now. Someone spat on me and I drowned in the spittle.

MARIANNE: Do you know what I think, Johan? I'm in the process of becoming free from you.

JOHAN: Allow me to congratulate you.

MARIANNE: I don't know why I'm saying this. And I suppose it's pretty callous of me to say it now, after what you've just told me. I've considered you far too much. I think consideration killed off love. Has it struck you that we never quarreled? If I remember right, we considered it vulgar to quarrel. No, we sat down and talked so amiably to each other. Do you remember after Karin was born? When we suddenly couldn't make love any more? We sat down so prudently and explained so prudently to each other that it was quite natural. That it was only to be expected after two pregnancies one on top of the other.

JOHAN: I find these retrospective expositions ridiculous and unnecessary.

MARIANNE: (*Shouting.*) You drive me crazy with your stupid sarcasms! Must you always be the one to decide what is suitable or convenient? I think it serves you right if things have gone wrong. I'm glad Paula has a lover. You can commit suicide for all I care, though I expect you're too much of a coward. Well, well, so there you sit with tears in your eyes. You're getting what you deserve for once. Now you can feel what I've gone through.

JOHAN: (*Calmly.*) Jesus, how I hate you really. I remember thinking it quite often: Jesus, how I hate her. Especially when we had made love and I had felt how indifferent and distracted you'd been. And we'd be out in the bathroom, with you sitting there naked on the bidet washing and washing away that nasty stuff you had got from me. You always used to say it smelled so awful. Then I would think: I hate her, her body, her movements. I could have struck you. I was itching to smash that white, hard resistance that radiated from you.

MARIANNE: Do you imagine I wasn't just as miserable about it as you were? I used to think: Does it really have to be like this for us? Does it have to be so bad? Then we'd console ourselves with the thought that after all sex was only of secondary importance, and that we got along well together in every other way. What self-deception, Johan! Nothing could be right when we could no longer make love.

JOHAN: You're forgetting a couple of things which it may be unpleasant to mention in this connection.

MARIANNE: Then perhaps you would kindly enlighten me.

JOHAN: Do you know what you did all along? You exploited your sex organs. They became a commodity. If you let me make love to you one day, the implication was that you'd be spared the next day. If I had been nice and helpful, I was rewarded with a lay. If I had been disagreeable or dared to criticize in any way, you got your own back by closing shop. What I put up with! It's grotesque when I think of the way you carried on. Christ! You were worse than any whore.

MARIANNE: But you wouldn't face the truth.

JOHAN: What goddamn truth, may I ask? Is it some sort of female truth? A truth with patent pending?

MARIANNE: (*Furious.*) You're crazy. I really think you're out of your mind. Do you imagine that you can go on wiping your feet on me indefinitely? Am I always to be a substitute for your mother? All that goddamn harping on how I neglected our home and put my job first.

JOHAN: (*Shouting.*) That's absolutely not true!

MARIANNE: Certainly it's true. During the first years of our marriage I was nagged by everyone—you and your parents and my own mother. All you succeeded in doing was to give me a bad conscience. I had a bad conscience at work and a bad conscience at home. Then I was expected to have a bad conscience because I didn't make love properly either. Nothing but grumbling and nagging and demanding and—*Oh!* you son of a bitch! And if I got my own back with my sex organs, as you say, was it so strange? I was fighting against hopeless odds all the time: you and my mother and your parents and the whole of this god-damn society. When I think of what I endured and what I've at last broken free from, I could scream. *Never again, never again, never again.*

JOHAN: Now you're being utterly grotesque.

MARIANNE: So what? That's how I've become. But the difference between my grotesqueness and yours is that I don't give in. I intend to keep on, you see. I intend to live in reality and take it just as it is.

JOHAN: I'm glad we don't need to feel sympathy any longer. Glad we can throw all our bad conscience on the garbage pile. We're getting quite human. The whole trouble was that you and I ever met in the first place. That we fell in love and decided to live together. What a glorious fiasco right from the start. So the sooner we sign this paper the better, then we have only to divide up the silver and old wedding presents and say good-bye, and a pity it was all such a ghastly mistake from beginning to end.

MARIANNE: Do you know what? You don't want a divorce.

JOHAN: (*Feels caught.*) I never heard anything so absurd!

MARIANNE: If it's so absurd then you can prove the opposite by signing the papers here and now.

JOHAN: All right.

MARIANNE: Johan! Be honest now! Look at me! Look at me, Johan. You've changed your mind? You don't want us to divorce, do you? You thought we might pick up our marriage again. You were going to suggest something of the kind this evening. Go on, admit it.

JOHAN: (*Loudly.*) Well, suppose I did have thoughts in that direction. Is it a crime? I confess I'm beaten. Is *that* what you want to hear? I'm tired of Paula. I'm homesick. Oh, I know, Marianne. You needn't put on that smile. I'm a failure and I'm going downhill and I'm scared and homeless. I was dependent on all those things that are called home and family and regular life and quiet everyday routine. I'm tired of living alone.

MARIANNE: Alone?

JOHAN: Loneliness with Paula is worse than real loneliness. I can't en-dure either of them. I can't talk about this.

MARIANNE: (*After a pause.*) I wonder how it would turn out.

JOHAN: I know that we would be much more concerned about each other. Don't you think so? Don't you think so?

MARIANNE: No, I don't think so. After a week or two we'd slip back into all the old habits. All our good resolutions would be forgotten. We wouldn't have learned anything.

JOHAN: How can you be so sure?

MARIANNE: I don't want you to entreat me. I'm not certain that . . .

JOHAN: We could try.

MARIANNE: (*Coldly.*) Do you remember when I begged and implored you to come back? Do you remember how I groveled and wept and pleaded? Do you remember our meetings and your pretexts and half-truths, which merely showed your complete indifference all the more clearly.

JOHAN: I didn't know any better then. You can't reproach me for that now.

MARIANNE: (*Angry.*) Reproach! What a fantastic word, Johan. Do you know what I think? I think you are feebleminded and naive. Do you suppose that I've gone through all I have and started a life of my own, just so I could take charge of you and see that you don't go to the dogs? If I didn't think you were so deplorable I'd laugh at you. When I think of what you've done to me during the last few years, I feel sick with fury. Go on, look at me. I'm proof against that gaze of yours. I've hardened myself. If you knew how many times I've dreamt I battered you to death, that I murdered you, that I stuck a knife in your ribs. If you only knew what a goddamn relief it is to say all this to you at last.

JOHAN: (*Smiling suddenly.*) You know, you're awfully pretty when you're angry like that.

MARIANNE: That's nice to know. (*More graciously.*) Though *you* just look comical. What's more, you have lipstick on your cheek.

JOHAN: If I understand correctly, you'd prefer to see the divorce go through.

MARIANNE: (*On the verge of laughing.*) That's exactly how I'd like to sum up what I've already said.

JOHAN: Some more brandy?

MARIANNE: Heavens, we've nearly emptied the bottle! It's not surprising that I feel emancipated and a little peculiar. How do *you* feel?

JOHAN: Oh, not so bad. I think my cold has gone. At any rate, I haven't coughed for some time.

MARIANNE: Well, to talk sensibly . . .

JOHAN: So what you said earlier wasn't sensible?

MARIANNE: It wasn't sensible, but it was true and necessary. To say something reasonable, you should be glad I've made myself free and that I want to live my own life. I think you should do exactly the same.

You should free yourself from the past, every bit of it. And start fresh under completely different conditions. At this very moment you have a marvelous chance.

JOHAN: Will you answer me something?

MARIANNE: Now you're sounding all pathetic again.

JOHAN: What's the use? I mean, to start fresh, as you say. I have no desire to.

MARIANNE: What do you mean now?

JOHAN: Only what I've already said three or four times this evening, though you haven't bothered to listen. I have no desire to start fresh, I have no curiosity about what's ahead of me.

MARIANNE: (*Beaten.*) You're only saying that because you're depressed and have had setbacks. You just want sympathy.

JOHAN: You've hit the nail on the head, or whatever the hell the expression is.

MARIANNE: Well, what shall we do about that supper?

JOHAN: I'm too drunk to go anywhere. Can't we sit here together for a while longer?

MARIANNE: Why not. As long as you don't make me sentimental.

JOHAN: Can't we go home?

MARIANNE: You mean home to my place?

JOHAN: Of course I mean home to your place.

MARIANNE: No.

JOHAN: (*Drunk.*) Why not?

MARIANNE: Because I have a man who is sitting waiting for me, and he's going to be pretty upset that I reek of brandy and that I'm so late and that the papers aren't signed.

JOHAN: Is he jealous?

MARIANNE: Not particularly. (*Smiles.*) But he knows my masochistic nature. Do you know what he said before I left? He kissed me and said: "You and your husband will make love. And you'll come home with a guilty conscience and you won't have signed the papers. And you'll give me up."

JOHAN: Are you going to tell him we've made love together?

MARIANNE: No. (*Smiles.*) No, I don't think I will.

JOHAN: God, I'm tired.

MARIANNE: (*Matter-of-factly.*) We've had too much to drink. If we were sensible we'd go for a brisk walk in the fresh air before going home to our respective soulmates.

JOHAN: You really are fantastic.

MARIANNE: No, I just have an incurable passion for what's healthy. Come along, my dear. Let's go.

JOHAN: Don't go!

MARIANNE: It's late. Can I call a cab?

JOHAN: You must dial zero first, then you'll get an outside line.

MARIANNE: (*Phoning.*) Good evening. Will you send a cab to University Drive forty-six, please? It's coming at once? Marvelous. (*Puts down the receiver.*) Can I give you a ride? You'd better not take your own car. You've had too much to drink.

JOHAN: I'll stay for a while.

MARIANNE: No, don't Johan. Come with me now. It's not good for you to sit here alone brooding.

JOHAN: Never mind what I do.

MARIANNE: Come along, Johan.

JOHAN: I think you should stay a while longer.

MARIANNE: I don't want to stay any longer.

JOHAN: Don't go. (*Locks the door.*)

MARIANNE: Please don't start that, Johan. You're just tired and drunk.

JOHAN: You mustn't go!

MARIANNE: Let me past!

JOHAN: I'm not letting you go.

MARIANNE: Don't be a fool!

JOHAN: Don't be a fool yourself.

MARIANNE: Even in our marriage we never behaved in this stupid way, Johan. Don't let's start now. Please give me the key.

JOHAN: I don't give a damn what you say. Now I can see Marianne's well-ordered brain clicking away! What do I do now? Has he gone mad? Is he going to hit me?

MARIANNE: If you really want to know, all I think is that you're screamingly funny.

JOHAN: Oh, funny am I? Then why don't you laugh? I think you look scared if anything.

MARIANNE: At least let me call and cancel the cab. (*She starts to dial, and he prevents her.*)

JOHAN: Why? It will wait for ten minutes and then drive off. Sit down and take it easy. This is going to take a long time, I promise you.

MARIANNE: All right, I don't mind. Well, what do you want to say to me?

JOHAN: Nothing. I just want to look at you.

MARIANNE: Go ahead. As a matter of fact, it's just what I might have expected from someone like you. I wonder how many times I've warned wives seeking a divorce against being alone with their wronged husbands. I must confess I never thought I'd find myself in that situation.

JOHAN: Shut up!

MARIANNE: Do you think I'm afraid? If you want to know, I couldn't care less about what you're going to do.

JOHAN: Shut your mouth, I said! (*He strikes her.*)

(*She strikes back. A fight breaks out. A brutal, reckless vicious brawl. JOHAN grabs MARIANNE by the throat. She frees herself and runs terrified out of the room. JOHAN follows her. Screams and blows can be heard from the next room. Suddenly there is complete silence. After a long pause, MARIANNE reappears, crosses the room, walks to the worktable, and signs the divorce papers. JOHAN follows her to the table, lays the key on it, and also signs.*)

JOHAN: Are you all right?

MARIANNE: It was my own fault. I'll see that the papers are filed in court as soon as possible.

JOHAN: Thank you, I'd appreciate that.

MARIANNE: So long.

Interlude

JOHAN: In reality, these scenes from a marriage could end here, with the signing of the divorce papers. But we would like to perform an epilogue.

MARIANNE: Seven years have now passed. On a sunny afternoon in August, the two meet in their old summer house. They are married again, but not to each other.

JOHAN: One more thing: their respective spouses are away traveling. Marianne finds this fabulous; Johan, though, thinks it's a bit indecent
. . .

(*As they speak, the furniture for the previous scene is removed and is replaced, for the last time, by the large double bed.*)

Epilogue

(JOHAN *and* MARIANNE *lie on the double bed, their heads toward the foot end.*)

MARIANNE: Do you realize it's been almost a year now?

JOHAN: Has it?

MARIANNE: Nearly to the day. The eighth of September, the day before my birthday. And today's the twenty-eighth of August.

JOHAN: Did you ever go back and see the second act of that play?

MARIANNE: No. It must have looked odd when we sneaked off like two criminals at the intermission.

JOHAN: And now we're celebrating our first anniversary.

MARIANNE: No.

JOHAN: What do you mean?

MARIANNE: We're celebrating our twentieth anniversary. We were married in August twenty years ago.

JOHAN: Twenty years. So we were.

MARIANNE: A whole lifetime. We've lived a whole grown-up lifetime with each other. How strange to think of it.

JOHAN: What is it? Why are you crying?

MARIANNE: You're so touching, that's all.

JOHAN: Touching, am I? I'll be damned!

MARIANNE: Yes, you are. Dearest little Johan. You've somehow grown so small. You're much more handsome than before. And you look so gentle and kind. You always had such a tense look before, sort of anxious and on your guard.

JOHAN: Oh, really?

MARIANNE: Are people beastly to you?

JOHAN: (*Smiling.*) I don't really know. If anything, I think I've found my right proportions. And that I've accepted my limitations with a certain humility. That makes me kind and a bit mournful.

MARIANNE: (*Tenderly.*) And you with your great expectations.

JOHAN: No, you're wrong. It was my father who had the great expectations, not I. When I was little I had very modest and pleasant ideas as to what I would do when I grew up.

MARIANNE: (*Smiling.*) What were they?

JOHAN: I had an old uncle. He had a little store in Lund that sold books and toys and stationery. Sometimes he and Aunt Emma let me help them in the store. I liked that more than anything. My dream was to own a store like that. There you have my ambitions. To my wife it makes no difference at all whether I'm clever or not. She says she feels secure with me. She doesn't want any other man. It's totally unbelievable.

MARIANNE: Do you love her?

JOHAN: This eternal woman's question. I think she's kind, intelligent, pleasant, clean, well-mannered, presentable, and sexually attractive. I like having breakfast with her.

MARIANNE: (*Another tone of voice.*) You've had luck with your lottery ticket, Johan!

JOHAN: Then I suppose I shouldn't be unfaithful to her with you.

MARIANNE: Perhaps you love both of us.

JOHAN: I suppose you have to have a gift for feeling love. I don't have that gift. I have found it very hard to understand that I'm a child with genitals. A fabulous combination when it comes to women with maternal instincts.

MARIANNE: I've certainly known that all along.

JOHAN: And Henrik—?

MARIANNE: With Henrik and me, it was foolish to get married at all. We looked on it more or less as a joke. It was a purely sexual thing.

JOHAN: Oh. I see.

MARIANNE: Henrik is very, how shall I put it, convincing on that point.

JOHAN: How interesting.

MARIANNE: But today I'm no longer dependent on him. I live with him. That's fine. I live with you. That's fine. If I meet some other man who attracts me I can live with him too.

JOHAN: And you call that liberty?

MARIANNE: For me it's liberty.

JOHAN: Well, then everything's fine. Just fine. Tremendously good. It's just that I can't stand it.

MARIANNE: I knew you didn't want to hear the truth.

JOHAN: (*Fiercely.*) What do I care about your orgasms with this goddamn sex athlete? You're welcome to them. I'm full of admiration for your total emancipation. It's most impressive. You should write a novel about it. I can guarantee you the applause of the high priestesses of Women's Lib.

MARIANNE: You can't mean to be as stupid as you sound.

JOHAN: I'm telling you I don't give a damn about it all.

MARIANNE: But suddenly it seemed to matter so terribly.

JOHAN: No, not really. It's just a little bit of all the wonderful things life has to offer. Think of all our knowledge! Think of all the wisdom and awareness that we've arrived at through tears and misery. It's magnificent. Fantastic. We've discovered ourselves. It's crazy. The one sees that he is small and meaningless. The other discerns her greatness. What could be better? Here we sit so sensibly, talking pure rubbish about our better halves. They're almost with us in the room. We wave to them. It's mental group sex on the top level. It might all have come from a textbook on lifemanship. It's incredible, Marianne. Analysis is total, knowledge is boundless. But I can't stand it.

MARIANNE: (*Sad suddenly.*) I know what you mean, but I don't think it's as terrible as you do.

JOHAN: There you see. That's the big difference between us. Because I refuse to accept the complete meaninglessness behind the complete awareness. I can't live with that cold light over all my endeavors. I want something to long for. I want something to believe in.

MARIANNE: I don't feel as you do.

JOHAN: No, I realize that.

MARIANNE: Unlike you, I endure it all. And enjoy doing it. I rely on my common sense. And my feeling. They cooperate. Now that I'm a little older I have a third coworker: my experience.

JOHAN: (*Gruff.*) You should be a politician.

MARIANNE: (*Serious.*) Maybe you're right.

JOHAN: Good God!

MARIANNE: I like people. I enjoy negotiations, prudence, compromises.

JOHAN: You're practicing your election speech, I can hear it.

MARIANNE: You think I'm difficult?

JOHAN: Only when you preach.

MARIANNE: I won't say another word.

JOHAN: Promise not to tell me any more homely truths this evening?

MARIANNE: I promise.

JOHAN: Promise not to harp on that orgasm athlete?

MARIANNE: Not another word about him.

JOHAN: Do you think that for just a little while you can restrain your horrible sense of superiority?

MARIANNE: It will be difficult, but I'll try.

JOHAN: Can you possibly, I say *possibly*, ration your infinite female strength?

MARIANNE: I see that I'll have to.

JOHAN: Come on then. Let's go to bed.

> (*Pause. They lie in bed. Suddenly* MARIANNE *gets up and stands in a corner of the room, very frightened.* JOHAN *awakens and discovers her standing there.*)

MARIANNE: Why do I have such terrible dreams? What do you think causes it?

JOHAN: Maybe you ate something that didn't agree with you.?

MARIANNE: Do you think so?

JOHAN: Or else, dearest Marianne, in your infinitely well-ordered world there is something you can't get at.

MARIANNE: What would that be?

JOHAN: How should I know?

MARIANNE: Put your arms around me. I'm so terribly cold. Do you think I'm catching something? The children have just had the flu.

JOHAN: (*Gently.*) There, there. You'll soon feel better. Do you remember what frightened you?

MARIANNE: You and I and the children—we have to go along a dangerous road or something. I want you others to take my hands so that we can hold on to each other. (*Frightened.*) But it's no good. I no longer have any hands. I only have a pair of stumps. At that moment I begin sliding in soft sand. I can't get hold of you. You're all standing up there on the road and I can't reach you.

JOHAN: (*Tenderly.*) That was a horrible dream.

MARIANNE: Johan!

JOHAN: Yes, my darling.

MARIANNE: Do you think we're living in utter confusion.

JOHAN: You and I?

MARIANNE: No, all of us.

JOHAN: What do you mean by confusion?

MARIANNE: Fear, uncertainty, folly. I mean confusion. That we realize secretly that we're slipping downhill. And that we don't know what to do.

JOHAN: Yes, I think so.

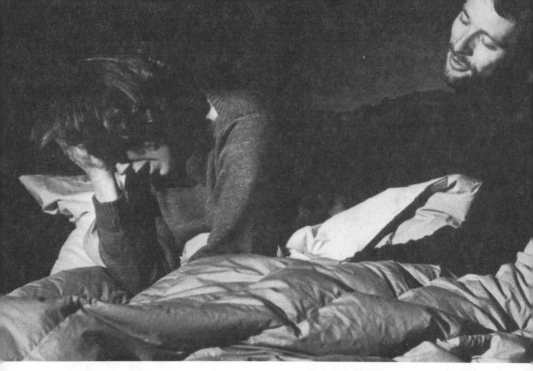

"That was a horrible dream." Johan (Hallhuber) and Marianne (Dohm) in the last scene from their marriage.

MARIANNE: Johan!

JOHAN: Yes?

MARIANNE: Have we missed something important?

JOHAN: All of us?

MARIANNE: You and I.

JOHAN: What would that be?

MARIANNE: Sometimes I know exactly how you're feeling and thinking. And then I feel a great tenderness for you and forget about myself, even though I don't efface myself. Do you understand what I mean?

JOHAN: I understand what you mean.

MARIANNE: Johan.

JOHAN: Yes?

MARIANNE: Sometimes it grieves me that I have never loved anyone. I don't think I've ever been loved either. It really distresses me.

JOHAN: Now I think you're being a little bit hysterical, Marianne.

MARIANNE: (*Smiling.*) Do you?

JOHAN: I can only answer for myself. And I think I love you in my imperfect and rather selfish way. And at times I think you love me in your stormy, emotional way. In fact, I think that you and I love one another. In an earthly and imperfect way.

MARIANNE: Do you really think so?

JOHAN: You're so damned hard to please.

MARIANNE: Yes, I am.

JOHAN: But here I sit with my arms around you, without any fuss, in the middle of the night in a dark house, somewhere in the world. I can't honestly say I have any great insight or fellow-feeling.

MARIANNE: No, you haven't.

JOHAN: Presumably I don't have the imagination for that.

MARIANNE: No, you're rather unimaginative.

JOHAN: I don't know what the hell my love looks like. I can't describe it and I hardly ever feel it in everyday life.

MARIANNE: And you think I love you too?

JOHAN: Yes, perhaps you do. But if we harp on it too much, love will give out.

MARIANNE: We're going to sit like this all night.

JOHAN: Oh no, we're not!

MARIANNE: Why not?

JOHAN: One leg has gone to sleep and my right arm is practically dislocated. I'm very sleepy and my back's cold.

MARIANNE: Well then, let's snuggle down under the covers.

JOHAN: Yes, let's.

MARIANNE: Good night, my darling.

JOHAN: Good night.

MARIANNE: Sleep well.

JOHAN: Thanks, the same to you.

MARIANNE: Good night.

(*The light on the double bed fades to black.*)